Through The Years

MEMOIRS:
A COLLECTION OF LITERARY WORKS

BY PATT ABRAHAMSON

small
point
publishing
escanaba, michigan

sand
point
publishing
escanaba, michigan

PATT ABRAHAMSON
PO BOX 344
ESCANABA, MI 49829
pattabe@charter.net

Printed in the United States of America.
This book is printed on acid-free paper.

Abrahamson, Patt, 1933-
    Through The Years
    Memoirs: A Collection of Literary Works / Patt Abrahamson

    ISBN 978-1-60402-242-1

Memories

MEMORIES: They are what sustain us in our "Golden Years." We thrive on memories created *Through The Years*.

MEMORIES: Of our childhood, of our family, of our town, of local history, of historical events and of personal relationships

MEMORIES: Happy memories with laughter, sad memories with tears. We all have them. They define who we are.

MEMORIES are our legacy - proof that we have been here. The generations before us have touched our lives - just as we will touch the lives of the generations to follow...with MEMORIES.

~ Patt Abrahamson ~

Dedication

Ironically, two of the most important people in my life share the same birthdate: March 28.

To my husband Gary - my partner of 57 years, my soul mate and my personal cheerleader. Without his enduring support, vast knowledge of subjects and photographic memory of the past this book wouldn't be possible.

His love of history whether it is Escanaba, a historical person, a historical place or a historical happening has been the impetus for many of the articles.

Together our lives were intertwined with history and rekindled in several of the articles *Through The Years*. Together we relived the nostalgic past of years gone by.

For my grandmother, Laura Derouin Cotnoir who showered me with her love and wisdom. Today she lives on in my memory - what better legacy.

Laura Derouin Cotnoir
1878-1949

Contents

Acknowledgements

First and most importantly my humble and deepest gratitude goes out to Rick Rudden, Editor of the Escanaba Daily Press for recognizing my writing, my style and possibly what a senior writer with a wealth of experiences could contribute as a columnist. Without Rick's belief in me as a writer and without his thumbs-up for me to write a weekly column - this book would not be happening.

My husband, Gary, has been supportive and instrumental in suggesting topics of interest and supplementing me with his vast knowledge of local and national history. He is always there for me - to garner his opinions, his critic and his praise - when he exclaims, "Yes, Patt that's it." I go with it.

Laced throughout the book are photos provided by the Delta County Historical Society Archives. Their dilligent effort to preserve local history has also served to enhance my book.

My readers have become a huge part of my life. Their head nodding takes many forms: phone calls, letters, E-mails and approaching me in the community to affirm their appreciation of my column and the subjects I write about. So - a huge THANK-YOU to all of my readers!

This book was a combined effort with the folks at Richards Printing: Jeff and Ray Richards. I worked daily with their graphic artist, Tre Branstrom. Between us we came up with a cover design, photo placement and text format. Her knowledge, unique style and help were invaluable.

GRANDMA PATT'S JOURNEY "THROUGH THE YEARS."
WRITTEN BY MARY PAT ABRAHAMSON (AGE 17)

Grandma Patt, If at all possible, teach us what you, wiser than we, know about our country and the life you lived as a successful American from hard youth.

What is there that I do not understand because of my short time on this earth?

Fill me with your thoughts and your wisdom.

"Heather, Mary Pat, Kelly and Gabrielle my precious granddaughters, I haven't lived a life known as perfect. Nor have I been an angel to my Father, God, who has guided me through these long-lived years. I can tell you of my mistakes and of my hardships, but, above all, of my strength in overcoming the struggles in life.

Now shush your impatient, glossy lips and sit; I will tell you a tale of my journey. Let your youth listen to my wisdom during this short story. I will be filling your young minds with stories from generations gone by.

As a child I knew poverty because of the times. It was after the Depression when keeping food on the table for my sister and brother and me was in itself a chore. Living a life in my shoes as a youngster made me feel like you could never succeed and maybe would die in the same circumstance. A negative outlook to be sure, but the tales of my life will break the mold for the possibility of success in the eyes of those who think education or some success is impossible."

Here is Grandma Patt's journey *Through The Years.*

Her years as a child were more like that of an adult: Her mom's babies kept coming, dishes to be washed, worn linoleum to be scrubbed, school work to be done, mouths to be fed. Time for curiosity had already come to a halt. At age, 12, it was the start of her adult life. Changing diapers, feeding babies and helping with the meals left no time for growing and learning. Rather she was learning to become a mother and housewife.

Education in a woman's eyes was unnecessary during such times. Women tended to the children, made meals and cleaned house. That was their everyday job. There were no aspirations for more. But to Grandma Patt it was everything. Enlightening her mind was her first priority. Her duties at home were to come first;

no woman needed an education past high school. School slowly and steadily became a low priority. She stayed home frequently from school to help tend to her baby brothers.

Her mother, Edna, was struggling with a life that Grandma Patt would pray that she would never endure - the same as all the rest. Edna's unoriginal story was typical. Perhaps the saddest part of growing up was her constant witnessing of the abuse of hard working Edna. The times were difficult in the thirties and forties; lots of mouths to feed; money was scarce; drinking was an escape and with it came arguments and terror. It was typical - just so damn typical.

At the end of the day it had been said - her first dream, at a young age, of becoming an educated mind and being more than a typical woman had failed: her one chance to avoid being different than a statistic set by society during those years.

Through these rough times she found her love for the arts. She loved dancing, painting and anything that hinted of creativity. Any time of day was a day of song and dance for her. The music was her home like no other. It was her time to escape from it all. Club 314 was a place of gatherings for young-hearted dancers looking to show their practiced moves to *In the Mood* and *Hawaiian War Chant*.

Club 314 became the always-remembered meeting place of the love of her life, Gary Abrahamson. They say 'twas dancing that brought them together. Whispers of fate and destiny surged through them as they danced the night away.

Dancing was the beginning of their undying love for each other. Only a child at heart, still in her teens, they were wed. He was her reason for living; her escape from the mundane. She was to feel more special than any other being by his side. He was just as amazing as she had dreamed as a child: handsome like the men in the movies; dreamy. And he was madly in love with everything she was about.

As the journey continued the union produced their first child, Gary Junior. His parents were still just kids. Two more babies would follow - their family now complete. A new home and three children; those were wonderful years!

But she had a burning desire for more. She became an entrepreneur and opened the first tanning salon/exercise center in Escanaba. Times were different - more prosperous. She didn't feel stifled or boxed-in like her mother; with no way out. Now poverty was a mere distant memory from youth.

Everything good was building up much higher than skyscrapers could be built. Soon it would tumble down into the streets of her family all over again.

Gary Junior, first son to be held in her arms: athletic, charming, handsome and humorous suffered a cardiac arrest while jogging at age, 37. The result of being without oxygen was brain damage. Life for him and those who loved him would never be the same. She had to reconcile that he would never again be a productive member of society. It would surely be the most difficult of life's blows to face.

She wouldn't consider an institution; she took him home to care for him. Diversions from her caretaker duties were competing in the Ms. Senior Michigan Pageant - she walked away with the title in 1997. She entered college as a diversion; and graduated cum laude from Northern Michigan University with a bachelor degree in social work. Her dreams of an education were finally realized. She was age 59.

Her story was to be shared by those willing to listen. She wrote of her struggles with Gary Junior in a journal. That wasn't enough - she wanted to share what she had learned. Her experiences, struggles and ideas were published. *Brain Injury: A Family Tragedy* sold in stores and in other countries - read by many. Her experiences and struggles would touch those families who had suffered the same fate.

She continues to touch lives with her experiences and wisdom in her weekly column in the Daily Press - the object of her second book, *Through the Years*.

"Now, my darling granddaughters, I feel most strongly that I have had some impact on the lives of others. I have fulfilled my goal of not being "typical."

My journey, my mistakes, my successes and my life: Let it be your guide to lead you on your path. I've filled not only you, but also others with my thoughts and wisdom. You must remember education is key; fulfillment in yourself is key, so pass on all that you know and it will travel in generations to come - just as it has been passed down in generations gone by.

Heather, Mary Pat, Kelly and Gabrielle you have heard my journey "Through The Years". Now, my precious young ones, it is time for you to live in the moment..."

St. Anne's Church Afire

Photos Courtesy Delta County Historical Archives

HEADQUARTERS

"Centennial Belles" 1863-1963

EXHIBITION BUILDING

Farmers Market

The Coliseum

The Roundhouse

Chapter 1

Local History and Memoirs

Two Miles Worth of Memories   June 2, 2006

Let's begin our Ludington Street tour down memory lane at the House of Ludington; a hosteler dating back to 1864 with a nationally-known reputation. The transformations since then have been many, but perhaps the most colorful owner was Pat Hayes, an Irishman from Chicago who purchased the hotel in 1939.

His eccentricity and stories of ghosts and spirits roaming the halls are fodder for an exclusive story in the future. And who could forget his specialties; Chateaubriand with duchess potatoes and that famous House of Ludington sandwich.

Located off Ludington Street on Fourth Street and First Avenue South was the Coliseum owned by Dutch Flath. We spent every Saturday roller skating to pipe organ music; kids of all ages. We danced on skates and skated with partners. At Christmastime one of the biggest treats was the holiday variety show and, of course, the arrival of Santa Claus. Everyone received a jumbo bag of Christmas candy and a popcorn ball.

Dutch Flath and his popcorn wagon was a fixture for years on the corner of North Ninth Street and Ludington. People strolling leisurely and those attending the movies across the street purchased his popcorn. There was no concession at the theatres back then.

My husband remembers walking with his little old grandmother (in her 80s) to the Michigan Theatre to see *Gone With The Wind*. She was so impressed with the movie she bought the booklet sold at the theatre. The theatres had drawings at that time and she once won a beautiful silver tray and toaster. Never used it though; just displayed it. She liked her toast made the old-fashioned way; over the gas stove.

I accompanied my grandmother to *Going My Way* with Bing Crosby. We walked there and she wore one of her elegant hats while hanging on to my arm. She was deeply religious, reciting the rosary on her knees by the sofa everyday. Bing Crosby was a priest in the movie and the reason she wanted to attend.

Hoyler's Tea Room, across the street from the Delft Theatre, was a popular spot in the '30s. The bowling alley was upstairs, next door to the theatre. Young boys set the pins; there were no automatic pin setters.

On the corner of 10th and Ludington stood the Boston Sweet Shop operated by the Prokus and Rouman families who emigrated here from Greece. Both families - mom, pop and kids -

worked in the store. A specialty was their famous olive and nut sandwiches. And homemade taffy! Five cents bought a big bag of it. They broke it off of a huge round slab with a silver hammer.

There were three dime stores, all on one block. Across the street was City Drug. The soda fountain was a Mecca for teens. Up the street was Sayklly's; another popular hangout for teens. Their soda fountain boasted every flavor of coke and ice cream treats.

Before the era of McDonald's, we had Tommy's Lunch. Next door to Sayklly's in a Quonset hut (a remnant from World War II) stood Tim and Sally's. After a dance at Club 314 everyone flocked to Tim and Sally's for chocolate milk and french fries. Not many could afford a hamburger. On occasion my mother would bring home hamburgers from Tommy's. They were six for a quarter.

Fairmont's ice cream store, across from Sayklly's, featured two dips for a dime. A family outing was a ride in the car up and down Ludington Street and Lake Shore Drive with everyone (young and old) licking on an ice cream cone.

The Street Car Lunch was across the street from the Junior High School. It was an old street car converted into a lunch counter. Street car tracks were still evident on some streets.

And who could forget the Ludington Street parades? The town lined up at the curbs three deep. There was the Smelt Jamboree, the Forth of July Parade, the Memorial Day Parade, and the Homecoming Parade. I remember Paul Bunyan on stilts taking part in parades along with the elaborate floats.

The parades were huge. I was a majorette in the high school band and one Memorial Day Parade two of us did cartwheels with our batons all the way down Ludington Street. Wow! To be young again and full of energy and flexibility!

Ludington Street may be only two miles long but it holds a million miles memories.

CHANGING FACE OF ESCANABA   May 4, 2007

The changes in Escanaba from the late 1800s to the present are phenomenal, yet, interestingly, the population has remained relatively the same. In 1927 the population was 13,103. In 2002 it was 13,140, a mere gain of 37.

The evolution of the physical town and the types of businesses have undergone many changes since the incorporation of Escanaba.

Bill Mulvaney, lifelong Escanaba resident, researched a wealth of facts and approached me about doing a column relevant to his findings. I found his information extremely interesting and agreed it should be shared.

In 1892 the population of Escanaba was about 8,000. The ore docks being the largest on Lake Michigan, shipped out over 4 million tons in one year on about 3,000 shiploads. They operated 24 hours a day averaging nine or 10 ships a day.

By 1921 the population had grown to 14,652. It regressed to 13,103 by 1927. Not much variation since then.

In a quote from the 1927 city directory: "Escanaba as a home is one of the most delightful cities in the Northwest. The moral and religious tone of our community is excellent. Sunday is emphatically a day of rest in our city. Business of every description is suspended and citizens willingly co-operate with the authorities in the enforcement of the Sunday law."

That in itself is quite a change. Today you can shop for just about anything on Sunday from groceries at supermarkets to clothing, shoes, building materials and other items.

The 1927 directory predicts: "It is as certain as anything in the future that [Escanaba] will become a manufacturing center and its population will become doubled within the next 10 years and quadrupled within 20."

Of course, that prediction fell flat. The size of the city has remained basically the same since 1927. The prediction was based on having ore, flux and fuel for iron smelting furnaces and unrivaled opportunities for manufactures of wood.

Another interesting fact: In 1908 there were 84 saloons in Escanaba; 55 of them on Ludington Street. From 9th street to 14th Street there were 30 saloons, or an average of six per block.

How about this fact: In 1907 the old senior high school was built for $150,000. Astounding isn't it? For those of us that attended school there we remember matriculating around the creaking and groaning inside running track above the gym to get from one side of the building to the other - of course, minus drug sniffing dogs, police and hall monitors.

Thoughts of teachers like Miss Brennan, Miss Irons, Mr. Loveland, Mr. Schram, Mr. Ruwitch, Mr. Wylie, Mr. Edick, Mr. Rouman and Miss Blizel bring us back to those enchanting memories in the old high school.

The 1927 city directory states: Escanaba is the only city in the United States owning its own water, light and gas plants. It has

35 industries, some of which are the largest of their kind in the world.

My husband Gary's family had integral positions within the city. For many years his father, Stanton, was superintendent of the gas and steam plant and his uncle, Hugo Lillquist, was superintendent of the electrical department.

The 1927 directory also cites industries: The Woodenware Co. on the 400 block of Stephenson Avenue (former Harnischfeger building) made more toothpicks, clothespins and wooden dishes than any factory in the world. There was also a maple flooring plant, a pole company and stump puller company that all claimed to be the largest in the world.

In 1927 there were 43 grocery stores. Most were family-owned neighborhood stores. Escanaba also had three cigar manufacturers and 15 dressmakers.

In 2004 we had eight grocery stores: Nelson's, Viau's, Elmer's, Super One, Sav-Mor, Kobasic's, Gary's South Side and Wal-Mart.

I wonder what my grandma would have thought of an adult book store or a tattoo parlor? Yet, some of today's younger grandma's even have tattoos.

I took the concept of a sun-tan center back home from Florida and opened the first one in Delta County called Hawaiian Sun Fitness Center in 1980. Today there are scores of them. Many businesses have nail technicians where you can have artificial nails applied and receive facials and massages.

Wonder what grandma would have thought of that? Probably useless, very narcissistic and a waste of money! Their hands were truly work hands: gardening, cooking, baking and canning.

My grandma, donned in her housedress, apron and a bun secured with a hairnet, would sit me down for a piece of her famous orange cake drizzled with orange glaze hot from the oven. Yummy! She will always be my perception of what a "grandma" is all about!

I remember my grandmother talking about certain streets named after women: Charlotte Street, Hattie Street, Carrie Street and Mary Street. Lincoln Road was 23rd Street since I can remember. For years, after it was renamed Lincoln Road, many of us still called it 23rd Street.

On the corner where Carne's Station is located was Smitty's Gas Station. Behind it on 23rd Street was the Blue Roof Cabins and next to that Kallio's Restaurant. Down the road a bit was Degrand and Brisbane Oil Co.

Behind the present high school were all fields and hills where we picked blueberries when I was a kid. It is also the location where our house stands now.

Time marches on and changes are inevitable. And reminiscing about those changes is so much fun! It seems we always look back with rose colored glasses - remembering mostly the good.

A WALK DOWN MEMORY LANE   October 13, 2006

Memories through the years take center stage in the life of seniors. A person that loses a spouse is left with memories. For some that may be all that is left. When you hear a particular song it can conjure up memories of what you were doing when that song was played at some other time in your life. I can bring you back where you were and your feelings at that time - even decades later. A historical event can do the same.

So, take a walk down memory lane with me. Where do the songs of yesterday place you? What were you doing? Is it a romantic memory? How about a powerful historical event?

Let's begin with a favorite song of mine: *Sweet Caroline* (Neil Diamond). Jean Cote called me after reading one of my columns reminiscing about dancing to the combo of Jean and Pat Henderson at the Ludington. "Hey Patt, thanks for the memories," said Jean, "but you didn't mention your favorite song: *Sweet Caroline.*" How could I ever forget?

Every Friday and Saturday night when we entered the Ludington, Jean and Pat automatically began to play *Sweet Caroline.* Even before we sat down we were swinging on the dance floor. What I wouldn't give to experience one evening like that again!

Sweet Caroline is also a favorite of the Red Sox fans. For over nine years *Sweet Caroline* has been the Sox anthem during the eighth inning at Fenway Park in Boston - much like the Cubs traditional seventh inning anthem at Wrigley Field: *Take Me Out To the Ball Game.*

Neil Diamond's *Sweet Caroline* is a catchy song - mid-tempo, middle-ground and middle-aged! Everyone sings along at Fenway Park. One guy said when he listens to a ball game at home he plays *Sweet Caroline* too. It really has nothing to do with Boston - just one of those things that started, caught on and is now synonymous with a Red Sox game.

What memories do you have that coincide with historical happenings?

1941 The Japanese bomb Pearl Harbor: Gary was listening to the radio on a Sunday afternoon when the broadcast was interrupted. "My brother Stan, who was in the Marines, was home on leave from Pearl Harbor," Gary remembers. "Stan was reading a book and jumped up shocked and distraught."

Songs popular were *Amapola, Boogie Woogie Bugle Boy* by the Andrew Sisters, and *Chattanooga Choo Choo* which was featured in the movie *Sun Valley Serenade* with Sonja Henie.

1945 VJ-Day (victory over Japan). I remember the huge street dance held in front of the House of Ludington. It seemed like the whole town turned out; hundreds were there dancing and singing with fireworks lighting the sky.

Let It Snow, 'Till the End of Time and *The Gypsy* by the Ink Spots were hits in '45. I remember others in the '40s like *Near You, To Each His Own, Linda, Far Away Places, For Sentimental Reasons, In the Mood,* Bing Crosby's *Don't Fence Me In* and the happy, fun song *Zip-A-Dee-Do-Dah.*

1963 President Kennedy was assassinated. We were living in the Sault. I was hanging clothes outside and a neighbor ran over screaming, "the president has been shot!" Later we watched Walter Cronkite on TV announce the death of the president. Grief stricken he took his glasses off and wiped away his tears. The country mourned the death of JFK.

Gary and I were watching TV on Sunday morning and actually witnessed Lee Harvey Oswald, Kennedy's assassin, being shot by Jack Ruby as he was transported through the jail. We were as confused as most of the country watching who just couldn't believe what was happening - on live TV.

Some of the '60s hits were *I Want To Hold Your Hand* and *Hey Jude* by the Beatles, *Pretty Woman* (Roy Orbison) and *Beyond the Sea* (Bobby Darin). Another favorite was *Stranger on the Shore* (Acker Bilk). It was the first British song to hit no. 1 on the U.S. billboard.

1969 Man landed on the moon. The country was glued to their TV sets as we watched Neil Armstrong making history: the first man to step foot on the moon, bouncing in a state of weightlessness. Top songs for '69 were *Proud Mary, Honky Tonk Women* and *Whole Lotta Love.*

1980 Reagan was elected president. Many will remember

the end of the Cold War and Reagan's words: "Mr. Gorbachev, tear down this wall!" Two top songs of 1980 were *Do That To Me One More Time* and *Working My Way Back To You.*

1985 the space shuttle blew up. On that day as commentator of a fashion show at the Ramada Inn I initiated a minute of silence and prayer. The mood was solemn, shocking and sad.

Wow! I am beginning to lose touch in the song department. The top song in '85 was *Careless Whisper* by Wham - who is Wham? *Say You, Say Me* and *Separate Lives* held the number two and three spots. All Greek to me! And probably not the humming kind.

2001 9/11 terrorists destroy The World Trade Center. We were having breakfast when our son called us from Washington, D.C. "Turn on your TV," he said, "a plane has just crashed into the World Trade Center."

Then we witnessed, live, the second assault with another plane crashing into the second tower - and the horror and chaos that followed. As it turned out, our son had passed the Pentagon on his way to work at the Treasury Department when a short time later another plane crashed into the Pentagon. These are visions of horror we will never forget.

Not much in the way of song memories though - at least not for me. *Lady Marmalade, I'm Real* and *Family Affair* were the top three songs in 2001. My age is really showing now! I can't remember or relate to any of those - hits?

Elvis has always been a favorite of mine. Guess it was in the '80s when pop music left us yearning for the music we used to enjoy, that we really started to appreciate country western music. It was something we could relate to.

Willie Nelson's *On the Road Again* in 1980 was a top hit. In 1982 Willie won the best Country Male Vocalist Award with *Always on My Mind.* Then in 1984 the number one song was Willie's *To All the Girls I've Loved Before.*

Hip-Hop music? No way! And lap dancing? What's that all about? I can only say that the drastic changes in music and dancing through the years leave me cold! No wonder I listen to "The Music of Your Life" on WDBC. Pure nostalgia!

A Look Back at the Streamliner

May 5, 2006

From the 1930s, to the 1950s, the train depot in Escanaba was a hub of activity. The Peninsula "400," also known as the Streamliner, made the daily 400-mile trek from Chicago to Ishpeming and back, stopping at many little towns in-between.

The Daily Press sent a reporter every morning to interview travelers for a column on the society page about who was traveling where, and why. A typical news item read, "Mr. and Mrs. John Doe and their daughter, Mary, traveled to Green Bay to visit relatives for the day." Big news in those days!

The wooden plank platform that lined the train tracks was filled with well-wishers and people waiting for the conductor's "All Aboard" call. During the war young men and women in their uniforms from all branches of service were either departing or coming home. It was an emotional time for families.

Travel on the Streamliner was exciting. A round-trip ticket to Chicago was $9.85. Advertising slogans included "400 miles in 400 minutes" and "The train that set the pace for the world."

A club car was added in Green Bay and boasted fine linen and club sandwiches. The bar car surely shortened the trip for many who enjoyed a cocktail or two. The dining car featured elegantly served cuisine. On the return trip you could almost tell time by the Streamliner's near midnight arrival from Chicago. Its shrill whistle could be heard throughout the town miles before the train screeched to a halt.

The highlight of the summer for my husband as a young boy was the trip with his father to Chicago to see the Tigers and the White Sox play a double-header. Sometimes on the return trip the train was so filled that many passengers had to stand until they reached Milwaukee. He still remembers the excitement of the train ride and dining in the club car.

Many of our ancestors who came from Ireland and Canada in the late 1800s were employed building and working for the railroad. It was a viable occupation and the largest employer.

My grandfather, Frank Kidd, started working for the Chicago and Northwestern Railroad when he was in his teens. By the time he retired he had worked his way up to the well-respected position of Yardmaster.

The railroad tracks also attracted tramps, bums or hobos as

they were called in those days. Today they would be "homeless people." They hopped trains for free rides. It was not unusual for a person to be killed or maimed by slipping under the wheels of the train while trying to hitch a ride.

My maternal grandparents lived in the 1700 block of Ludington Street during the '30s - three short blocks from the train station. My grandfather, the Good Samaritan that he was, enjoyed feeding bums and tramps that came to the door begging for food. He would give them breakfast on the porch, and the bums would share their good fortune with one another. Before long a steady stream of tramps was knocking on his door.

After my grandfather died in 1938 my grandmother, who was deaf, was not comfortable with the tramps and bums knocking at her door. She discouraged their visits.

Of course, nobody locked their doors in those days. One day she was petrified to discover a bum in her upstairs bedroom sleeping. Apparently, he had knocked at the door, received no answer and ventured upstairs for some much needed rest. Poor man - he was awakened by my uncle who lived nearby, shooing him out of the house with a broom.

Sometime in the '60s passenger trains were discontinued in the area. Train travel was lost to posterity as auto and plane travel became the mode of transportation. The train station was eventually dismantled.

Public Safety now graces the land that was once a hub of the community: The Train Station.

It Was the Best of Both Worlds May 19, 2006

Times were not so prosperous in the '30s and '40s. Jobs were scarce, and most mothers didn't work. Today's technology and prosperity have set the stage for a totally different life; it's almost like a being on a different planet.

As I look back, there was no television, no cell phones, no computers, no McDonald's and no discretionary dollars for today's "toys." Yet, I wouldn't trade my youth for the perks of today.

We enjoyed simple things like jumping rope and playing hopscotch. In the spring we played jacks and marbles. We made our own kites and flew them. We walked to school and wore snow pants and babushkas. There were no buses. And we were skinny for the most part.

We roller skated and made scooters out of old roller skates. Our hair-dos were concocted with pin curls or curlers. Hairstyles from a beauty shop were nonexistent.

Most of our mothers were home when we came from school. Moms wore aprons and seemed more matronly. Our daily evening meal consisted of meat and potatoes and dessert with everyone home and around the table. And dishwashers - well, they were the kids.

Most grocery stores were of the Mom and Pop variety. They delivered the groceries right to your kitchen table and charged it to your account.

Milk was delivered in glass bottles by local dairies. Ice was delivered on trucks by the ice-man. He shaved the ice out on the street to fit it in the ice-box. Refrigerators weren't prevalent. In the summer kids gathered around the ice truck, picked up the ice shavings, brushed off the sawdust and sucked on them. Kind of like a cheap Popsicle.

Friday fish fries were abundant on Ludington Street. Sandbergs and the Peoples were popular spots that specialized in dollar fish fries with a dime beer. Other popular places were the Michigan Hotel on Stephenson Avenue, Tom Swift's in Bark River and Potvin's in Schaffer.

Coal was used to heat homes. Everyone had a coal bin. The fire was banked at night and sometimes went out. Sometimes you could see your breath in the morning, and your nose and feet were cold. No one had carpet. Linoleum covered hardwood floors; you could buy them for $4 at the dime store.

Club 314 at Third Avenue and 14th Street was the pinnacle of social life for yesterday's teens. During the week there was ping pong, stained-glass classes, free tap dance lessons, crafts, basketball, pool, and just gathering with friends. The dances on the week-ends were worth waiting for.

And my favorite activity! We jitter-bugged to the bands of Ivan Kobasic and Chet Marrier. *In the Mood* was a favorite along with the *Hawaiian War Chant*. And the slow tune you wanted to be dancing with that someone special was *Dream*.

I lived in Chicago when I was first married in the early '50s. I remember signs in the windows of bar businesses advertising free TV. I had no idea what "free TV" meant - nor did I know what pizza was.

My husband attended college and I worked at a night club/vaudeville lounge where I met George Goebel and Patti Page when they performed there. Being from Escanaba and exhibiting the naivety of a young girl from the U.P., I remember hearing the word lesbian and thought that was a nationality (Lebanese)!

Although I wouldn't want to trade my youth with the youth of today - or my Escanaba naivety for that matter - I realize progress and technology have had a significant impact on the quality and comfort of life today. I feel extremely fortunate to have been born and raised in Escanaba during that era...and equally fortunate to be an adult in today's times. Television, computers, travel, and medical technology are just a few examples of today's perks. I have had the best of both worlds!

LIFE HAS CHANGED SINCE THE '40S   July 14, 2006

In many respects the '40s decade was defined by World War II and the end of the Depression era. However, sometimes the most trivial of life events are so important because it gives us a greater appreciation of how life has changed: Some changes for the better; some not so good.

One thing I do remember was Saturday night baths. Yes, Saturday night was reserved to bathe the kids. Hot water was a luxury. My mother would build a fire in the laundry room stove and all of the kids bathed in the same water. I was the oldest so I had the privilege of being first to bathe. Quite a bathtub ring after kid number three finished bathing. A shower wasn't experienced until junior high school.

Mothers did the wash with a wringer washer and a scrub board. The clothes were all washed in the same water; one batch at a time, then put in a tub of rinsing water. The washer was drained by a pail and thrown in the laundry tub. Clothes were either hung in the basement or outside to dry. It constituted an all-day job - and drudgery for mothers.

Diapers were made of cloth, rinsed in the toilet and washed over and over. There was no such thing as throw-away diapers. And there was no Kleenex until the early '50s. Handkerchiefs had to be laundered. Rags were used when someone was sick so they could be thrown away.

Entertainment was the radio. Some of the favorites were Charlie McCarthy, Jack Benny, Fibber McGee and Molly, Bob Hope, and Red Skeleton for adults. The kids enjoyed Little Orphan

Annie, Jack Armstrong, Captain Midnight and The Lone Ranger. Movies and magazines also headed the entertainment list.

Clothing was drastically different than today. There was more conservatism, although during the war the skirts were short. Ladies wore hats. And there were specialty hat stores. After the war we wore long ballerina skirts, Gibson girl blouses, long straight pencil skirts, and bobby socks with saddle shoes. There wasn't much skin showing.

Today, the bare-skin area is huge and the clothes - covered area is skimpy. They pierce their tongues, noses, ears, lips and belly buttons. And tattoos! They were reserved for sailors who visited foreign sea ports - thought of as being seedy. Only a circus woman might have had a tattoo.

And make-up!

Eye shadows of all colors, mascara, false eyelashes and false fingernails painted dark are considered cool today. In the 40's, girls in school might have worn a little lipstick but that was it. Older ladies wore rouge - we call it blush today. Ladies wore red-red lipstick. Today you have gazillion choices of lipstick or lip gloss.

Kids grow up so much faster today. I was dumbfounded last week when my 12-year-old great-granddaughter visited with lip gloss and eye shadow. She could have easily passed for 18. She is taller than I am now and very mature. It's like they can't wait to grow up.

And hair.

The girls today iron it straight. Or they crimp it with a tool. Or it is all different lengths sticking out all over. I am not sure what that is called. The bobby-socks girls of the '40s mostly had long hair devoid of style - just hanging with a barrette. The guys of the '40s had cookie-cutter crew cuts. Today many of the guys shave their heads. The so-called sexy Telly Savalas look has become a "neat" look and a God-sent for those without much hair. A lollypop would complete the Kojak look.

Fast food restaurants were virtually non-existent except for A and W drive-ins. Mothers prepared food from scratch. My mother baked bread every other day. Kool-aid was the drink. Kids didn't drink soda like today. We all became entrepreneurs selling Kool-aid at sidewalk stands for 2-cents. We didn't sell much, but enjoyed drinking it ourselves. Most adult takers just donated a few cents and didn't want the drink.

I worked my teen years at the U.P. State Fair for Conrad's

Southern Fried Chicken. My pay was $35 for six days, 12 hours a day. I used my earnings to buy all of my school clothes. In today's world of designer name brands $35 would not even buy a sleeve.

It seemed every third tent was a beer tent. When I finished working at 11 p.m. there were people drunk and some arguing in front of beer tents; some staggering up and down the midway - not too wholesome. Thank goodness in later years alcohol was banned from the fair.

A favorite place for kids and adults alike was the picnics just about every week-end at Pioneer Trail Park. The Labor Day picnic was especially big. There were all kinds of games and races for the kids. I remember practicing for the three-legged race and the gunny sack race. Prizes were strange though - at least for a kid: A 25-pound sack of flour (my mother loved that one), a ton of coal, gas or groceries.

Pioneer Trail was rustic, family oriented and interesting. Adults played ball, bingo and of course there were the beer, pop and ice cream tents. Seems we always took a stroll up the hill to view the Indian cemetery surrounded by an iron fence to protect it. It was eerie and yet fascinating to kids.

Looking back at the small, almost inconsequential events of life in the forties is not only reminiscent of simpler times, but serves to remind us of the significant changes that have occurred over time. Why is it for most of us the nostalgic past is always remembered with such great affection and leaves us yearning for the "way it was?"

SHARED MEMORIES ARE THE BEST   September 15, 2006

My husband and I often exchange memories of the past: some include family memories. I might start a conversation about something I remember and invariably he chimes in with a similar memory.

For instance, our grandmothers had a language all of their own. My grandmother, a French Canadian, called the closet, the "clothes-press." And Gary's grandmother called his bike a wheel. "Take your wheel and go to the store for me." she would say. My grandmother called a tavern a 'saloon.' Her father (Ferdinand Derouin) during the late 1800's was the original owner of a Bark River saloon, later known as Tom Swift's.

I went to live with my grandmother at age 5 when my grand-father died. She was deaf and didn't want to be alone at night. She was nineteen when her horse was spooked by a train whistle at a railroad crossing in Bark River. The horse bucked and she was thrown against a telephone pole; an injury that eventually caused her deafness.

I was just a young girl of 8 or 9 when, on rare occasions, she would send me to a near-by tavern (saloon) on Ludington Street to purchase a quart of beer. I couldn't even reach the bar. Yet, Fern, the bar-tender knew what I came for and would put it in a bag and send me on my way. Grandma didn't have a refrigerator so she kept her beer in the "clothes-press." I think beer was about 25 cents a quart then.

Gary remembers at age 11 or 12 his dad sending him to the Hob-Nob on the week-end to get two bottles of beer at a time. Of course, the liquor laws were in place, but times were different then - more innocent. The proprietors knew we were buying the beer for my grandmother and Gary's father. That would never happen today. In fact today's youth might even be buying it for themselves.

Gary's Aunt Ruth from Florida visited us every summer. She identified with the Prohibition Era. We could sense her discomfort whenever we took her out to dinner: She didn't like being in an establishment that served liquor. We still had our glass of wine or beer and tried to ignore her less than subtle disapproval.

I suppose you could liken it to this scenario: If marijuana became legal today - how would we feel if our grandchildren and everyone around us in a restaurant was puffing on or sniffing "dope" as we call it. Now, in retrospect, I can at least appreciate how she might have viewed any alcohol consumption.

Communicating has really changed through the years. If you are younger than fifty you probably won't remember telephone party-lines. Very few people were privileged to have a private line. Sometimes there were two and four parties on one line; each having a different ring. You would pick up the phone and your neighbor might be talking. Some folks were amused at listening in on the conversations of others.

When you made a call, a central operator would say: Number please. You talked to a real live person. There was no automation - no dial up. We didn't have a phone when I was young and I remember the lady downstairs yelling up the stairwell for us to come to the phone: that she had received a call for us.

Later when I was in high school we did get a phone. I remember going down to the Michigan Bell telephone office on the corner of Tenth Street and First Avenue to pay the monthly bill. It was $4.35.

Long distance was extremely expensive. Only emergency calls were made. We communicated with family and friends mostly by mail. Everyone wrote letters and anticipated an answer by return mail. Stamps were 3 cents and post cards were a penny.

Western Union delivered telegrams. If you received a telegram it was usually bad news - like someone died or needed to borrow money. We discovered through the city-directory in the early 1900s that Gary's Uncle Harry was the office manager in Escanaba for Western Union. Gary's dad, who was Harry's younger brother, delivered telegrams when he was 10 years old.

Interestingly, Gary's dad only went to the forth grade. One day his dad asked him if he could read and write. He replied, "Yes." "That's enough of that foolishness," his father said, "now get out and get a job!"

Today, letter writing is almost a lost art. Love letters were written and preserved by many of our presidents and their wives. They were eloquent and beautifully written. George Washington wrote endearing letters to his wife, Martha, whom he called Patsy.

So much of history is recorded in letters. Ronald Reagan was known for his love letters to Nancy. He called her Nancy Pants, Nancy Poo, and Muffin. My husband has pet names for me too like, "dumpling" or "dunce" and a few other endearing names I chose not to share!

Today, Western Union is primarily used to transfer money. Long distance phone calls are readily affordable. Seems everybody has a cell phone now. Even the kids have cell phones of their own.

Letter writing has taken a different form. Much of today's communicating is done on the computer through e-mail. I am no longer stuck in the age of "snail mail." However, my kids are still perplexed as to why I don't have a cell phone.

RECOLLECTIONS OF SCHOOL AND TEACHERS   August 25, 2006

Memories of our journey through school days can be quite colorful - especially if you look back sixty plus years. The female teachers we had in grade school came from an era where they weren't allowed to be married - as if that would interfere with their ability to teach. In today's society that would be considered gross discrimination and grounds for a law suit.

By today's standards some of the tactics teachers used to discipline years ago were quite harsh. Some of the treatment would have bordered on a misdemeanor today. Time-outs were unheard of and corporal punishment was used quite readily - especially when we reached junior high and first experienced male teachers.

My husband remembers coach Pucklewartz in Junior High. If you messed up in gym class, you had to endure crawling through the legs of 40 plus kids paddling your behind. That was dubbed his famous "spanking machine." He also grabbed kids by the hair and pulled it or used excessive exercises as punishment.

I remember chewing gum in Miss Ladd's gym class. My punishment? I had to wear the gum on my nose all during gym class. And Mr. Starr, an English teacher would draw a line on the blackboard and make kids (boys) hold their chin up high above it for the entire period.

In Junior High I remember being embarrassed because we had so many babies at home and my mother couldn't attend a Home-Ec tea. Then in tenth grade I purposely misspelled a word when two of us were left standing during the spelling bee contest. I was petrified with the thought of advancing to the finals being held on stage in front of the student body.

Escanaba High School was always a conservative school. Majorettes wore trousers when other schools had short skirts for uniforms. As head major in my junior year I agreed to approach Mr. Lemmer (superintendent of schools) and ask if we could wear skirts in lieu of trousers for uniforms. I was, of course, intimidated by him and had no response when he explained: That wearing short skirts was not the policy in our conservative school district - and boys didn't need another reason to give them ideas. We were also one of the last schools to have a lighted football field. Mr. Lemmer felt afternoon football was more wholesome - so no short skirts and no night games - but we survived and Esky's reputation as a conservative school was perpetuated.

Fast-forward forty years.

In 1988 I entered college at age 55. It served as a diversion after my son's tragic brain-injury and helped to keep my sanity. As it turned out I couldn't wait to attend classes. I graduated from Bay College and decided to attend NMU to work toward a bachelor's degree.

The most logical way to accomplish this was to rent an

apartment on campus for the three of us; my husband, son and me. Soooo - we applied for student housing. Can you believe we had to produce our marriage license to prove we were married? "This is my 40 year-old son and we have been married 40 plus years!" I exclaimed. Common sense didn't prevail. Our license was still required because school policy dictated it.

My husband also enrolled in classes - and had some funny but frustrating experiences. "I am the only one with white hair in my political science class," he wailed. Then to add insult to injury, as a project, each class member had to look up their birth date and report what was the news of the day in Michigan. He found a newspaper article, dated March 28,1931, announcing that the State of Michigan would soon require a driver's license to operate an automobile - quite a contrast from astronauts landing on the moon! This really did make him feel like a relic.

Gary, the patriot, was bothered by the revisionist ideas that surfaced in his political science class. He complained that the professor constantly criticized the U.S. role in history and detested his "blame-America-first" philosophy. After a while he dealt with his frustration by joking about it. He lamented that the instructor didn't even like the Green Bay Packers, as if that was some kind of a litmus test.

The instructors in my classes often remarked that I was an "interesting" student because of my "unique analogies." Hmm - rather a flattering way of addressing my age difference. Truly though, I enjoyed the young student's perspectives and the opportunity to interact with them immensely. I did graduate from NMU at age 59 with a bachelors degree in social work (BSW) cum laude: A feat I will admit I am most proud of. My husband, kids and grandkids attended the graduation ceremony. They beamed, whistled and screamed when I walked across the stage to receive my diploma. Gary, my son with the brain injury said, "Way to go Mom," and for that shining moment he was fully aware; those four little words touched my heart more than anything.

DANCING THROUGH THE YEARS...   August 11, 2006

Our mutual love of dance is what brought my husband, Gary, and I together. The place: Club 314 during the summer of 1948. I don't recall the name of the song playing when he first asked me to dance, but it should have been "Could I have this dance (for the rest of my life)?" because that is exactly what happened.

Step back in time. Gary remembers his parents reminiscing about dancing to the Wayne King Orchestra who performed in Escanaba in the '30s. And I remember my mother talking about her and my father winning a dance contest - so you might say our mutual love of dance was handed down.

Wayne King was the called "Waltz King." The waltz was a popular dance originating in Austria. Wayne King, a popular band leader in the '30s, has been compared to Lawrence Welk and Fred Waring. His theme song was *The Waltz you saved for me*. Some of the more popular favorites were *I Don't Know Why (I Just Do)* and *Melody of Love*.

Frankie Yankovic was considered the Polka Maestro. The Polka has always been a popular dance in this region. In the '70s, my son, Jeff, played in the rock band Clinton in this area. When playing wedding gigs they always had to play the obligatory polka songs, including *She's Too Fat For Me*, *Beer Barrel Polka* and *In Heaven There Is No Beer*. The U.P. is synonymous with polkas - like hot dogs are to baseball.

The Charleston was the dance of the Roaring '20s. The Charleston has the beat and flamboyance of a theatrical performance. I chose the lively Charleston to perform in my bid for Ms. Senior Michigan in 1997 - and won! People seem to clap spontaneously when they see the unique, showy dance movements with the brilliantly colorful fringed costumes flapping to the Charleston's distinctive beat. It's a dance that seems to transcend all generations - a real showstopper!

Big Bands were the craze in the late '30s and '40s. There was Tommy Dorsey, Glenn Miller and Harry James, to name a few. In 1935 at the Palomar ballroom, Benny Goodman, a popular band leader played an arrangement of *Stompin' at the Savoy*, and the rest is history. A new dance-craze swept the nation

Depending on where you lived it was called Jitterbug, Jive, the Lindy Hop or Swing. An all-time favorite jitterbug tune is *In The Mood*. Each generation since has discovered the "fun" of Swing.

We have a huge collection of Big Band albums dating back to the '50s. Our youngest son, Jeff, discovered Swing in the late '80s. He really appreciated that we had preserved all of those great albums. He and his wife were taking Swing lessons at the time, so he packed up some of the albums, took them home and they are now part of his Swing collection.

Swing was called Jitterbug in Escanaba. Swing is contagious! Swing is the most uniquely American of all dances with its carefree movement. Great features were "breakaways" and "swing outs." You could interject a lot of individuality by improvising, and only a handful of guys from our era were really good at it. Most girls were naturals - so they danced with one another.

My husband was stationed in Cheyenne, Wyoming, when he was in the Air Force. We took the bus to Denver one weekend to see Eddie Howard, who was performing at the Elich Gardens. We were thrilled to dance "under the stars" to the great sounds of Eddie Howard. Some of his famous songs were *Careless, Dream, To Each His Own* and *I Love You for Sentimental Reasons.*

A few years later when we were living in Chicago Eddie Howard was a staple at the Aragon Ballroom. Again we danced to his great music. The Spanish-motif ballroom was magnificent and we relished the opportunity to dance in such splendor.

The famous Trianon Ballroom was located on Chicago's Southside. During that era dance bands were featured on radio right from the ballroom. It was a common technique to gain more exposure and become better known. People had their ears peeled to the radio while toe-tapping to the Big-Band sounds around the country.

In the '60s there were many short-lived dance crazes that swept the country. The Twist was one of them. Chubby Checker made the Twist famous with his Twist record. He also recorded *Let's Twist Again like We Did Last Summer* and *The Peppermint Twist.* Its debut on the Dick Clark Show in 1960 got the whole world twisting. It was because the Twist was so simple it became a craze - even across generation gaps.

Other fad dances in the '60s that burned out quickly included the "Monkey," the "Swim" and the "Funky Chicken." They all included the "no touch partner" dancing. In the '70s Disco became popular - remember John Travolta?

We frequented many places to dance in the Escanaba area over the years; among them were the Dells, the Terrace, the Lake Bluff, Holiday Bowl and the House of Ludington. For years we were fixtures at the Ludington every Friday and Saturday night dancing to the combo of Jean Cote and Pat Henderson. Some of the songs they played were *Has Anybody Seen My Sweet Gypsy Rose, New York, New York, San Francisco* and *Memories are Made of This.* I could go on and on. Those were the days!

Today dancing is still our passion - although I hate to admit time has slowed us down. Last fall we danced at our grandson's wedding: They even cleared the ballroom floor and cheered us on while we took center stage and high-stepped to a favorite tune - *New York, New York.*

COMMUNITY CHANGES ARE INEVITABLE   June 29, 2007

Many years ago when our ancestors migrated to the Escanaba area or if you were born in Escanaba during the late 1800s chances are you didn't stray afar. Cars weren't even a figment of the Ford family's imagination. The streetcar ran down Ludington Street and over to Gladstone. My grandma talked about taking the streetcar to South Park for a family picnic.

Society wasn't mobile like it is today. One thing hasn't changed. If you live in or are connected to this community you care about changes that are proposed whether it is a new garbage collection system or angle parking versus curb parking.

Everyone that weighs in on the proposed changes at city council meetings has to be respected. They care and they are willing to attend council meetings to voice their opinion. Different opinions are what helps the council decide what their ultimate vote will be on any given issue. Some residents have more passion in their expression than others. I would just like to see respect and dignity when the folks offer their opinions - not grandstanding or denigrating individuals.

Some grumble to one another down the street and at restaurant coffee klatches - and certainly this is, no doubt, quite normal. No change will ever get a 100% green light. If you were handing out 100 dollar bills some would find reason to complain. Think of national politics. Take the presidential race for example: 55% to 45% vote would be considered a landslide. So why would it be any different in local politics or decisions?

In the past I have criticized both the Mayor and the council in letters to the editor. My concerns were viable - to me. I am but one voice - still as an interested member in the community I will more than likely offer my opinion again in the future. Remember, I am a political junky!

If truth be told I really have admiration for all of the elected government body. They undoubtedly must take their work home. They can't escape irate residents. They hear both sides of the issues and must do their homework to make tough decisions.

It takes a certain individual to be able to stand up to public criticism, to be a public servant - and lest we forget, they have families, jobs and other responsibilities. The pay is certainly not commensurate with the duties and decisions to anguish over - not to mention the verbal abuse. We may not like certain personalities, but we have to applaud their dedication.

I also commend the folks that are appointed and so willingly dedicate their time to serve on the various committees.

To be sure there may be decisions made that splash "egg on the face" of the decision makers - but they are human and do what they think is best with the knowledge presented at the time. They can't get it "right" 100% of the time. Nobody can! Personally I would not want the job!

One issue that is being jostled around is angle versus curb parking on Ludington Street. I found some interesting photos at the Delta County Historical Society Archives that show parking both ways over the years.

In the early 1900s when cars were a real luxury - not a necessity like today - there were very few - so curb parking was adequate. Then, as cars became more prevalent in the '30s and '40s angle parking became necessary to accommodate more shoppers.

Turn of the Century

Those were the days of the meter maid. The city of Escanaba bought up properties on first avenue north and south to alleviate the parking problem on Ludington Street. But that all changed with the opening of the shopping center in the 1970s. Business migrated out to Lincoln Road.

The meters downtown were removed and thought to be a deterrent - the mall parking was free. Since then parking has reverted back to curb parking to gain a wider main street. That's where we are now!

And there is surely going to be controversy as to where we go. That, my friends, is called "Human Nature."

1920's

CLEAN UP
- PAINT UP

Views of Ludington Street with parallel and angle parking.

1950's

MONTGOMERY WARD

⭐ ⭐ ⭐ ⭐

HISTORY WAITING TO BE REDISCOVERED

June 8, 2007

Ludington   Wells   Stephenson

I spent several hours at the Delta County Historical Society Archives yesterday researching photos to include in my new book of columns called *Through the Years* - to be published this summer. I could have spent days there if time permitted and if a cot were available. What a treasure of local history at our finger tips. I guarantee you I will be back.

Lori Rose works there. She is knowledgeable, personable and oh, so helpful. I came away with pride in our community to know that so many hundreds of people have contributed to the interesting files: a road map, if you will, of our area history from the beginning of the early 1860s.

Many people are only familiar with the Historical Society Museum: another place to spend hours looking over their wonderful exhibits, but many folks are unaware of the rich information available in the archives. The buildings are right next to one another

I was absolutely mesmerized at the old photo of Delta County lumber barons: Daniel Wells, Isaac Stephenson and Nelson Ludington. Interestingly, in reading the abstracts from a couple of homes we built west of Lincoln Road, Nelson Ludington was the first title holder of the raw land.

At one time the only route to Escanaba from Green Bay was by boat. In 1867 a group of gentlemen including the afore-mentioned men are pictured sitting on the dock at Menekaunee, at the mouth of the Menominee River near Marinette waiting for the arrival on a boat of the directors of the Chicago and Northwestern railroad.

They would advocate for an extension of the road from Green Bay to Escanaba. They successfully got the extension of the railroad within a year. And that railroad helped put Escanaba on the map!

The Escanaba depot and the Streamliner, also called the "400" (the miles it traveled from Chicago to Ishpeming) will always be etched in the minds of the local senior community. The depot was a hub of activity: It bustled with people coming and going daily. Even the Daily Press had a reporter there every morning to report in the Briefly Told column about who traveled where and why - whether it was a shopping trip or a visit to a relative in Marinette, Green Bay, Milwaukee or Chicago.

We lived only a few short blocks from the depot where kids loved to hang out - including me. I remember the young men in service uniforms and their tearful families hugging and kissing as they either left for the war or returned from the war. My father, Francis Kidd was one of them. He served with General Patton's Army in Europe. Sadly, he died of a massive heart attack in 1946 just three months after his discharge. He was 33 and I was 13.

The depot also served as a deposit for mail. Folks would rush to get their mail there before the Streamliner arrived to pick up the mail, therefore hastening letters to their destinations. Many were wives and parents of servicemen during World War II.

Weather never affected the Peninsula "400" schedule: snow, sleet, rain or thunder storms. You didn't have to buy a ticket in advance - just go to the ticket master's window and purchase a round trip ticket to Chicago for less than ten dollars Certainly security checks were unheard of - no security police there to monitor for terrorists. Most of us had never even heard of the word "terrorist."

Speaking of Nelson Ludington, one of the area's pioneer lumber barons - his wonderful gesture of paternalism has been and is enjoyed by everyone who has ever lived here or visited the area. Escanaba's founding father had his chief engineer lay out the town's 120-acre park when he platted the town with its wide streets in 1863.

Think of how great his foresight was in this north woods frontier at the time when the urban parks movement was just starting to be launched in the United States a la Teddy Roosevelt.

Hence, the name for the House of Ludington, Ludington Street, Ludington Park, and the town of Ludington in lower Michigan.

The town of Wells is named after Daniel Wells, speculator, businessman, politician and congressman who eventually made his home in Milwaukee. He speculated in land, grain and lumber. As early as 1847 he acquired a lumber mill in Escanaba eventually controlling vast timber holdings.

Plan a visit to the Delta County Historical Society Archives if you want to spend a delightful, informative and interesting afternoon.

Wow! History! Nostalgia! Don't ya just love it?

THE STREAMLINER IS "HUGE" IN DELTA COUNTY HISTORY

July 13, 2007

I received many e-mails, phone calls and people in the community talking about their experiences with the Streamliner - the "Peninsula 400." So I felt it warranted another column - and I stand to be corrected on one point.

"400 hundred miles in 400 minutes," represented the 400's slogan. The mileage from Chicago to Ishpeming is 396 miles. So the consensus was that was where the slogan originated from. Not so!

The original "400" traveled from Chicago to Minneapolis - ironically a distance of 428 miles according to Gary Stiles, a member of the local U.P. Central Model Railroad Club.

The club meets every Thursday at 7 pm at the Eighth Street Coffee House. They have a humongous train with running sessions the third Thursday of the month. Open house for people interested in viewing their elaborate set-up is the first Saturday of the month.

The trains coined the "400" were actually a fleet of trains traveling to different areas.

The Chicago and North Western Streamliner that traveled to the north woods of Upper Michigan was splashed with North Western's traditional and identifiable yellow and green. She was well-blended with the rest of the 400 fleet. Inaugurated in 1942, The Peninsula 400 raced north to communities such as Marinette, Escanaba and Ishpeming.

And the stories it would tell if it could talk! It provided service from a lone fisherman, to shoppers visiting the Windy City, to college kids traveling to and from Chicago, and the many, many World War II heroes as it slammed through snowdrifts scooping snow off of the tracks.

My husband's mother always knew if her kids came home late during high school years. She gauged time as to whether it was before or after she heard the streamliner rumble into town, vibrating the ground and screeching to a halt. It usually arrived between 11:00 to 12:00 midnight and blew its shrill horn that could be heard all over the city.

One morning at the breakfast table she questioned, "Gary, you came home pretty late night. I know because it was after the Streamliner whistle."

Gary wiped his brow and said meekly, "Yeah Mom, it was a little late." Little did she know it was 5:00 AM! Just for the record he wasn't with me!

Sadly, in 1969 the end came when the train was cut back to Green Bay, Wisconsin. But the memories and stories persist. So do the images of the "400" rushing toward Escanaba with the strobe of its beacon headlight oscillating back and forth; lighting up the town. And that unforgettable horn announcing, "It's me - the "400!" I'm back!"

Denny Grall, Sports Editor wrote: "Patt, I enjoyed your item on the CNW, the 400 and the depot."

The CNW had particular significance for Denny - his dad worked for the company for 47 years.

"I rode the 400 to Escanaba with my dad once, when I was in high school in Marinette," related Denny. "We spent the night at the Delta Hotel - for all of about five hours. We arrived on the late night train and left on the early morning train, number 209 northbound and 214 southbound on the schedule. My dad spent 47 years with the CNW, working his way up to road master with just an eighth grade education.

He retired in 1972. I worked for him on the summer extra gang for two years and I sure got a different view. He was always firm with me at home, but it stepped up a notch or three on the job and it was obvious, in a good way, to all of the workers that his son was not going to be coddled at work.

I also remember him showing a friend of mine, who was 18 years old, how to drive a spike into the tie. My buddy could not get the hang of it and my dad, who was 58 at the time, grabbed the hammer and in two swings had the spike embedded.

He zipped off four more spikes, handed the hammer back to Ken and said, 'Son, that's how it's done.' Talk about pride in your dad! I'll never forget the astonished look on my buddy's face as he took the hammer and tried to follow suit. That was the topic of conversation for some time."

Gary remembers happy and sad times riding the Streamliner. Happy was when he went to the Tiger/White Sox game in Chicago with his dad every summer as a youth. Sad was when he returned home on the train from Texas while in service to attend his father's funeral. He was 19.

Trying to get a photo of the Peninsula 400 was almost as difficult as getting an Audience with the Pope. I exhausted local venues such as the Delta County Historical Archives, the library and Gary Stiles, from the U.P. Central Model Railroad Club, among others - all to no avail.

The demise of the stellar system in the central Midwest of a proud railroad, CNW, ceased in April 1995. So I called Chicago and another railroad. Personnel referred me to a CNW web-site. Voila! I managed to find several photos of the Peninsula 400, but with strings attached. They were copyrighted.

I didn't stop there. I wrote to the photographer who holds the copyright: TED ELLIS. He also gave me permission to publish the elusive photos in my upcoming book of columns, Through the Years - along with the green light to give copies to the Delta County Historical Archives and the library.

Now the visual of the Peninsula 400 will never ever be lost to time! Nor can you erase all of those precious happy (sometimes sad) streamliner memories. The "Peninsula 400" will always play a "huge" part of local history.

LOCAL SALOON HAS RICH HISTORY
FAMILY SECRETS BURIED FOR OVER A CENTURY

July 20, 2007

Many shocking stories in my quest to recreate what happened in my family over one hundred years ago came to bear out that - "Truth is stranger than fiction."

Through the years my mother always told me that the restaurant/bar in Bark River, namely, Tom Swift's was originally her grandfather's saloon - the Derouin Saloon in the late 1800s.

In the '50s my husband and I lived in Chicago for a few years and how we looked forward to a summer vacation in Escanaba: Especially the delicious Friday fish fry at Tom Swift's in Bark River - Price $1.00

Being young and engrossed in raising a family at that time I really never had the interest to ask questions or know more about my family's history. I do remember hearing that my Grandmother's brother, Tim Derouin, lost the saloon in a poker game one night. It sounded far-fetched! Was it hearsay? I was about to uncover what transpired.

About 8 years ago while researching my mother's maternal family background the first of many documented stories came to life.

Ferdinand and Adelaide were from Quebec, Canada. I acquired their nuptial record dated 1864. No one in the wedding party could read or write. It stated they could not sign.

I am sure that they were in love and like most couples excited about beginning their married life together. Sometime in the early 1880s they migrated to the Bark River/Schaffer area where many French people had settled. By then they had four children: Fridolin, Mary Alice, Tim and my grandmother, Laura.

Ferdinand Derouin, my great-grandfather, started the Derouin Saloon in Bark River. He owned several properties and was considered a successful business person - however, in 1889 he began to act strangely. He was age 45.

At age 48, in 1892, records show Ferdinand was declared insane. The following is taken from court records:

"During the last three years he has had frequent attacks at regular intervals of insane delusions - was formerly given to running after women; his principle delusion consists in thinking that the husbands of women with whom he has had [affairs] are chasing him to kill him; thinks they are concealed in the cellar of the house at which he stops. Ran away from home three months ago; threw himself out the window of a passenger coach; goes about nights; threatens to whip attendants; gets ugly; threatens to kill himself; carries an axe with which to protect himself."

Sadly the records show Ferdinand spent 10 years at the Northern Michigan Asylum for the insane in Traverse City. There was no asylum in the U.P. at that time. In 1902, Ferdinand's horror came to an end. Records reflect he died from drowning by his own hand.

None of this was ever talked about and I doubt my mother even knew the revelations now coming to light through documented research. I was able to search the saloon chain of ownership at the Register of Deeds office: With the gracious and patient help of Rob Buchler we were able to piece together the saloon history.

Tim, Ferdinand's son, bought out his siblings who inherited the saloon and ran it until 1906 when he lost the saloon to his sister Mary's husband - his brother-in-law, Modeste Hurtubise in a poker game. That fiasco affected many lives.

Berniece Lambert, daughter of Tim, recalls how the family lived poorly and never prospered. Her brother, Palmer Derouin, one-time fire chief in Escanaba and Berniece grew up with resentment toward their father - and so did their mother! Lost the family livelihood in a poker game?!

Bernice says, "My mother scrubbed 25 shirts a week on a board; starched and ironed them for Anthony and Son to supplement the family income." Her dad, Tim, worked sporadically in the woods after losing the saloon.

Modeste Hurtubise sold the saloon six months later to Peter Newhouse for a handsome profit and it changed hands a few times, even owned for a time by the Richer Brewing Company. The Tom Swift family bought the saloon in 1942.

Tom Swift Sr moved his family from Kenosha to take the job as bar manager of the Delta Hotel around 1937. He yearned to go into business for himself.

When his wife, Tootie, viewed the saloon he was interested in buying she wasn't impressed at all. It was dirty with spittoons lined up all along the bar where the cronies hung out - where they drank whiskey, chewed snuff and spit! Mr. Swift received the down payment to buy the bar from none other than a priest friend from Kenosha.

Tootie dug in, cleaned up the place and threw out the spittoons. She was warned that business would dwindle if the spittoons went. But that didn't happen. She introduced fish fries with home cooking made from scratch: home baked beans, homemade rolls, pan fried fish and coffee from the Jewel Tea man made in a big pot with a couple of eggs thrown in. The price at that time for a fish fry was 35 cents.

She added her stamp of class to the place. China cabinets were built and held her beautiful antique dishes. They served 200 on a Friday night in a dining room that held less than fifty. People waited for hours to be served - believe me, it was worth waiting for!

Tom Swift Jr. told me about the slot-machine they kept in the back room of the bar - possibly from Moon Oberg's gas station on Lake Shore Drive. Tom related, "A guy won a lot of money and came back to win more - he lost his paycheck and his wife called the sheriff. They raided the place and removed the slot-machine."

Jack Krause recalls his father frequenting the saloon years before and claimed it was a place where heavy gambling and drinking took place.

Tom Swift Jr and his wife, Barb, ran the bar for ten years after his father died. "The hours were long and they just got burned out," says Tom. They sold the business to the Carsons. Of course there was no resemblance to the original Derouin saloon - but the Swifts created a real landmark and great memories for many folks.

Ron Hurtubise, grandson of Modeste died last month. His wife, Martha, aware of my interest gave me the saloon ledger from 1906 when the Hurtubise family ran the saloon for a few short months. The bottom of the yellowed pages seemed to be nibbled by mice - but the crudely written information is a real gem.

It lists familiar family surnames and charges for 10 and 20 cents plus bartering with potatoes, hay and boarders paying 20 cents for a meal. It records purchasing jugs of whiskey for $1.50. I would say one hundred years later the "walls have talked!" And can there be any doubt that "truth is stranger that fiction?"

The saloon in Bark River rich in history still stands and is now called Cal's Corral.

Ferdinand and Adelaide Derouin
25th Anniversary 1889

Tim and Mary
Derouin
Wedding Photo
1902

Derouin's Saloon
1880's

The Ledger
from 1906

Tom Swift

Tom and Tootie Swift

Chapter 2

World War II Remembered

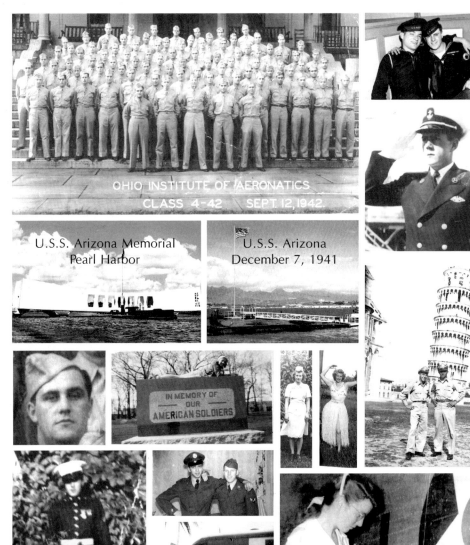

OHIO INSTITUTE OF AERONATICS
CLASS 4-42   SEPT. 12, 1942.

U.S.S. Arizona Memorial
Pearl Harbor

U.S.S. Arizona
December 7, 1941

IN MEMORY OF
OUR
AMERICAN SOLDIERS

War: Similarities and Differences   April 24, 2006

The year is 1943. The United States is at war with Japan and Germany. I am 10 years old and in the fourth grade. The war is evident everywhere... and frightening. In school we had air-raid drills and practiced hiding under our seats in event the school was bombed. The movies portrayed the horrors of war. Homes displayed banners in the windows with stars depicting the number of family members in service. The memories of how I felt can be still dredged up today. Why now? Why me? I thought I may not live to grow up, get married and have children. In my limited self-absorbed world I was consumed with frightening thoughts about bombs and the war.

My husband-to-be was 12 years old. His perspective was entirely different. His brother, Stan was in the Marines and Gary dreamed of someday wearing a uniform and being a soldier. He enjoyed playing soldier games and using play guns with his friends. To them the war was fun and filled with excitement. The movies were filled with war stories and young impressionable boys ran home to play act them out.

My father served in the army under General George Patton in Europe. I remember getting V-mail from him. Victory mail was censored from the war zone. Photos of the mail were taken, transferred to reels, shipped to their destination, and then developed.

I remember going door to door collecting newspapers, binding them and getting paid in defense stamps. We pasted them in a book until we had $18.75 needed to buy a war bond. I remember ration stamps. Coffee, sugar, meat, and gas were rationed. The bigger the family the more tokens you received. We didn't need gas stamps because we didn't even own a car. I remember my sister and me pulling our rusty wagon down to the Relief Office to get free commodities like grapefruit... even dresses. My son asked me recently how I felt about being so poor. I didn't realize we were poor; most families were in the same boat.

The Government requisitioned the Terrace Gardens (Terrace Bay Inn) to house the Coast Guard personnel stationed here. Their mission was to guard the ore docks against potential saboteurs. Iron ore was essential to the war effort and used to make steel for tanks, trucks and bombs.

My husband's father was a volunteer air-raid warden. The look-out post was on the roof of the Delta Hotel (the tallest building at that time). His job was to scan the skies looking for the remote possibility of German enemy aircraft. Wow, that seems really far-fetched today. German prisoners of war were incarcerated in several locations around the U. P. Occasionally, a prisoner escaped but was quickly apprehended. My husband witnessed the capture of one in Escanaba near his home.

Hitler, Germans and Japanese conjured up ill-feelings that weren't dispelled for decades. Now the Germans and Japanese are our friends and Allies. During the war the anti-American Muslims sided with Germany against us - not much has changed!

However, the way wars are fought has changed dramatically. Terrorists have found a way to circumvent traditional methods of combat. They don't need armies and they kill innocent people in the name of God.

Today the threat of one person planting a bomb in our schools is played out in crank calls all over the country. Sadly, we have experienced recent bomb threats in our own community schools. For a day off of school some of own children (citizens) are emulating acts of terror against their peers.

Today's youth do not seem to be traumatized by the current conflict like children of my generation. Daily life is pretty much "business as usual." Perhaps that is a good thing. But in years to come will bomb threats, visions of 9-11 and possible future terrorist atrocities haunt the children of today? Will feelings of ill-will toward Muslims be perpetuated for decades to come? Only time will tell.

Bronze Star   Purple Heart
World War II Medals of Stanton Abrahamson Jr.

SURVIVING WORLD WAR II IN HOLLAND   July 7, 2006

Kees DeHaas was born in Hilversum, Holland (20 miles from Amsterdam) in 1937. He married my childhood friend, the former Joanie DeGrand. The following story is about Kees' World War II survival experience.

Kees was only 3 or 4 years old when the war broke out. "My first recollection was hearing big guns and running to the corner to look for the guns - the sounds were from miles away," relates Kees. His father, a Dutch baker, and his mother, a Hungarian, married in Holland. Kees was the second born of four children. Their family, like thousands of others, would struggle to survive.

The war progressed and Germans occupied the city. Things went from bad to worse. Germans applied sanctions. Water was rationed. Food was scarce. Electricity was shut off. "And we had to go to the woods and cut trees to provide heat," said Kees, with a far-away pained look as he relived the atrocities his family and country experienced.

"Thousands of people didn't survive. They starved to death. 1944-45 was the worst winter. There was no food. I remember the hunger most. We ate tulip bulbs. There were soup kitchens, but you never knew when they were in the neighborhood. The soup smelled awful - you could smell it from the street. Everyday children (who were) holding hands knocked on our door begging for food; some so young they couldn't speak. Signs hung from their neck begging for food," Kees remembers.

"Toward the end of the war, you could smell and see death and devastation everywhere," relates Kees sadly. "People were skin and bones; you could see death looming in their sunken eyes."

Kees' father was a baker, but there were no supplies. A German city ordinance prohibited bakers and butchers to leave the city. Germans closed off the streets in a raid. All males over 18 were picked up and brought to an assembly place (the local soccer stadium). From there they were sorted and shipped to Germany to work at ditch-digging jobs, etc. His father was allowed to return home at night.

Kees' mother left her young children for a week or two at a time to procure food for the family. She bicycled up north to barter with the farmers. She would knit articles to exchange for food and brought home bacon and eggs in the huge basket on the front of her bicycle. Her mission to provide food for her starving family was fraught with danger.

Kees was arrested by the Germans when he was 7. The older boys boosted him through a small window to steal some bread. While reaching for the bread, the row of shelves fell and alerted the Germans. He was taken into custody overnight until his father came to rescue him. Later on, he was shot at while trying to steal pieces of coal off of the ground.

"The Germans were ruthless. If I see a Nazi fanatic today, I still feel resentment," declares Kees, "It reminds me of what we went through." Seeing the North Koreans and their "goose-stepping march" on TV is another reminder of what he witnessed and experienced in Holland.

Holland supports a monarchy. The Queen and the Prince and their cabinet fled to England for safety. The national color is orange. During the war Radio Orange was broadcast from England. The Germans confiscated the radios or the tubes out of the radios - no one was allowed to listen to a radio. Kees' family hid their radio in the rafters. Neighbors would gather to hear the broadcasts. Strange codes such as, 'the fish swam through the net,' were relayed to the Dutch underground.

Kees remembers a Jewish family who lived across the street. "The young boy, about age 10, played the piano beautifully" recalls Kees. "All Jews had to register and display the Star of David on their person. One day I saw the Germans take the family away, never to return. They were undoubtedly taken to an extermination camp."

"We were starving," exclaims Kees. He reluctantly added, "And a neighbor brought meat to cook." Kees' family invited another neighbor lady to share their dinner. What they perceived as "rabbit" was Mimi, the neighbor lady's pussy cat that went missing. She never knew.

One neighbor ingeniously lit their house with bicycle lights all through the house. The family took turns peddling a stationary bike with a generator on the wheel. Kees' family used oil lamps with wicks. There were curfews and everyone had dark paper in the windows to block out any light at night because of the Allied bombings.

Things slowly began to get better. A Dutch and German armistice allowed food to be dropped from planes by the Swedish Red Cross. Each person in the family was allowed one loaf of white bread. "I can still taste that wonderful bread today," remembers Kees. "If it weren't for the food droppings one-half of the population would have died."

In 1962 Kees, at age 25, immigrated to the United States with $60 in his pocket. A church in L.A. was his sponsor. His cosponsor lived in Pasadena. He got his first job as a draftsman, which was his occupation in Holland. His first purchase was a car, then a TV which helped him learn the English language. He went to college nights and obtained an engineering degree. In 1967 he became an American citizen.

Kees and his wife, Joanie, live near Ventura, Cal. They visit Escanaba and the huge DeGrand family every summer. Two years ago they purchased a home in the bluff area to retire in the near future. Kees loves the area. "It is so peaceful and tranquil here." He says the landscape reminds him of Holland.

Joanie and I have been friends since second grade and reminisce about our childhood: playing paper dolls, building doll houses out of shoe boxes, going to movies, roller-skating, going to the beach and dances. Wow! The life we experienced as youngsters was surely a far-cry from Kees' world, his struggle to survive, and the indelible mark left on his psyche.

ROSIE THE RIVETER: ELNORA VADER   July 15, 2006

Elnora Vader has worn many hats during her 89 years: Wife, mother, educator (taught Government at Escanaba High School), esteemed Delta County Commissioner and civic leader. Tucked away in her past is a hat that not many are aware of. That is until now. Joining the World War II war effort in the forties on the home front, Elnora was an original "Rosie the Riveter." For the younger generations unfamiliar with "Rosie," she was a character icon memorialized in a 1942 song "Rosie the Riveter," on postage stamps, and in posters with her flexed biceps and polka-dot bandana proclaiming, "We Can Do It." Over 6 million women joined the work force between 1940 and 1944 filling jobs that had been exclusively held by men. Elnora Vader was one of them.

The World War II Memorial dedication in Washington D. C. has raised consciousness and interest about our men and women who so gallantly and courageously served their country whether at home or abroad. Tom Brokow appropriately coined them "The Greatest Generation."

Alert, bright eyed and articulate it was evident Elnora delighted in reminiscing about her early years, the war years and her family. Born in Fife Lakes near Traverse City, the second of 5 children, Elnora's mother died when she was age 7. During high school she had visions of being a journalist - but her Dad, who owned a Chevrolet Dealership, told her to get that out of her head - girls were either teachers or nurses.

She graduated from High school in 1932 and knew she would have to earn her way through college. "I told my aunt (now my stepmother) I wanted to go to beauty school to help earn my way through college. The family vetoed that plan and arrangements were made for me to go to County Normal School in Traverse City where I lived with a relative and earned a rural teaching certificate. I boarded with a Catholic widow with five children while teaching rural school - but knew I would eventually have to get a BA degree. I even considered nurse's training. I applied to the Traverse City State Hospital but was too late for acceptance into the nursing class. Ultimately I was hired in the hospital section of the Insane Asylum. A correspondence course gave me enough credits to enter Western College (later named Western University) as a sophomore." Elnora was destined to meet her husband, Leonard in college. He graduated in 1938 and Elnora in 1939.

Leonard was drafted into the Army shortly after graduation. Marriage just wasn't affordable yet. She was teaching school and barely making ends meet. "I made thirty-five dollars a month, and Leonard made thirty dollars a month. On the weekend I would make a pot of chili and eat that all week" exclaims Elnora. "At one time, when I was teaching country school (a one-year teaching certificate was all that was required to teach in the country at that time), I even considered being a nun. I was struggling." An education with free room and board seemed enticing to Elnora. (That was before she attended the University and met Leonard). "However, my dad was vehemently opposed to that idea — so, out of respect, I promised him if I considered it further I would discuss it with him again."

Leonard was assigned to the Great Lakes Coast Artillery near Chicago and occasional weekend visits to Kalamazoo were what kept the couple going. It was rumored that eventually Leonard's unit could be transferred to Panama with the threat of Germans bombing the Panama Canal. Elnora was teaching English and History at Fennville High School. "We made a hasty decision to marry the summer of 1941 because only wives, not girlfriends, could visit in Panama. I fully intended to continue teaching at Fennville until I could join my husband in Panama. In the fall, much to my dismay, I was informed they didn't hire married teachers."

Elnora distinctly recalls December 7, 1941. "My husband and our good friends were about to have a piece of pumpkin pie I had made - when someone said, 'The Japs bombed Pearl Harbor!' Instantly, the two men, both stationed at Great Lakes knew they would be sent somewhere else. "That very week the fellas got orders to go to Iccland. They would embark out of New York," recalls Elnora. But when they arrived in New York, a German submarine had been sighted in Long Island Sound - so they were assigned to Ft. Lee, New Jersey." At Christmas time Elnora and her friend went to New York to spend Christmas with their husbands.

Leonard, who had no aspirations of making the army a career, realized with the onset of the war his service time would be extended. He decided to apply to Officer's Training School. He was accepted and sent to Panama. Meanwhile, Elnora found a teaching job at a business college in Kalamazoo. Evenings were spent in class learning riveting in preparation for a job in a factory. She went to work in a defense plant at Willow Run. "The plant operated by Ford motor Company employed 40,000. There were many blacks and people from the South. "The pay was $1.25 an hour. Big money!" exclaims Elnora. "We made B-24 bombers. I worked on the center wing section. Two people worked together: one held the bucking bar and I riveted the two sections of wings together with an air driven rivet gun. At the end we were turning out one plane an hour." She remembers war rations on gas, meat, sugar, and coffee and receiving extra rations for gas because she worked in a defense plant. The fabric of the workplace in America would be forever changed as thousands of women like Elnora experienced earning power, independence, confidence and competence.

Leonard and Elnora moved to Escanaba in 1951. Leonard was employed as a State Veterinarian earning $2000 a year. Elnora was busy raising their family of five - four sons and a daughter. She beamed with pride when I asked her about their vocations. Virginia, the only girl was a veterinarian for 15 years and went on to the University of New Mexico to become a doctor. She lives in Oregon. Charles is a retired Escanaba schoolteacher.

Dan lives in Escanaba with his wife - both are practicing attorneys. John Paul is a doctor and lives in Switzerland. Tom is a doctor (anesthesiologist) and lives in Washington near Whidbey Island. And she is equally proud of her 12 grandchildren and 6 great-grandchildren. One of her grandchildren lives in Israel.

In 1963, Elnora applied for the History instructor position at Escanaba High School. Mr. Baltic said the position was filled but offered her the position of government teacher. She taught until 1981. In between she managed to get her Masters degree at Utah State University. In 1978 she sold her home and spent a year in Switzerland with her son's family and getting to know her grandchildren.

She has been active in the Democratic Party, The League of Women Voters, held the position of Delta County Commissioner from 1975 to 1985, and was appointed by Governor Blanchard to the State Children's Trust Fund for the Prevention of Child Abuse and Neglect. In 1958 she was the first woman to run for a political office in Escanaba running for City Council against Harold Vanlerberghe. She lost. But she has been a winner ever since.

Today, she lives in her own apartment at the Bishop Noa Home, modest and comfortable. Rocking in a favorite chair while watching the humming birds feed outside her window, she reminisces about her early life, the war years, her family and the many students she has taught over the years. A computer nearby keeps her in contact with her family members. Numerous pictures of her grandchildren (received via e-mail) sit beside the computer. Many are from Switzerland. Elnora Vader is one incredible lady— rich in experiences, family and memories. Her positive influence in our community and the lives she has touched lives on.

REIDUN (RY) BARRON:
WORLD WAR II ARMY NURSE

July 16, 2006

Ry was only 4 years old when her sister, Rangfred, age 6, her brother, Martin, age 3, and her mom, age 29, booked passage to America. The immigration register listed three infants. The SS Bergensfjord departed from Stavanger, Norway on April 11, 1926 - final destination for the Sviland family would be Escanaba where Svrre Sviland anxiously awaited their arrival. "I remember being told we traveled first class," recalls Ry, "and that meant we didn't have to go through Ellis Island. None of us spoke English and Dad, who worried about my mother making the trip, always claimed he paid a small fortune for us to travel first class." Ry, even at age 4, vividly remembers her first sight as the ship maneuvered into the New York harbor - the Statue of Liberty. The Svilands would have one more child, Betty, born in Escanaba.

Ry graduated from Escanaba High School in 1939, and enrolled in nursing school at Northwestern University in Evanston, Illinois. "I was a student nurse when the war broke out. I remember my mother calling me and being very upset. She had heard that immigrants without citizenship papers were going to be deported. Whether that was true or not - I'll never know, but I immediately applied for and became a proud citizen of the US in Chicago. Most of my 1944 graduating class went directly into the army because nurses were sorely needed and had not been replaced." Ry and Betty Jaeger (now Jurmu) were among four gals sent to Hawaii. "We really lucked out," says Ry, "the war was winding down, the accommodations and the weather was great - it was like an extended paid vacation trip to Hawaii. Ray Jurmu flew to Hawaii to marry Betty. We all attended their wedding and reception." Shortly after Ry remembers the huge celebration held in downtown Honolulu when the war ended.

In 1946 Ry was transferred to Guam. "It was extremely hot and like a jungle there. Of course there was no air-conditioning. Everything was very primitive, including the shack-like hospital with rickety wooden steps. The nurses didn't have to wear stockings, and our shifts were short because of the heat. Day nurses worked from 7am to 1pm and 1pm to 7pm. At night it cooled off so nurses had to work 12 hour shifts." In the afternoon either an ambulance or jeep would take the nurses to the beach and pick them up. With a mischievous twinkle in her eye, Ry related how the patients loved to have their picture taken with the nurses. "One patient claimed he wanted a picture with her to send home to his wife."

A high wall surrounded their living quarters. Guards were stationed around the complex even though the war had ended. "We had to be very careful and always double-dated for safety." recalls Ry "There was still a threat of Japanese snipers - so the men carried guns." The Japanese philosophy was to fight until you die. There were cases of Japanese soldiers in the jungles for months and even years unaware the war had ended.

Finally, Ry's tour of duty was over. She was on a plane headed for the United States, and ultimately Fort Sheridan, Illinois where she would be discharged as a First Lieutenant. Suddenly the plane developed engine trouble. "We lost an engine over the Pacific and we were told to put on our Mae West (life preserver). It was frightening and scary!" said Ry. "Then we made an emergency landing in Hawaii. We spent the night in Hawaii while repairs were made." The remainder of the flight proved uneventful.

Ry worked for a short time at the University of Michigan Hospital upon returning to the states. She eventually returned to Escanaba where she was hired at St. Francis Hospital and worked in the Pediatrics Department.

The time was the late 1940's. CJ's bar downstairs of the Delta Hotel was a popular nightspot and gathering place of young people during that era. Bill Clark, (radio announcer for WDBC) played piano along with other local singing talent - Bernard and Mim Ammel (eventually Mrs. Ivan Kobasic.) It was at CJ's where Bob Barron proposed to Ry. "On the first date!" exclaims Bob. "Not quite," says Ry. "I had known Bob forever from school years. But I think it was three or four dates before he asked me to marry him. I asked him the next day if he remembered what he had said last night. 'Of course,' he said, 'I asked you to marry me.'"

Bob attended Michigan State University and was in the ROTC program when the war broke out. He left the day after Pearl Harbor for duty in the states and eventually spent two years in Italy as an Intelligence Officer earning the rank of Captain. Ry and Bob were married when Bob returned to college to complete his senior year after the war. Upon graduation Bob worked for General Motors in Bay City - until he was offered a job from Mead. He was Personnel Director at Mead for years. His career with Mead took the Barron's to North Carolina, Cincinnati and back to Escanaba where Bob eventually retired.

Bob and Ry are the parents of three children; Chris, who lives with her family in a suburb of Memphis, Tennessee and Bob and Mark, who both work for Mead in Escanaba. The Barrons also have two grandchildren. Ry, now 83, enjoys coffee get-togethers with her neighborhood friends. Like any typical Scandinavian household - there is always fresh coffeecake and the coffee is always on!

STORIES FROM THE FRONT STILL HAUNT

May 29, 2006

Tom Hanks' gut-wrenching portrayal in *Saving Private Ryan* garnered him an Academy Award. The movie won the 1998 Best Picture Award and also served to reignite interest about World War II. Tom Brokaw's book, *The Greatest Generation* has preserved many of the personal stories about the great heroes who fought in that war.

My cousin, Don Jacobs, was one of those men. Here is part of his story. Don graduated shortly after the Japanese bombed Pearl Harbor. He, like many of his classmates, walked directly off the Escanaba High School graduation stage and into the war. He enlisted in the Marines and traveled by train to San Diego to begin boot training. He was just 18.

Raised on a farm, and carrying a rifle from the age of 10, he was no stranger to fire arms. He began training in the Rifle and Sharpshooter division. His experience in the Marines would change him and his outlook forever. War is Hell - and the horrific memories of blood-spilling among his buddies and the enemy has been forever seared in his mind.

Don's division was involved in many hard fought campaigns including the battle of Okinawa in the Ryukus Islands located right below the southern end of Japan. "We were knocking on their back door," Don related. "The battle of Okinawa was the most costly casualty battle of the war. It took six months to take that island."

After regrouping and more training his unit went on some much needed liberties and rested up for their next maneuver. From there they boarded ship again for a rendezvous about 300 miles off the coast of Japan. An attack force was being formed that included battle wagons, cruisers, destroyers and troop ships to be in the initial assault wave on Japan at the port of Nagasaki. They were within hours of beginning the assault when suddenly a message came over the ship's loudspeaker system.

"'HEAR THIS, HEAR THIS! THE WAR IS OVER!'" Don said, "Our initial reaction was what kind of a joke is this? We were up on top of the deck hollering and talking, confused by the message, when we were stunned by another message."

"'HEAR THIS, HEAR THIS. WE HAVE CONFIRMATION - THE UNITED STATES HAS DROPPED A SECOND ATOMIC BOMB ON THE PORT OF NAGASAKI. THE WAR IS OVER'"

No one had heard the term atomic bomb. They were trying to make sense of the message. Even the chemists and those schooled in physics in the unit could not shed light on the word "atomic." Finally the realization set in that the war must be over. Guys began dancing and celebrating on the deck.

Now, instead of being an invasion force, the Second Marine Division became the first occupation troops to hit the shores of Japan. For the first two weeks they slept on a concrete slab in the bomb crater. None of them had ever heard the term "atomic" and consequently were not aware of radiation and its deadly effects. Perhaps our government didn't even realize the long term effects at that time.

The slab of concrete was all that was left intact of an old railroad station. "As far as you could see there wasn't a wall standing. What few people that were alive stood along the streets at attention - rigid as a board." relates Don. "They never moved a hair having been told we were going to kill them all. They had been brainwashed by the Japanese military."

The Japanese survivors of the atomic bomb were petrified and frightened. Death and destruction was everywhere. The marines started handing the kids candy and whatever they had in their pockets. Finally the people realized the marines were not there to hurt or kill them. And they immediately started trying to clean up, pick up the pieces out of the rubble and erect some kind of shelter to lie under.

"It was the saddest sight I had ever seen," recalls Don. "I watched a Japanese carpenter with next to nothing as far as tools trying to put things together. I marveled at his cleverness. My opinion of the Japanese people was shifting dramatically. Going into war I, like my buddies, inherited a dislike of the Japanese and couldn't negate the reason why we were there: The sneak attack and bombing of Pearl Harbor.

Conversely, the longer I remained in the occupation force in Japan the more admiration I had for them as a truly amazing people. Living proof of their ability to rebound is evident on the world stage today in their economy, their technology, and their work ethic."

Chapter
3
The "Golden" Years

SENIOR STATUS: THE 'GOLDEN YEARS'? March 30, 2007

Seniors that reach the "Golden Years" can consider that achievement a real privilege. Shouldn't they? More people than any time in history are reaching their 70s, 80s and 90s. I am not convinced "Golden Years" is a true representation - it might instead be a bit of a stretch! Many seniors have an overwhelming list of problems related to health, depression, loneliness, changing living arrangements, financial problems and end-of-life decisions.

Health problems head the list. You may be a caregiver to a spouse with a terminal illness or be seriously ill yourself. More seniors suffer pain, like arthritis and degenerative diseases, than other age groups. Pain management clinics were unheard of years ago - perhaps because people didn't live as long.

Depression is real. And so is loneliness. Many problems are bearable if you have a partner to share concerns with. But in many cases seniors are isolated. We live in a mobile society, so children and family members are scattered all over the country.

Seniors may have lived all of their life in one home. Changing living arrangements can be devastating. They miss their "things" and "treasures" that have surrounded them throughout their lives.

They want to bring all of their "treasures" with them to senior housing, but it's impossible. Their world becomes smaller and smaller. In many cases assisted living is next. No one could possibly know how these changes affect the psyche until they are faced with similar decisions.

At one point some folks are transferred to a nursing home. The dependency alone has to be depressing. Finances dictate what type of facility is available to them. Certainly, thoughts of dying haunt many elderly seniors. How can it not?

Some people put off decisions like funeral arrangements and purchasing a burial plot and other end-of-life choices. I probably would have been in that category except for the constant nudging of my husband.

Ten years ago he wanted to purchase a burial plot. After many discussions we couldn't agree on the cemetery. The indecision went on for four years. Finally, as my husband relates: "We compromised and bought a plot in the cemetery of my wife's choosing. Some compromise!"

The headstone was next. We agreed on that purchase. And it is comforting to have those housekeeping choices tended to. I have seen families who leave the choices up to their children, and instead of a headstone the kids may enjoy a trip to Hawaii. Then others just don't want to deal with their own mortality - so they don't make any decisions.

Choices are many: cremation, conventional burial, memorial service or no services at all. My husband has a great outlook for when he departs. In fact, he acts like he is hosting a party. He is busy choosing the music he wants played at his funeral: *Through the Years*, by Kenny Rodgers and *Could I Have This Dance for the Rest of My Life* by Anne Murray and *Years* by Barbara Mandrel. I might as well write his obituary and put it in a file.

It reminds me of when Ray Sabuco died. Ray knew he was terminally ill and arranged his own "memorial service" by invitation only. It was held at Marco's Stardust Lounge, which he owned. The drinks flowed freely and the food was wonderful. Yes, it was a unique party and maybe raised some eyebrows!

The host, Ray, was on the huge screen talking to all of us. He talked about his wonderful life, his family and his hobbies. He loved hunting. He told us not to mourn, that he had a great life and wanted everyone to have a happy time: Drink, eat and be merry!

At the time it seemed so surreal, but in retrospect, his way of saying goodbye has left us with good memories of him and his departing party to which we were invited. Not a bad idea!

Of course young people think they are invincible. I remember when we were first married and living in Chicago. An insurance man knocked at our door and wanted to schedule an appointment to pitch life insurance. I was 19. "We don't plan on dying!" I smugly told him. "Nobody does." he said. Ahh, youthful naivety can be bliss!

We try to keep it lighthearted at our house. Our retirement life is busy and filled with appointments: doctor, x-rays, blood tests, eye exams, podiatrist, dentist and cardiologist. Occasionally, there is a trip to the emergency room or a stint in the hospital. And many, many trips to the drug store.

Conversations are caught up about health: Who has what illness, how are they treating it, and how are you feeling now? Who is your family doctor? Seems you just get comfortable with a doctor and he leaves the community. Not like years ago when doctors made house calls and were fixtures in the community forever!

Choices for health insurance coverage are more complicated. Most seniors need help. Seniors need to take a pro-active posture in medications prescribed to them and seek second opinions about recommended surgeries. All of these decisions become overwhelming when memories and abilities may be on the decline.

Then there is the question about wills. We have had a will since 1975. It has been updated twice. It is on our to-do list to update again. Insurance policies should be updated if a beneficiary dies. Look at the Anna Nicole Smith fiasco. When her son died he was her only beneficiary. Then she had a baby and five months later when she died, her will had never been updated - yet she was surrounded by lawyers.

Wills should be updated when there is a change in circumstances. Of course we should all have a living will or directive. Wishes need to be in writing to avoid being kept alive with artificial means if that is not your choice. The same is true if you do not want to be resuscitated.

Ahh, so much for the Golden Years!

SENIOR FUN AND FRUSTRATIONS   September 1, 2006

Senior power! We are the fastest growing population because of advances in medicine and technology. According to the 2000 Census there are 35 million older adults in the U.S., representing 12.4 percent of the total population. What is interesting is that we are so much alike about how we think and feel.

Many seniors detest changes - especially men. Try moving their favorite chair. Some of the more daring seniors have braved the computer - not mastered it mind you - but like me have learned enough to navigate a little. Many others want nothing to do with it. My daughter insisted I get a computer about seven years ago. She spent a few days visiting, helped me shop for one, and then proceeded to teach me the basics. For a year or so I wondered why I let her talk me into this thing that just used up space in my office. Now I wonder how I could possibly live without one.

It took my husband a little longer and a bit more frustration, but he has also learned to do basics: Pull up sports scores, check the weather and news, pull up sports scores, read e-mail, and pull up more sports scores.

My mother was so proud when she became a senior citizen. Being a product of the Depression, she raved about the 10 percent off perks. Yet, the first time someone asked me if I was a senior citizen at a theatre in Florida, I thought, "How dare you to ask." Was she implying that I looked like one?

Technology does get complicated and frustrating at times. We waited for our grandson to visit so he could set our clocks or fix the VCR. He was 6 years old! My 12-year-old great-granddaughter is still teaching me computer skills.

Most seniors will be able to relate to the following:

We used to begin our evening out on the town at 10 p.m. - and stay out until 4 a.m. Now we have inverted those numbers - we rise as 4 a.m. and retire at 10 p.m.

I walk into a room and can't remember what I was looking for. I grope for names of people I have known for years and for words to explain something. I am up all hours of the night - for bathroom breaks and just for ... well, nothing. I take a nap in the afternoon. It seems like we revert to babies, except we don't need a bottle or a pacifier.

Some of us may be good at telling stories, over and over and over. Some of us are aware that other people's grandchildren are not nearly as cute as ours. Some of us are not really grouchy - we just don't like loud music, traffic, crowds, waiting, politicians and unruly kids.

Some favorite senior statements are:

Your mind makes contracts your body can't keep.

Your favorite part of the newspaper is "20 Years Ago Today."

Your knees buckle and your belt won't.

Your children begin to look middle-age.

You're 17 around the neck, 42 around the waist, and 96 around the golf course.

You look forward to another dull evening.

And you look forward to another dull evening. (We also repeat)

And the nicest thing about living in a small town:

When you don't know or remember what you are doing someone else always does.

Think about this: In about 40 years we will have millions of old ladies running around with tattoos. Somehow I can't envision my grandmother sitting in her favorite rocker with tattoos all over her body and body piercing. Can you?

Wear your senior status with pride! It is not the senior

citizens who took the great melody out of music (try humming today's songs), the pride out of appearance (the more sloppy and hole-riddled jeans, the better), the courtesy out of driving (young people giving the finger to seniors), the romance out of love (lay down - I want to talk to you), the commitment out of marriage (one in two end up divorced), the nativity scene out of our cities, civility out of behavior, and God out of our government and school. Think of it! God has been excommunicated!

Some of us may be saggy, lumpy and wrinkled, but we do understand and honor the real meaning of patriotism. You will see tears in our eyes and pride swelling in our hearts when we stand at attention on Veterans Day and on the Forth of July, our great country's birthday.

The greatest thing about senior humor is that we seniors laugh the loudest and longest at all of the jokes about us. We take it in stride because so much of it rings true.

Recently, on the computer that I was against purchasing and now can't live without, this Prayer for Senility caught my attention.

"God grant me the senility to forget the people I never liked anyway, the good fortune to run into the ones I do, and the eyesight and hearing to tell the difference."

LOCAL CASINO DRAWS 'THE GRAY ARMY'   April 19, 2006

For years people have been traveling to Las Vegas for gambling, night life, and great entertainment. Including me! A check on the Reba Mc Entire Show in Vegas recently had a price tag of 400 dollars! Crazy—yes, but that's a fact. And Celine Dion's performance goes for anywhere from 175 dollars to 400 dollars.

The Island Casino right in our own back yard offers great top-notch headliners at a fraction of the price. Some headliners that have been here in the past were Lou Rawls, Bobby Vinton, Englebert Humperdink and Kenny Rogers. All seats were 20 to 45 dollars! Unbelievable!

The Casino is presently undergoing a huge renovation that includes enlargement of the "show room." The draw of headliners similar to what Vegas offers will only get bigger and better.

And then there are the slots! I am most familiar with them. For me it is kind of a diversion from my caregiver duties to go out there and push the buttons or pull the lever for hours at a time.

What's more - you can go alone and not feel conspicuous. Yet, I never frequented the Casino until recently.

Sometimes I win a jack-pot. That is most exciting! Your light goes on, flickers and red seven's or some winning combination is displayed. All wins on some machines over 250 dollars are hand pay. People walk by and 'oh' and 'ah' with envy while you wait for the pay attendant. Other times I lose. We don't talk about that.

It is amazing how many white-haired folks are regulars. They stream off of buses from all over and stay a minimum of four hours. Some are in wheelchairs. Some are pushing walkers. Some have canes. I truly find the people that frequent the casino fascinating. I have secret names for some of them.

First, there is Betty-Bah-Humbug. She has been there whenever I am and just walks around in a glum mood and complains, "The machines are turned off. No one is winning anything." If I tell her I just won a jackpot she will say, "Well, you must be getting special treatment."

Then there is Inquisitive-Irene. She will pull up a stool at the machine next to you and demand to know how long you have been there, and whether or not anyone has "hit" anything on the machine she is contemplating playing.

Keith-Know-It-All gives everyone advice. "Vary it! Play one quarter, then two. Trick the machine. Professionals stick to one machine until they "hit." Play the end machines only: They get more play."

One-Coin-Connie isn't unique. There are dozens of them. She goes from machine to machine with her bucket and plays one coin hoping to hit it big. Sizzling-Sally plays only the Sizzler machines.

Tom-Tells-It-All plunks down at the machine next to you and proceeds to tell you his life story: married four times and will never do it again. "Of course, I picked the wrong women," he whines oblivious to the fact no one is listening or responding...or even cares.

And how about Irritating Irma or Ivan who hovers behind you waiting for you to leave the machine they want to play.

Every now and then you can hear screams of excitement from the Blackjack tables or the pounding beat to music in the bar. The Wheel of Fortune hits and spins. The aroma of mouth-tempting food sometimes permeates the air mixed with the occasional smell of smoke. The loud speaker calls out a warning of buses about to depart.

The landscape changes: During the week the Casino resembles a large "PLAY-PEN" for seniors with a sprinkling of younger folks. The week-end draws younger people mixed with the usual kaleidoscope of white hair, wheelchairs, walkers and canes.

Many ladies are widows and look forward to the hustle and bustle of being around people, and playing the slots. It adds excitement to their lives. They no longer sit at home in a rocking chair with a "poor me" attitude. They don their canes and walkers and become part of the Casino scene. I think it is a good thing. Of course, that is, provided a person can handle it and gamble sensibly.

AGING: CHALLENGES, OR OPPORTUNITIES?   June 23, 2006

I enjoy writing. It's creative and my way of relaxing. And the acceptance from readers has been overwhelming. Thank you for the e-mails and phone calls. The nostalgic articles really hit a note with many of you. Then it occurred to me that not only do I think about the past and enjoy talking and writing about it, but I think about the future, too, in terms of aging and yes, mortality. Yet, I don't write about that.

When I was young, I would check out the births and weddings in the paper. Now I hear my peers say the first thing they read is the obituaries - just like me. Conversations with our age group usually go like this: "Did you hear John Doe had a heart attack? Or, Jane Doe has cancer." Men undergoing heart surgery is most common. And just about every other person I know has had a hip or knee replacement. So it is only normal to think about possible infirmities and our own mortality as we age.

The way we think begins to change. Yesterday I was taking my morning walk at the high school track. It is convenient because we live near there and it's fun to keep count of my mileage. My husband heard an ambulance go by our house and imagined I might have collapsed while walking. By the time I returned home he had worked himself into a frazzle.

Or like the time I was shopping in Florida. My husband and son waited patiently in the mall at a designated place. I didn't realize there were two mall entrances to this huge department store. Consequently, I went out the wrong one. I waited for two hours frantic that either my husband or son must have met with a heart attack or worse. I checked with security who inquired if I had checked the other entrance.

Other entrance?

There they were sitting, half worried that something might have happened to me and half upset that I had shopped so long. Recently my husband read his medical report and was dismayed at being referred to as an *elderly* gentleman. One time when he went to a Rose Bowl game in California he had to rush to board his connecting flight. He heard an airline employee call ahead about an elderly gentleman. He turned around to see who was behind him - then realized *he* was the elderly gentleman being referred to.

He was shocked!

And he is amazed at how many people open doors for him. White hair or a lack of it has its advantages. I guess inwardly we don't equate our age with the outward aging of our bodies. In our mind we can and want to mow the grass, shovel snow or dance the night away - it's our body that rebels.

He remembers the time when he was about 60 and a customer who frequented our dry cleaners always called him "sonny." The customer was in his eighties. Now my husband refers to sixty-year-olds as kids. He bantered back and forth with a clerk recently, and mentioned proudly that he has been married for 56 years. She replied in shock, "to the same woman!?"

My husband has been through some really serious health issues in the past year - and survived. Now we consider each day a gift. It is not always easy, but for the most part we tend to look at the glass as half-full rather than-half empty.

Think of the wisdom our age group has gained through life experiences. It's wisdom we can impart to our children and grand-children. Life's lessons cause mellowing to occur through the years; some folks (hmm, mostly men) that were as rigid as an oak tree in the beginning become willows and sway and bend. Hey, that's a good thing!

Mostly, it is good to realize that basically we are all alike. As we age we have many of the same concerns. The trick is to keep busy, develop interests, exercise if you can, encourage social contacts and try to think positive. Faith helps too!

My husband pointed out that my writing is a gift, and then referred to Jean Nicholson's (friend and artist) painting as a gift. I should have replied, "Your gift is far greater than a talent; giving empathy and encouragement to your friends in need."

Instead, I flippantly asked him what his gift was. His reply:

"Having you for a wife!" Now how sweet can that be?

ART LINKLETTER:
GET READY FOR THE NEXT PRIME OF YOUR LIFE!

January 5, 2007

Art Linkletter isn't letting any grass grow under his feet. Together with Mark Victor Hansen, co-creator of the *Chicken Soup for the Soul* series they spawned a new exciting book: *How to Make the Rest of Your Life the Best of Your Life* published in July 2006.

Art Linkletter is 94 years young. He was born in Canada where, as an orphan, he was adopted by a Baptist evangelist minister. Shortly, thereafter, the family moved to Massachusetts and eventually ended up in California. Art graduated from San Diego State College in 1934.

Most will remember his long running shows: *House Party* (25 years) and *People are Funny* (19 years). He has written 23 books. Among them are *Old Age Isn't For Sissies* and *Kids Say the Darndest Things*, one of the top 14 best sellers in American publishing history.

After reading his newest book I am convinced that it is a must read for every senior. Personally, I couldn't put the book down. Not only is there ways to improve your health and stay fit, keep your memory from fading, enjoy sex through your senior years and keep a vibrant spiritual life, but there is humor abound.

For example: A husband and wife, both sixty years old, were celebrating their thirty-fifth anniversary. During their party, a fairy appeared to congratulate them and grant them each one wish. The wife wanted to travel around the world.

The fairy waved her wand and poof! - the wife had tickets in her hand for a world cruise. Next the fairy asked the husband what he wanted. He said, "I wish I had a wife thirty years younger than me."

So the fairy picked up her wand and poof! - the husband was ninety.

Art Linkletter and his wife Lois of 70 years have had their share of tragedy in their lives. In 1969 their daughter, under the influence of LSD jumped to her death from her sixth story apartment. They have also lost a son and have dealt with a life threatening illness of another child.

Those were tumultuous years for the Linkletters. They had to go on - and they were able to overcome the heart-ache. Art went on to become a professional lecturer on drug abuse, positive thinking and gerontology. He schedules 75 lectures a year: Incredible considering his age.

Art says, "Don't ask me if I am going to retire. Retire to what? I love what I am doing because I think it matters. And I think this book can matter to anyone"

As I mentioned the book is filled with wonderful information and a good dose of humor.

You know you are getting older...

...When happy hour is a nap.

...When your idea of a night out is sitting on the patio.

...When your idea of weight lifting is standing up.

The architects of the book believe that age 60 is the new 40, the new middle-age - and age 80 is the new 60. And I have to agree. Our grandparents seemed older than the grandparents of today. Today's more youthful grandmothers might wear jeans, sport a tattoo (ugh), run a marathon, start a business, write a best seller, mountain climb, sing, dance and entertain and the list goes on and on.

Not exactly the stereotypical grandmother of yesterday when grandmothers looked tired and older than their years, wore housedresses covered with an apron, a hair net and for the most part did not work outside the home - nor did they have washers, dryers and the myriad comforts of today that make life easier.

There are many myths and misconceptions about how we age - lifestyle or genetics? On the chapter that addresses this question the final score may surprise you: Lifestyle 70, and genes 30. But think about the diseases we bring on ourselves by what we put into our bodies.

The list is lengthy. Dietary choices, obesity, smoking and alcohol are culprits that cut years off of our life expectancy - not to mention the quality of life and energy sucked out of us from poor choices. Exercise also plays a huge part in delaying our destiny with the Grim Reaper.

I love the humor in the book:

Two old men had been best friends for years. They both lived to their early 90s when one of them fall deathly ill. His friend visits him on his deathbed, and they're reminiscing about their long relationship when the friend asks, "Listen, when you die, do me a favor. I want to know if there is baseball in heaven."

The dying man said, "We've been friends for years, this I will do for you." And then he dies. A couple of days later, his surviving friend is sleeping when he hears his friend's voice. The voice says, "I've got good news and bad news. The good news is that there's baseball in heaven."

"What's the bad news?"

"You're pitching Wednesday."

Did I mention how great laughter is for our well-being?

Three elderly men are at the doctor's office for a memory test. The doctor asks the first man, "What is three times three?" "274" is his reply. The doctor rolls his eyes and looks up at the ceiling and says to the second man, "It's your turn. What is three times three?" "Tuesday," replies the second man.

The doctor shakes his head sadly then asks the third man, "Okay, your turn. What's three times three?" "Nine," says the third man. "That's great," said the doctor. "How did you get that?" "Simple," he says, "just subtract 274 from Tuesday."

You've got to love this one!

A reporter was interviewing a 104-year-old woman: "And what do you think is the best thing about being 104?" the reporter asked.

She replied: "No peer pressure."

Art says, "Get ready for the next prime of your life! Make the 'rest of your life the best years of your life'."

Many Senior Frustrations Deal with Either Health Issues or Technology
November 17, 2006

It seems seniors must deal with many frustrations, and they mount up as the years go by. Health issues top the list, but there are others. Today's technology can leave us confused and adamant that we will not waste our remaining brain power on trying to figure out digital cameras and other mystery marvels of today.

HEATH ISSUES: We have a special calendar to keep track of doctor appointments: cardiologist, general physician, optometrist, dentist, podiatrist (it gets difficult to bend to clip toe nails). Multiply those appointments by three - my husband, son and myself - and the calendar gets filled very quickly. Often we make an appointment at the doctor's office only to get home and realize that day is already occupied with other appointments.

Then there are the constant lab work-ups: A fasting blood test and an early-morning visit to the lab to draw blood to check cholesterol and thyroid levels, potassium, sugar, calcium and triglycerides among a host of other blood screening tests and urine analysis. Then there is my yearly trip to the x-ray department for a mammogram. Sandwich in-between my husband's bout with congestive heart failure that lands him in the hospital for a couple of days to get everything back on track again, or even the occasional visit to the emergency room with heart palpitations.

The ambulance has been at our doorstep four times in just over a year. A five-week trip to Houston for heart surgery almost proved fatal. One time the medics literally scooped up my husband who collapsed in the parking lot of an Escanaba restaurant, but the "cool cat" with nine lives prevailed and golfed regularly this past summer. He's like the Energizer Bunny - he keeps on going and going and going!

Medications are endless. One day is reserved to fill pill boxes. Gary takes 12 pills everyday, Gary Jr. takes four and I take three, with one being an aspirin. It's not all bad though. We socialize and meet our peers during these trips to the drug store and the doctor's office. We discuss operations, what pills we are taking and how we are feeling. We talk about other peers and their infirmities: Who had a hip replacement, a knee replacement, a recent hospitalization, who is dying or who recently passed on.

Insurance choices become overwhelming. Finally we sit down with staff at UPCAP in Escanaba for much-needed advice. We have three people and umpteen plans to consider. We file away insurance papers, print-outs of lab work and other important documents. Then our senior moments take over. Where did we put this or that? Did we pay that bill yet? When I can't locate whatever I'm searching for I blame Gary for throwing it away. Then it shows up somewhere. Oops! Sorry!

It seems like light years away from our younger years when we were in the mainstream: Raising a family, our jobs, involved with the kids activities and sports, clubs and politics, dancing the night away, energy to burn the candle at both ends and on and on. I wish we could have bottled some of that energy!

Years ago we remember elderly family members complaining about aches and pains, and perhaps thought they should get a life! At the time I was jogging on Lincoln Road and entering races for people over 50 - and winning! Now here we are at the same stage in life with our aches and pains. Rich in experiences and memories, we can dredge up what happened 50 years ago, but what happened two weeks ago might be a mystery.

Sleeping should be natural at night. Wrong! As you age your bladder must shrink and cause sleep disturbances. Sometimes bathroom trips occur three or four times a night. Afternoon naps become a necessity needed to sustain energy.

The hospital personnel know Gary Sr. on a first-name basis. Ah, the joys of living in a small town! Everyone knows you and everything you need is relatively close: Doctors' offices, hospital, drug stores and funeral homes.

TODAY'S TECHNOLOGY: Sometimes I wonder if they invent things just to stump seniors. I had my digital camera for over a year before I called the company and finally mastered it - somewhat. And, for example, consider our car: There are gadgets and buttons I still haven't discovered what they are for. I still can't set the clock in the car. That takes a trip to the dealer. Even the dealer is unsure of some of the gadgets. Whatever happened to on and off?

And how about items you purchase that say, "some light assembly required." You open the package to discover 50 parts and 300 nuts and screws with instructions that require a Ph.D. A recent TV purchase drove us wild: "Are you interested in HDTV, black or silver, what size, resolutions, wide screen or not, floor set, wall mounted flat panel or table top? What about DLP, plasma, LCD, front or rear projection, surround sound, inputs, controllers?"

The president signed into law that all (OTA?) television programming must be broadcast digitally by 2009 - a new TV is in your future - so you might as well get it over with. Or should we wait to purchase until 2009? We may not even be here! In that case the only choices are simple: Where will I be buried, cremation or casket?

We gambled on being here in 2009 and finally purchased a HDTV 60 inch widescreen. It's great for watching ball games! Now we just need to figure out how to operate all the buttons on the remote.

NEVER STOP DANCING!   May 11, 2007

We strive for longevity, yet we fear many of the changes that are associated with advancing age. We worry about a loss of independence or perhaps a decline in our memories. We try to "hang on" to our physical attractiveness.

Even at a young age we search for signs of wrinkles. Wrinkles, hair color and hair loss along with weight gain are all multi-million dollar businesses: They include plastic surgery, creams, hair color, diet pills and diet books. Weight loss alone is a 30 billion dollar a year business. We think the greatest compliment we can receive is that we do not look our age.

The term "golden years" creates much black humor among the old about the losses that accompany advancing age. I can remember my mother being so proud when she became a "senior citizen" like it was a badge of honor. She liked the 10 percent off perks.

There really does seem to be an underlying resentment between generations. Jokes are rampant about incompetence of the elderly such as being too old to drive or of being absentminded. It is probably difficult for the young to envision what they eventually will become. I am sure when I was young I was oblivious to being old one day. That time seemed light years away.

The other side of the coin is that the elderly become intolerant of the behavior and tastes of succeeding generations. They don't like their clothes, their music, their behavior, their lack of manners or for that matter - their values.

For example: When I go to the super market young checkers are more interested in conversation with the person packaging the groceries. Thank you seems to be a word that has escaped their vocabulary.

You may get a canned response like, "have a good day" or "there you go" with barely any eye contact. They may even just plunk the receipt and the change in your hand and say nothing. What an ultimate put down to our humanity at any age: To be ignored.

I just celebrated my 74th birthday and feel very fortunate to be in relatively good health.

My daughter, Vicki (Victoria as she now likes to be called) sent me my usual gift; a book. She knows I am an avid reader with my nose in a book every chance I get. The book, *And Never Stop Dancing* must have been written for me!

It is a book that imparts great wisdom, humor and common sense. One chapter addresses loss as an inevitable consequence of the human condition. And the truth is if we survive long enough we will encounter many losses. Grieving, unfortunately, is part of life. One who has experienced a loss and knows the heartache is better equipped to console others and offer hope.

The ultimate message is *And Never Stop Dancing!* Even in the face of adversity!

What does that mean? It means that even though we are in a world where bad things happen unexpectedly or even routinely we need to develop resilience when tragedy occurs to protect us from feelings of despair. Some things we must accept - there is no choice.

Eleanor Roosevelt once said, "You have to accept whatever comes and the only thing is that you meet it with courage and the best you have to give."

We have heard many times that life is for the living. Life is a precious gift. Getting up each morning with courage is a matter of attitude. And this is where we have a choice.

There are chapters with much humor: Take for example, "Marriage ruins lots of relationships." Most of us choose partners when we are very young. Looks and passion are usually the main attraction for men. If it works out you are in the minority today.

If it falls apart Dr. Livingston, author of the book, says, "When I ask what they fought about, it's always the same: children, money, sex, in-laws, and all the things that consume a marriage when partners don't love each other anymore."

Why is it so hard to get it right? Once divorced the adventure of looking for that "soul mate" starts again. Livingston states, "Not much is learned in the whole painful process from the fact that second marriages have a higher failure rate than first marriages."

But do we stop dancing? No! We have a romantic idea that we will find the person that completes us.

Author Dani Shapiro, *Picturing the Wreck* says: This is the tyranny of marriage: the vows which bind us together allow us to become our worse selves. Thrown dishes, slammed doors, faces contorted like an infant's - all part of the contract. No one tells us this.

"No one tells us that the only unconditional love is between parent and child...But passion between a man and woman is finite. If it lasts a thousand days, count yourself lucky."

That, I might add, is a somewhat pessimistic view point with maybe some elements of truth. I am sure most of us have experienced slammed doors or worse - silence and indifference, the ultimate put down. But the message is: Never stopped dancing! You maneuver through the mine field of married life and persevere.

Physically and figuratively I hope I "never stop dancing."

Life can't possibly be all "peaches and cream!"

57 years later I am blessed with a wonderful caring family and a soul mate - someone with whom I have experienced the pain of adversity and the pleasure associated with the years of shared great memories.

Life is about never giving up. NEVER STOP DANCING!!

THIS COLUMN IS ABOUT...   June 22,2007
OH, DAMN IT, I FORGOT!!!

Have you ever walked into a store and could not remember why you had gone there? Or walked into a room to get something and wonder what it is that you wanted? Or not being able to find a word that you use frequently in that great computer we call memory? I have even been driving someplace in town and have had to stop and think: Where am I going?

When these memory glitches start to happen it is frightening. Sometimes I can't remember a phone number I call often -- like the drug store. Many of my peers say they experience similar memory glitches. Of course with people living longer and the prevalence of Alzheimer's, our first thought is: Am I beginning to show signs of something more to come?

Yes, for years we just take our brain for granted and assume our memory and thinking will always be there for us. The most common type of change involves trouble recalling someone's name.

Joan, my best friend since second grade is here for the summer from California. The four of us were dining when a more recent friend stopped by out table to chat for a moment. I started to introduce them: "This is -dah, I couldn't remember the name of my friend of 65 plus years."

I looked at the friend who stopped to chat. Silence! My mind drew a blank. I couldn't think of her name either. Finally they introduced themselves and saved my pride.

My husband has trouble remembering faces. He can see

someone and not recognize them even though he may have seen them weeks or months before. He has always had trouble with names.

One example: When we owned several dry cleaners he would occasionally wait on a customer. Then he recognized faces but couldn't remember most names. One day a gentleman (good customer) walked in with an arm full of clothes to be cleaned. The conversation went like this.

Customer: "Hi Gary! How is it going today? What did you think of the Packers last week?"

Gary: "Busy day today, you know how it is - everyone wants their clothes for the week-end. Farve had a great game - blah, blah, blah."

Now Gary is struggling to remember this guy's name - He begins to write on the invoice and in an effort to conceal his lack of memory he says to the guy, "How do you spell your name again?"

That blew Gary's cover. The guy says exasperated, "Smith, the name is Smith. S-M-I-T-H."

Yet, ask him the starting line-up for the 1945 Detroit Tigers. He will recite the name of every player. Or ask him about a football game he played in 1948 and he can recite a play by play of the game: who caught a pass; who made a tackle or who carried the ball on a particular play.

He loves Jeopardy. Most often he can answer the history questions that the contestants miss. And music! Name an old song and we can both attach a memory to it.

Memories from the past are similar to a photo album. Just thinking about a wedding, a birthday or some special event we can retrieve all of the photos or snap shots of that event.

Attention is important. How many times have we parked our car at a super market and have had to search like crazy when we wheel out our cart of groceries?

Once after a mall shopping excursion in Florida I could not locate my car in the parking lot. Convinced it had been stolen I contacted security. They rode me around on a cart until we found it - on a totally different side of the mall than where I had told him I had parked.

Some of my memory problems I am sure are due to multi-tasking - doing too many things at once. Memory can also be affected by stress or just plain fatigue.

A quote from *Our Bodies, Ourselves* states: Intellectual functioning involving all aspects of the brain's ability to work with information steadily declines with age. Not all aspects change equally and there is much variation from person to person."

So, unfortunately the longer we live the less quickly our brain is able to function. We have witnessed it in our older relatives and friends: older information is more easily remembered than new information.

Hmmm - I wonder if that is the reason so many of you tell me you enjoy reading my column; we all love to reminisce and we remember yesterday better than today. Seriously, when I am out and about I do truly appreciate all of your comments.

For most of us the most troubling change is trying to recall names and numbers. This is not a sign of a "dementia." It is more than likely simply a sign of age.

Many of our friends talk about writing everything down—but then some complain of not remembering where they put the list. I file everything but then wonder where I filed it. Is it my system or my memory?

If I can't find something I blame my husband: he either threw it away or can't remember where he put it.

We have a weird existence as a family of three. Our son, Gary, who has a brain injury, remembers the words to every Beatles song and all of the artists from his generation like James Taylor and the Rolling Stones. He remembers most of his youthful past, his family and friends.

Yet, he can eat a meal and five minutes later ask, "What's for supper?" Or, "what year is it?" Or, "how old am I now?"

He does encode recent memories now, but need cues to help him retrieve those memories. He has learned to live without knowing what went on last month, last week or even a day ago.

So here is an excerpt of a typical day at our house: Gary Jr. happily sings his Beatles songs along with his CD. I am either on the computer or constantly looking for something that has been misplaced: my keys, my sunglasses or some document.

Then again I am very versatile - I could be doing domestic chores like making out a grocery list, washing clothes, preparing a meal or - changing diapers. And of course, Gary Sr. is his usual defensive self saying, "I never touched it or saw it! I didn't have anything to do with it!"

All kidding aside - Gary Sr's help with all of the chores are invaluable! It takes the both of us to run our, at times, wacky household.

If any of this sounds familiar - you're normal!

TIME FOR A REUNION REALITY CHECK　　　　July 28, 2006

Summertime is filled with high school reunions. As the years float by change is inevitable. Bodies change. Faces change. Priorities change. And reunion attendance numbers change due to health issues or death. Many would never miss a reunion; others would never attend.

For most classes the 10-year reunion is the initial gathering. Careers and marriage head the list of conversation. Our generation dressed to the hilt; cocktail dresses and suits were the norm. And party drinking at that age tends to lean toward the heavier side.

By the 25th reunion the conversation still touched on careers and family; number of children, and by now grandchildren. Guys reminisced about their high school sports activity, teachers and coaches; gals talked about their school memories, their families and how others have changed.

Men with premature hair loss were teased and talked about. Body sizes were observed and discussed. Some looked "good" for their age and for others the years haven't been as kind, creating fodder for even more conversation.

Of course every class has a few members most would like to dodge: There is Boring Bob, who thinks a conversation is a monologue delivered by him. And how about Bragging Bill? He never shuts up. Then there is Jack the Jock who relives and embellishes every touchdown he ever made in high school.

Sneaky Stan runs around dishing out backhanded compliments - in jest of course. Name Dropper Donna is busy spreading her stories of important friends while Spiteful Susie looks for the worst in everyone. And every class has at least one Vicious Vivian and a Jealous Jane. But oh, how we look forward to those reunions!

Reunions continue in most classes every 10 years - but by the 50th the class begins to dwindle. Death and health begin to enter in and attendance shrinks. The conversation changes drastically. Retirement talk is prevalent; who retired when and to where. People still reminisce about the past; but now much of the conversation focuses on illnesses, operations and general health concerns and who has died since the last reunion.

Reunions now began to be scheduled every five years. Dress code is whatever you want it to be; for many, more relaxed and casual. And drinking is minimal.

We had a recent gathering of classes '48, '49, '50 and '51 at the Elks Club. While searching for a place to display a board of memorabilia Tom Ammel, manager, pointed out a great place and then added, "If this was a 10-year reunion that is where the guys set up their kegs of beer." Guess that tells it all! Perhaps Geritol, Ex-Lax, Viagra and vitamin pills would be more appropriate now for our age group. Two nights of partying was the norm in earlier reunions; now one night (that ends early) seems more than adequate.

There are many other facets of class reunions that undoubtedly occur. For instance, out-of-towners come from thousands of miles away, not to mention expense, to see their classmates. Yet some people who live in town fail to attend. Why? I can only speculate. Perhaps some didn't have positive memories of school days. For them school years may dredge up memories they have long ago put to sleep.

Some have attended and are turned off by the same cliques that prevailed during high school. The cliques tend to congregate in their select groups and don't reach out to other class members. That can be a turn off. Some worked after school or were bus students and weren't involved in extracurricular activities; therefore, they didn't bond with classmates, so attending isn't a high priority. Some have baggage I am unaware of and I am sure there must be a ton of other reasons.

For those that attend regularly their perception of a class reunion is totally different. They look forward to attending and getting up to speed on classmates. For the most part these were the active members of the class: those involved in sports, band, choir, debate, cheerleading, plays, service clubs and other social activities.

I did observe, in our recent get-together, a greater display of affection; lots of hugging and lots of laughing. At our age pompous airs are dropped and pretentiousness is virtually nonexistent. People seemed more open in their demeanor and discussions of life in general.

The gathering was casual and people came from as far away as California, Colorado and Texas to return to their roots and enjoy a fun-filled evening with classmates.

We talked about how many couples in our generation have celebrated their 50th anniversary. Our generation tended to stick together through thick and thin - unlike today's generation in which 50 percent of marriages end in divorce, according to statistics.

The talk of a casual gathering every summer seemed to get great reviews. One wonders how many of us will not make it to the next reunion. It's a sad thought when bidding everyone good-bye. Will this be the last time we will see some of our classmates?

Yes, the years do take a toll on bodies and faces, but inside we are the same person - even better. Time and life experiences have mellowed most and in our hearts we hold a special affinity for the classmates we bonded with so many years ago.

GENEALOGY IS A FAVORITE HOBBY   July 6, 2007

I started a fantastic journey nine years ago: Researching the family trees of both my family and my husband's family. The impetus that got me started was to document our forefathers as Delta County Pioneers complete with a certificate from the Genealogical Society.

I had no idea I would become obsessed with this project. Nine years later the research is ongoing and family descendants show up "out of the blue" usually by an e-mail on the internet. I am listed as a source on the Gen-web under our family surnames. We communicate with new-found relatives in Wisconsin, Canada and Oregon.

A couple of weeks ago a lady e-mailed us and wanted to know if my husband was connected to the Elliott family, specifically, Valeria Elliott.

Valeria was my husband's grandma, who married James Elliott, first cousin to Thomas Edison.

I did extensive research on the Elliott side because of the Edison connection, but little was known about Valeria's family - even her parents name was unknown.

The lady, Patty, a librarian from Wisconsin explained she was planning a trip to the local casino with friends - could she meet us and bring some interesting family documentation? OK! We are excited!

Valeria came from Chippewa Falls, Wisconsin with a young son in the 1890s and eventually went to work as a domestic for Mr. Elliott who owned a store in the 400 block of Ludington Street. She was in her 30s and James Elliott was near 60 when they married and had Gary's mother. The family story handed down was that her first husband was killed on the railroad.

When you rattle around in family trees shocking branches fall out. Researching Valeria, we found that she was divorced from her first husband - in fact, one of the earliest divorces in Delta County. Divorce in the late 1890s was frowned upon. We discovered the name of her father, Joe Summers on all of the documentation we found. However her mother was listed as just Louisa. Just Louisa!

Then Patty appeared and oh! What a story she brought with her!

Many years ago the Sioux and Chippewa Indians were natural enemies. The tribal territory was separated by the Mississippi River. These tribes raided back and forth.

One day a party of Chippewa ambushed and destroyed a small party of Sioux. The Chippewa paddled up the Chippewa River and waved fresh scalps at a white settler along the river bank.

What the Chippewa's didn't know was that a large party of Sioux was following to avenge the Sioux who had been killed. The Chippewa party went up the river and camped on an island later known as Battle Island.

The Sioux surprised the Chippewas and killed them all except one old woman who was badly wounded and a six-month old baby who was left alive. After the Sioux left the island the old woman picked up the baby from the battlefield and made her way to Eau Claire, Wisconsin where she died of her wounds.

A white family adopted the baby and raised her. Apparently she gave up her adopted name and eventually did go back and live with the Indians. Of course that baby was Louisa!

And Louisa with no last name was Gary's great-grand mother. That makes Gary 1/8 Indian. If the family (Gary's mother) knew they never talked about it—-being Indian in that era was not something you wanted people to know - it was looked upon negatively like divorce. During that era Indians scalped their enemies - they were thought of as barbaric savages.

Patty, the new-found relative said "The Bad River Chippewa Tribe in Odanah, Wisconsin accepts membership based on proving descent. Some members of my family, including myself have become members."

Gary asked, "What is beneficial about proving decent?" "Well, you can hunt and fish on the land without a license." related Patty. Guess Gary won't become a member though. He doesn't hunt or fish or live in Wisconsin.

Gary's mother had dark skin, dark hair and brown eyes. Four of his siblings all resembled her. Gary, on the other hand, looks like his Norwegian father: Light skin, blond and blue eyes.

I tease him now and have anointed him my blond-blue-eyed Indian. His new nick-name: Chief! Instead of Abe. Our kids are fascinated by all of the revelations that keep coming out of the closet.

My friend Mary Pearson, who lives in Texas, wrote Gary a note recently when they were experiencing somewhat of a drought.

"Hey Gary, how about coming down here and performing a 'Rain Dance?'"

Ironically, shortly thereafter, they had a near flood in Texas where swimming pools overflowed and water lay on the ground. Mary said, "Hey Gary! You can stop the 'Rain Dancing' - we've had enough!"

Of course, the discovery of my family skeletons are for another story - another column.

Much of my research was done right here in the Family History Center at the Mormon Church. The volunteers who work there help anyone interested in researching their family history. They are dedicated and incredibly helpful. We have all of this information right in town, right at our fingertips. Yours for the asking!

They can access records from Salt Lake City, Utah and have them sent here. They can help you trace your family to other countries. We have traced ours to Germany, Ireland and Canada and Norway. What a treasure to have the Family History Center here manned with interested, helpful volunteers.

They get as excited as you when a "branch is discovered or uncovered!"

Go for it! Find out more about your ancestors; where you came from! Be ready for some surprising revelations!

Chapter
4

Sports Scrapbook

SPORTS EDITOR DEDICATED, DEVOTED
DENNY GRALL PROVIDES AREA SPORTS SCRAPBOOK

May 25, 2007

Everyone in this community who has been involved in sports to any degree including athletes, coaches, arm-chair quarter-backs, parents, and grandparents has heard of Denny Grall. Most of them know him on a personal basis.

Denny, who has been a Sports Editor for 37 years, has endeared himself to this community. He considers it a privilege to carry on the tradition that includes such notables as Ray Crandall, Jim Ward and Ken Gunderman.

By the same token the community at large feels that we are the privileged ones: To have such a dedicated devoted Sports Editor and fine journalist. Denny has been the Sports Editor of the Daily Press longer than any of his predecessors.

Denny knows and has made it his business to know the rich history of Delta County sports. His knowledge of sports coverage spans generations that include grandfathers, fathers and sons and grandmothers mothers and daughters.

He loves talking to the old-timers like Carl Dixon or Jack Beck who are walking encyclopedias of sports history in Escanaba. Both Carl and Jack have penned books on Escanaba sports history.

"Covering sports has been a wonderful experience," relates Denny. "It has enabled me to meet many outstanding people, from youngsters to coaches to fans, while remaining a kid who gets paid to have fun. I am basically providing a scrapbook of the area's athletic life and take that position very seriously."

Denny joined the Daily Press in 1970 after 15 months at WLST radio in Escanaba and worked here until 1980 when he joined the sports staff at the Green Bay Press-Gazette. He returned to Escanaba in 1984 when Keith Langlois took a sports writing job downstate. Lucky for us!

Denny is originally from Wisconsin but after all these years he qualifies as a full-fledged Yooper. Ironically, he almost moved to the Escanaba area in the eighth grade. His dad, Ed, was a road-master for the Chicago and Northwestern Railroad and almost landed that position in Escanaba in 1959.

Instead he went to Marinette and Denny attended eighth grade and then Marinette Catholic Central High School before graduating in 1964 when his family moved back to Manitowoc.

He was in the Marine Corps from 1966-68 and spent eight months in Vietnam where he was wounded twice. He served as a rifleman and radio operator in the same field company. Denny has received two Purple Hearts.

Denny and his wife Sally have been married for almost 40 years. According to Denny, "it has probably lasted because I am never home and she can't get upset with my goofy antics when I'm not around!"

Their son, Brian, pitched for the American Legion Escanaba Cubs and at Cardinal Stritch University in Milwaukee. He now lives in Menomonee Falls with his wife Debbie.

Denny has been inducted into the U.P. Sports Hall of Fame and has been involved for more than twenty years serving as secretary since 1992.

He has received numerous writing awards from the Associated Press and Michigan Press Association. He is also a member of the Delta County Softball Hall of Fame. Denny played softball here and in Green Bay and coached in Babe Ruth League and Little League in Escanaba.

What does Denny do in his spare time? He likes to play golf, take pictures and loves to travel. He says, "I've been in all 50 states and have seen pro ballgames or played golf in more than half of them."

Denny sums up his Daily Press experience, "I've enjoyed this job immensely and always tell people, including my boss, that I have the best job here by far. I wouldn't want any other position."

Denny knows how huge sports are in this area and says, "I just try to let everyone know what is going on in all of the activities and at all the schools."

We are so fortunate that we have a Sports Editor called Denny Grall - to most of us he is irreplaceable. He has an undeniable grasp on Escanaba sports history and does an admirable job!

Talking about how huge area sports are I received many, many e-mails, phone calls and comments from people in the community regarding the column I did on the Ptotenhauer-Gessner Award. People liked knowing about the rich history. However, I only focused on the Gessner history through 1991.

The following is from Sue Roberts:

"You wrote a very nice article (5-18-07) about the Ptotenhauer-Gessner award and I enjoy reading your weekly column but you missed out on a few other recipients that are relatives. (1992 to 2006)

There are at least two other sets of brothers. Charlie (95) and Chris (97) Detiege and Joe (96) and Rob (98) Freidhoff.

There is another brother-sister combo Jodi (92) and Spike (01) Houle. Also there is a sister combo that happens to be my two daughters, Amy (01) and Sara (06) Roberts and their uncle Jim Rodgers (76).

There are some cousins Jack (75) and Jim (89) Hirn, Nicole (94) and PJ (03) Fisher that I am aware of - those are some great names in sports at EHS. Again, you do a great job! Thanks."

Thanks Sue. The rich history of the Ptotenhauer-Gessner Award dating back to 1924 is not only recorded at the high school, and emerges in the scrapbook of the area's athletic life that Denny Grall provides - it also makes an indelible mark in the heart and mind of each and every recipient for the rest of their lives.

GEORGE RUWITCH AND 'HIS BOYS' February 2, 2006

George Ruwitch, a former school administrator, educator, and coach died January 13. He was 94. He fell in his apartment in Grand Rapids, broke his hip and died two days later from complications. He honed his extremely sharp mind playing the game he loved: bridge. Just two days before his fall he posted the top score in his bridge group.

Carolyn Ruwitch, one of Mr. Ruwitch's two daughters, traced the family history with her father's help. Harry and Ada, Mr. Ruwitch's parents, both illiterate and impoverished, emigrated from Jewish slums in Polish Russia (now Romania and the Ukraine) in the early 1900s. Destiny brought them together in the Upper Peninsula. George, born in 1911, was the eldest of four children. All had successful careers.

George Ruwitch received his degree from University of Minnesota and began his career teaching in a two-room country school in Faithorn during the Depression. He ended it as the esteemed Superintendent of the East Grand Rapids District. But his 21 years spent in the Escanaba school system would form special bonds with his students that would last a lifetime.

Coach Ruwitch left an indelible mark in Escanaba and in "HIS BOYS." And "his boys" as he called the many young men that played for him, left an indelible mark in his heart. His so-called "boys" are now in their '70s and '80s.

It is interesting to note George Ruwitch never really played football. At Norway High School he went out for football and broke his nose the first practice of the season. He said his parents wouldn't let him play anymore. Coach Ruwitch was a highly intelligent man. He studied the game and became a very successful coach with Upper Peninsula championship teams in 1939, 1940, 1941, and 1945.

Gary Abrahamson received a phone call from his coach several days before he broke his hip. He loved talking to "his boys" and had heard that Gary had been seriously ill. And Gary, being the history buff that he is, delighted in updating him about the boys, their lives and achievements. He told Gary he loved him and all of the "the boys." "I love you too coach!" Gary replied. Gary, who was always in awe of his respected stern coach with his 6-foot, 4- inch frame and booming voice, was humbled by his coach's expression of love. He often told Gary, "Isn't it time you called me George?" "Never," Gary replied, "you will always be Coach Ruwitch to me." Coach Ruwitch visited Howard Perron and Gary in Florida two years ago. Invariably, as always, they relived the game they lost to Menominee (13 to 12) in 1948. It was their only loss that season - by one point. And imagine—more than 50 years later team mates and coach were still reliving that game! Play by play!

Mr. Ruwitch was overwhelmed and grateful by the support and loyalty that had been shown to him over the years from "his boys." Jack and Bette Beck always hosted Mr. Ruwitch when he came to town. Jack was the catalyst in organizing special events and birthday parties for him throughout the years. Jack was also instrumental in establishing the scholarship in Ruwitch's name at Escanaba High School.

The following reflections are from members of the Class of 1949: They were the last team coached by Mr. Ruwitch.

HOWARD PERRON was hand picked by Mr. Ruwitch to be his business manager in the Grand Rapids district. Howard and his wife, Blanche drove the coach and his wife, Ruth to the U. P. for all the special events George's "boys" planned for him.

"Having known George Ruwitch for most of my life and also

working with him on a close and personal basis I found George to be one of the most honest individuals and a man of great personal character. His values were so high it is hard to imagine in this day and age that he walked among us."

DR. JOHN BEAUMIER "As I reminisce on my recollections of George Ruwitch, I think of him not only as a football coach - and a good one, but as an icon in the classroom as well. I had the privilege of visiting with him in Grand Rapids this past Thanksgiving and I was so fortunate to have spent an afternoon with him as he recalled his days of teaching, coaching and living in Escanaba for over 20 years. He paused quite often to emphatically state that he had received much more than he had given from "his boys!" He had no sons, but two daughters and several grandsons. Though a bit stooped with tremor of both hands, nevertheless, he was amazingly alert and conversed intelligently about current events at the tender age of 94! It was a memorable afternoon for me. I hugged him when I said goodbye and once more he said to greet "his boys." He was lonely after the passing of his wife Ruth and he reminisced about the great years they had together. In passing, we, "his boys" recall that tall giant of a man, and we will always remember him - Thanks George for the memories!

HERB NICHOLSON "George used to say, 'I was so thin I had to stand twice to make a shadow.' But I say that shadow made a lasting impression on all of us."

DON CARLSON "George Ruwitch was a special kind of man both as a coach and a teacher. I felt we had a bond of respect between us. He made me feel like I was special.

One day I stupidly called him to inform him I wouldn't be out for practice - because it was raining and I didn't have an umbrella. 'Baldy', he said, 'you aren't made of sugar - you won't melt.' I was dumfounded and embarrassed! After a few seconds of silence he said, 'I'll be over to pick you up in 15 minutes.' I always felt he admired our effort to play hard to win and we would always be high on his list of teams he loved. I have the fondest memories of a wonderful teacher, coach and man."

DICK BARRON "Coach Ruwitch was a wonderful inspiration to me and to many he came in contact with for that matter. He became aware of the fact that my mother had passed away a short time before we became acquainted. Though not my counselor, he gave me considerable guidance which was beneficial in school and in life. He was a wonderful friend. I know that I will never forget him."

NADIA DU BOIS, daughter: "I am so happy that (my dad) had such deep feelings for his football players. I know it sustained him in the last years of his life."

Yes, George Ruwitch was everything "his boys" said he was—larger than life! An ICON! He had a huge part in shaping "his boys" and he will live on with great fondness in their memories and in their hearts.

TOM SWIFT'S BASKETBALL TEAM IN THE '40S   August 3, 2007

Tom Swift's popular restaurant and bar in the '40s, '50s and '60s was well-known and appreciated for more than cavorting out to Bark River for great fish fries on Friday nights. Lined up behind the bar among the jugs of whiskey were myriad trophies won by the famous basketball team sponsored by Tom Swift. The men on the team were Tom Swift's pride and joy.

The year was 1946 and many of the young men that would make up Swift's team were just returning from the war.

Eddie Gauthier, one of the five surviving members of the Tom Swift basketball team, attended Michigan State University. He was in love with his high school sweetheart, Betty, and left school at Christmastime.

He knew he would be drafted and decided to sign up for induction into the Army in 1943. They were married in 1944 during Eddie's furlough.

Eddie was captain of the basketball team in high school. Not only was he an excellent athlete, winning eight letter awards, but he was a good student and proficient in his favorite subject: high math. He took a test and was chosen for Air Force Cadet training.

"At the time the Air Force was losing a lot of air crew in England - one mission lost over 70 planes with 10 guys in a crew,"explained Eddie. That is a loss of 700-plus men in one mission!

Subsequently, he became a navigator on an Air Force B-17 bomber. Some of the pilots were only 19 and 20 years old! Just kids! It is difficult to imagine young men right out of high school flying bombers.

Eddie was stationed in Italy and flew 10 missions in enemy territory. Ultimately he received the rank of Captain.

Eddie and Friends on Weekend in L.A.

Like most of the guys returning from the war - Eddie belonged to what they called the "52-20" club. That is, he received $20 for 52 weeks from the government. He supplemented his income working at his Dad's bar and hotel.

The St. Clair Hotel and Bar was located directly across the street from the train station - later known to many as Skinny's bar. The building still stands. Before Eddie's folks bought the St. Clair hotel it was a hospital: St. Clair hospital.

Eddie recalls the era of Prohibition: "We were busy making home brew. The Feds would make occasional raids, but the word got out they were in town. The net-work of local bar owners called one another to warn them of the Feds visit in advance."

Fun and relaxation for the guys returning from the war in the '40s was playing basketball, softball and hoisting brews at their favorite watering hole. Most of the guys were kicking back, enjoying normal life again with the camaraderie of friends after being in harm's way and seeing the atrocities of war.

Independent basketball flourished after the war. Tom Swift's team played in an Independent League that encompassed Northern Michigan and Wisconsin, The league included Munising, Negaunee, Stephenson, Hermansville, and Peshtigo, WI. Their biggest rival was the Hermansville Silver Foxes.

They played barnstorming teams such as the Harlem Globe Trotters, and an NBA team from Cheboygan, WI along with many others in the Junior High gym.

They played in tournaments in Green Bay and also the prestigious Gold Medal Tournament in Hermansville that still exists today. They won the tournament twice with both Tom Dufour and Bob Rangette each selected as MVPs on separate years.

Roy Johnson was the team captain. He was a fighter pilot during the war and subsequently head of the local National Guard.

Bob Anderson served in the Navy during World War 11 and was called back to serve during the Korean War.

They played three times a week to a packed house at the Junior High gym. They would congregate after the game at the Peoples Bar where they hoisted a few more - not exactly to the liking of the wives.

Five members of the team are still living: Marvin Palmgren, George Shomin, Ben Kleiman, Bob Ranguette and Eddie Gauthier.

Eddie says his grandson, Andrew, in the Marines now serving in Iraq and they exchange e-mails. He beamed when we talked about his granddaughter, Dr. Kimber Gauthier, who practices at Doctor's Park.

History and memories - it's what sustains us as we grow older. We reminisce, relive and reflect about our lives and the "golden old days." For most of us oldsters memories are a huge part of our interactions - although they play second fiddle to health "talk."

Tom Swift's Basketball Team (1946)

Standing: Tom Swift, sponsor, Marvin Palmgren, Don Dufresne, George Shomin, Ben Kleiman, Louie Kositsky, Stan Jensen, Manager

Front: Roy Johnson, Captain, Tommy Dufour, Bob Ranguette, Bob Anderson, Eddie Gauthier, Tom Swift Jr, Mascot

HONORS DAY EXCITEMENT BREWS!   May 18, 2007

Next Wednesday is Honors Day at Escanaba High School. Excitement is growing! Students speculate; they guess, they wonder and they surmise who the recipient of the Pfotenhauer-Gessner Sports Award will be. Those in contention for the award are on pins and needles waiting for the revelation. The recipients name is a highly guarded secret until the Honors Day ceremony. Who will it be?

The Herman Gessner Trophy is the oldest and most coveted athletic award at Escanaba High School. The Gessner Trophy through the decades has defined "who's who" of Escanaba High School Athletics. It originated in 1924. Herman Gessner, a pioneer Escanaba Businessman, and owner of the Fair Store was the original benefactor.

The trophy award with its rich athletic history and tradition continues today - with a name change. It is now called the Pfotenhauer-Gessner Award and funded by the Pfotenhauer family. Their intention was to retain and perpetuate the prestigious Gessner name and history that dated back to 1924. Both Don (1941) and Bob (1943) were recipients of the Herman Gessner Trophy.

Originally the award was presented to a senior male student athlete. Criteria included grade point average, service to the school, and a minimum number of award letters. In 1975 girls became eligible and it became a duel award.

The first recipient in 1924 was Ovila Savard.

There were three sets of brothers that won the award over the years: Don (1941) and Bob Pfotenhauer (1943); George (1942) and Richard Shomin (1951) and James (1967) and Bob Boyle (1978).

Additionally, John Tolfa (1981) and his sister Jean (1982) were the only bother and sister combination to win the award. However, there has never been a father and son or mother and daughter combination who has won the award.

The esteemed trophy holds a special meaning of accomplishment that is not diminished by the years. More than a trophy - it has been instrumental in shaping the lives of the young recipients.

BOB BARRON (1940) Bob's trophy was displayed among his treasured memorabilia up front and center at his funeral last year. Bob was one of only three individuals to ever win nine award letters before 1962. Until that time freshman couldn't compete in varsity sports.

The following quotes are from a few of the recipients:

GEORGE SHOMIN (1942) is the oldest living recipient today. George wrapped up his feelings about winning the trophy with a modest statement, "I was very proud!" When George was inducted into the UP Sports Hall of Fame, former coach Leon Schram (1929) Gessner winner stated George was the best all-around athlete that ever competed in sports at Escanaba High School.

GARY ABRAHAMSON (1949) "I became aware of the significance of the Gessner award as a young boy in the fourth grade. I would hear my two older brothers discuss sports and the trophy. I realized early on what winning the award entailed - and I was focused. Yet, when I won it I was overwhelmed. There were so many good athletes in my class. Winning the Gessner was one of the most memorable experiences of my life."

WARREN JOHNSTON (1952) "I was happy and pleased to win the Gessner Award. I never felt I had the talent that previous winners had - like Abe and the guys I looked up to. But I loved sports and I was a competitor."

JAMES BOYLE (1967) "I played sports all my life from the time I was a little kid. When I won the trophy I was surprised, happy and proud. I have it displayed in my home office."

MARY DULEK ERSPAMER (1977) "I still think about winning the award and what a great honor it was. It was exciting and I am very proud. I talk to my children about the rich history of the Gessner Award. They are very involved in high school sports. I tell them education is more important but you can link the two together. My trophy is displayed at my family home."

MIKE BEVERIDGE (1980) "I was very fortunate to have a class full of great athletes and I truly did not think I would have a chance to win this award. When the Gessner Award was announced and my name was called, I sat there stunned in disbelief. I remember the pride I felt walking up to receive the trophy. It was one of the most memorable nights of my life."

JOHN TOLFA (1981) "I remember feeling honored and very humble. I had known of the past trophy winners and always knew it was a great honor to be selected. There were many talented athletes in my class equally deserving of the award. I remember the happiness in making my parents feel proud. Athletics were a big part of my personal growth as a student in Escanaba."

JEAN TOLFA (1982) "I was thrilled to receive the Gessner Trophy because sports were such a big part of my life in high school. There were so many deserving female athletes in my class. The thing I remember most at the time of winning the trophy was how fun it was to receive it at the awards ceremony - dressed very girly in a long yellow dress. My mother always told me if I was going to act like a boy, look and conduct myself like a girl."

HOPE LAVIOLETTE (1983) "I was shocked, happy and really proud when I won the award. I was happy for my dad too. He cried when I won it because he was so happy and proud. The trophy is proudly on display at our family home."

NICK BINK (1990) "It is such an honorable feeling to be in that elite group of Eskymos that have won the award. I was lucky enough to be on good teams with team players. My trophy is still displayed at my parent's home."

1945 was the only year there was no Gessner Award recipient - but not because of a lack of talent. JACK MANNING informed me that many qualified athletes in 1945 left school before graduation to fight for their country during World War II- therefore were ineligible.

Previously the Gessner Trophy winners were displayed in the high school office. Now they are on display at the Historical Society among the precious artifacts to be viewed, preserved and maintained through the years - for posterity.

HERMAN GESSNER TROPHY WINNERS

| 1942 | 1949 | 1980 | 1991 |
| George H. Shomin | Gary Abrahamson | Mike Beveridge | Nick Bink |

ESCANABA'S FAMOUS LUMBERJACK   October 20, 2006

He proudly calls himself a "lumberjack." You will see him around town in his hiked-up jeans with suspenders, a red lumberjack shirt covering his Arnold Schwarzenegger physique, a twinkle in his eye, a wide smile   and a readiness for conversation.

You might meet him at a wedding, a funeral, a church picnic, a band concert, a grocery store, the farmer's market, a dance at the Rusty Rail or anyplace where people congregate.

Don (Bud) Jacobs, an Escanaba legend in his own time, is the epitome of a lumberjack. In the past I wrote about his World War II experiences but his early life is equally as interesting. Don was born in Escanaba in 1924, the second child of Phillip and Irene Jacobs.

His first 14 years were spent in Ralph, Michigan, a community about 55 miles from Escanaba where the family moved to operate the Quinn Ranch. At that time the narrow dirt road leading to Ralph was the end of the line.

As a young lad, Bud's father rented him out to work for 50 cents a day. If you had a healthy son this was customary. "Great money," says Bud, "considering family providers made one dollar a day in that era. Although most families would be considered poor by today's standards - they never knew it. Food was always plentiful. We picked wild blueberries, strawberries and raspberries - sometimes the bushes were six feet high."

Entertainment was simple and fun with not too many options. The entire family attended Saturday night dances at the town hall. Everyone learned to dance at a young age. Bud says, "During the Twenties my sister (Betty Keldsen, former owner of the Log Cabin) and I became quite proficient at a dance called the Flea Hop.

We jumped around and flapped our arms like a flea. It was the craziest darn dance! At the Saturday night dances the folks would all yell for us to do the Flea Hop. We had live music - most of the musicians were self-taught from the Smokey Mountains. My dad played the harmonica."

Some folks were fortunate enough to have a radio that played part of the time but there was no electricity in the back-woods until 1955. You had to run it on a set of batteries or a big car battery.

On Saturday Night they would all sit around the radio and listen to WLS Barn Dance from Chicago. Some of the stars of the show were Skyland Scottie, Lulu Belle and the Duke of Paducah. "During the Depression most people didn't own cars - so you walked," said Bud. "We had a team of horses and a sleigh and sometimes we went to school in the sleigh."

At age fourteen the family moved back to Escanaba. Bud relates, "Although I played basketball and baseball, I had only heard of football. I had never seen it played. In my junior year I played on the Junior Varsity and maybe a few minutes on the varsity.

In my senior year I became a full blown member of the varsity. We had a host of stellar players on the team and vaulted all the way to the U. P. Championship. We lost only one game that season to Marinette. We were leading 19-0 at the half then fell apart. They just outmaneuvered us. Many team members made All-UP and honorable mention. George Shomin made All-State and was awarded the coveted Herman Gessner Trophy."

Basketball wasn't an option for Bud. He loved the game but he had to work to help supplement his mother's income. There were three sisters at home yet. Coach Ruwitch recognized his need for a job and called a friend, Charles Gessner who owned the Fair Store. Bud was hired promptly to work in the produce department. Remember when the Fair Store had a huge grocery department in the basement?

Although Bud was like Little Abner - the strapping country boy in suspenders who came to the city - he wasn't all brawn and no brains. He managed to be inducted into the prestigious National Honor Society in his junior year.

Of course his life was interrupted like so many others when right out of high school he joined the Marines during World War 11. Bud returned to Escanaba married and had three daughters. He worked for Michigan Bell and has probably been in nearly every home in Escanaba.

At age 37 he became interested in log rolling and lumber-jack sports. His log rolling career spanned 40 years. His humble and modest personality would have you believe his incredible accomplishments were just a matter of fact.

He placed in the top three in the World Open Division Championship and placed first in the World Senior Division at the same time. And there is more! He went on to win 11 World Senior Division Championships - an amazing feat considering his late start in the sport.

In his self-depreciating tone Bud says, "I quit rolling at age 76. There comes a time when you just have to relent and give up."

He has been a widower for ten years. Thank goodness he loves life and people. You could run into him dancing at a rock concert - a rock concert at age 83? His charm, intellect, historical perspective and ability to relate to anyone on just about any level are what endear Bud to those who know him.

Bud has a humorous way of defining himself: "For the first eight years of my life I was kind of a rambunctious kid; the next 35 years I was known as 'The Fighting French Renegade' right out of the heart of the backwoods. Of course, I had to outgrow that, so the last 40 years I have been known as a partially reformed, partially self-educated, Christian lumberjack."

Surely they threw the cookie-cutter away when Bud, Escanaba's self-proclaimed lumberjack, was born! He is, without a doubt, one of a kind! Bud is my first cousin and makes me proud.

Don
'Bud'
Jacobs

Chapter 5
Hot Topics

"We have room for but one flag, the American Flag...We have room for but one language here, and that is the English Language... And we have room for but one sole loyalty and that is the loyalty to the American People.
≈ Theodore Roosevelt ≈ 1907

Religion

Immigration

Health Issues

Politics

Weight Control

Iraq War

AMERICAN, AND DAMN PROUD OF IT   January 19, 2007

"Good morning, welcome to the United States of America."
"Press 1 if you speak English."
"Press 2 to disconnect until you can"
This is a sample of the tongue-in-cheek messages filtering through the Internet. Overall, many people in our great country are fed up with those illegally entering our country, including those from Mexico. Even those who are here legally can't or refuse to speak English. The biggest insult is their resistance to learn the language. It is especially evident in border towns.

Our ancestors from Italy, Ireland, Ukraine, Poland, Finland, Norway, Sweden, Canada and a host of other countries - the building blocks of our great America - wanted to learn the language and fit in.

The ultimate insult happened last spring in Pioneer, California, where protesters flew the Mexican flag over the American flag as it flew upside down at Montebello High School.

President Ronald Reagan once said, "You can go and live in France, but you can't become a Frenchman. You can go to live in Japan but you cannot become Japanese. But anyone, from any corner of the world, can come to live in America and be an American."

And that is what is so great about our great country. But it has to be done legally. For years Mexicans by the thousands have been illegally sneaking over our borders. I might add it could also be an easy entrance for terrorists.

I understand why the Mexican people want to come to our country; they can find jobs here - even minimum wage is far better than what they can make in Mexico. For the most part they come for the same reasons our ancestors came for: A chance for a better life.

For example, my Irish ancestors came here because people in Ireland were starving when a famine resulted from the failed potato crop in the 1840s. However, they legally entered the country through Ellis Island and arrived in Escanaba in the late 1870s to work on the railroads. They became citizens and tried to blend in.

My French-Canadian ancestors spoke only French when they immigrated to Bark River in the 1880s. Their children quickly learned the language and they raised their kids to speak English. My mother also spoke French but only to her mother -

when she didn't want us to know what she was talking about!

I have my great-grandparents' Canadian marriage license. Neither they nor their attendants could read or write and signed their names with an "X." I have also obtained my grandfather's citizenship papers from Delta County. My mother said he was extremely proud of becoming an American citizen.

The Mexican people are good people. They are family-oriented, religious and good workers. They are good immigrants. I became much more familiar with Mexican people while wintering in Florida. I witnessed their work ethic. They are the folks doing the tough jobs that the average American does not want.

I observed firsthand Mexicans roofing homes in 90-degree heat and doing the heavy work of landscaping and housecleaning. Some are very talented. A Mexican man, fourth generation cabinet maker, built and finished our wall unit. It was beautiful. A woman artist from Argentina painted murals on our patio and in our home. They became our friends.

A man from Mexico upholstered a valance for us; another painted our home. The men who built our pool were all Mexican. I could go on and on. They are polite and respectful. I will admit they still spoke to one another in Spanish, but spoke broken English to Americans - some barely understandable.

The distinction is I am American of French and Irish decent. My husband is an American of Norwegian and English decent. Note we are Americans first and our ancestors amalgamated into our society as proud Americans. Is an ethnic-hyphen needed? Many include an ethnic hyphen and call themselves Mexican-American, Hispanic-American or Afro-American.

Many do not make an attempt to learn English. They insult us by re-writing our National Anthem in Spanish. Perhaps our country helps perpetuate the situation. Why do we facilitate bilingual employees in schools, businesses and government here in the U.S.? We put up signs in Spanish, print ballots in Spanish, most directions to assemble anything are in Spanish - even Folgers coffee directions are in Spanish. And yes, we have to Press 1 for English.

This is about nationality - not about race. Those coming into our country should only be here legally so we don't have to pay taxes to feed, clothe, send their kids to school and provide them with medical attention.

It is not to say that nationalities cannot celebrate fiestas, such as St. Paddy's Day or Greek festivals, or that we shouldn't have specialty restaurants featuring Italian, French or Mexican cuisine. But first and foremost we are Americans. We are here legally and speak our country's language - English.

My contention is illegal aliens should jump through the same hoops as our ancestors did. No one should benefit from illegal acts, surely not at the cost of American citizens. And if they enter the country legally, English should become their primary language.

HOT TOPICS: POLITICS AND RELIGION   July 21, 2006

Politics and religion can foster some great conversations and also some intense arguments. Especially in our family which is extremely political-over the top.

Even writing about those subjects can be somewhat controversial. So my treatise will tread lightly and try not to rile up the troops.

My earliest recollection of politics began in grade school. The teacher informed us we would have a mock presidential election that week. I asked my mother, "What are we; Democrat or Republican?" "Why, Democrat, of course," was her answer. So I voted Democrat. I do remember that there was only one Republican vote in the whole class. I thought that girl must be odd if she was the only one in the class that was Republican (whatever that meant). Republican must be bad.

Then I remember my grandmother talking about President Roosevelt like the sun rose and set on his very being. Of course he was Democrat and was instrumental in getting people back to work after the Depression. She loved him. So I grew up thinking Democrat was the way to go - not realizing a party philosophy entered in. Families handed down their brand of politics. That is just the way it was.

Fast forward to the year I got married. Lo and behold. I married a Republican. What was that all about? His father was a staunch Republican and a Roosevelt detester. We voted in presidential elections: Predictably, I voted Democrat and he voted Republican. As a young adult I didn't have strong feelings about either except hoping my candidate won - just so I could gloat.

Years passed and I was swayed by my husband's leanings. I became actively involved in politics. My mother, not very happy about my switched allegiance, exclaimed my grandfather would turn over in his grave; he, at one time, was party chair for the Democratic Party and I became a registered Republican and party chair for the Republican Party in Delta County. My mother, although secretly enthralled with Ronald Reagan's charm, wasn't too happy.

I was appointed campaign chair for then Congressman Bob Davis - a position I held for six years. And I was one of fifteen key people in the state chosen to meet with President George Bush Sr. to discuss strategies for his bid for the presidency in the upcoming election. And on and on.

Finally, after many years, I became disenchanted with politics. I studied the platforms and decided I was neither Democrat nor Republican. I am an independent. Therein is where the problem lies. My husband is still a Republican - although he prefers to be called a conservative. We have had so many heated arguments that we had to opt not to watch political stuff on TV together. The words were many and the volume was high. I couldn't keep my mouth shut - and he reacted.

My son is a senior attorney for the Treasury Department in Washington. In previous years he worked for three Republican congressmen. Needless to say he followed his dad's persuasion. He is analytical, but very fair; therefore having a difference of opinion with him is fun and with a bit more civility. His wife, a political appointee, has also worked for Republicans on Capital Hill and in the executive branch (Department of Energy) as a speech writer.

Enter in religion. I was raised as a Catholic. My husband was raised in the Protestant faith. As a kid I was not allowed to go into any church other than Catholic. His dad denigrated Catholics and didn't allow his kids to attend CYO dances. By the same token, some Catholic kids couldn't attend Protestant church hayrides - like perhaps the hot chocolate served afterward would cause them to switch?

Parents preferred that their children married in the same faith. Lines were drawn in both religion and politics and penetrated the psyche of the kids. That is just the way it was.

Eventually, I did join his church because I thought our kids would benefit. However, when the kids were raised I decided to return to my church. I missed the pomp, ceremony and belief system of the Catholic church. Then, without provocation, Gary decided to join my church taking six months of religion classes which he truly enjoyed. We exchanged our marriage vows again - this time in the Catholic church. My mother was soooo happy.

Jeff, my youngest son, married a Catholic girl and joined the Catholic Church. My oldest son remained in the Protestant faith and my daughter became a Lutheran. The two boys are strong Republicans and my daughter is an Independent. The girl (me) from the Democratic family became a Republican and the boy (Gary) from the Protestant family became a Catholic. The end result - we are one big mixed happy family and respect one another's choices.

PRESIDENTIAL HOPEFULS: A MIXED LOT   April 20, 2007

I recall in 1997, as a candidate for Ms. Senior Michigan, I answered questions posed by judges. The one question that stymied me was: "What is your opinion of a woman president?"

It seemed so far-fetched at that time that I hadn't really given it much thought. My answer was probably vague: "There have been capable women who have been heads of state in other countries. I
hope that a qualified female candidate will eventually emerge and someday become president - but I surely don't expect it to happen in my lifetime."

That was 10 short years ago. If the question had arose regarding a black person or a person of the Mormon religion as president, I would have had a similar reply, "Not in my lifetime!"

The slate of candidates today is very diverse, cutting across gender, race and religion. Perhaps that says something good about acceptance - and maybe even tolerance.

Take a look at front-runner **HILLARY CLINTON**. Her money-raising capabilities are phenomenal. She is expected to have $75 million in her war chest by the year's end. Hillary raised $26 million in the first quarter. In my opinion she lacks the charisma that hubby Bill exudes; pundits say he can only help her. And Bill would love to spend eight more years in the White House making history.

Bill is her biggest cheerleader. He would be "America's First Man." He personally has much to offer in the public sector. He is still young, smart, charismatic and cares about America and its people. Hillary jokingly says she can make "Bill ambassador to the world." Ironically, he is already playing that role through the William Jefferson Clinton Foundation.

She will get a huge portion of the female vote - especially

under 60. She has been named "Most Admired Woman" in the Gallup poll for five years running. My prediction is she will be our next president. She may or may not be the best candidate, but the timing for a woman president is here and now!

However, a possible roadblock and veritable threat she didn't anticipate burst on the national scene, namely **BARACK OBAMA**. He first gained national attention when he was selected to be keynote speaker at the 2004 Democratic Convention in Boston, and his star continues to rise. His first quarter fund-raising hit $25 million, making Hillary's party nomination no longer a given.

I read with interest his book, *The Audacity of Hope*. He speaks of being a child of a mixed marriage with a curious relationship to the '60s. Without the social upheavals of the '60s, Obama states, "My life would have been impossible, my opportunities entirely foreclosed." His reference: The civil rights movement.

He is gaining a close second in his bid for president. But can he overtake Hillary? You would think he would garner the majority of the black vote. Not entirely so! Many blacks feel he is not "one of them." He is articulate and can you believe many of the blacks are offended by that.

Enter **JOHN EDWARDS**. He has name recognition from the last presidential primary. Just recently he held a news conference announced his wife, Elizabeth, is once again fighting cancer. They explained their decision to continue his bid for president with Elizabeth by his side. Contributions and interest in his campaign surged after the news conference. I remember John as being very articulate and charismatic in his 2000 bid for the presidency. Wonder where that will go?

Settle back and get ready for an interesting ride. Of course, politics has always been a passion of mine, so I will find this primary and the 2008 election one of the most interesting ever!

Presently the top Republican contender is **RUDY GUILIANI**. As former mayor of New York City, he is most remembered for presiding over the 9/11 Twin Towers attack. He was also named "Man of the Year." A detraction might be that he is on his third marriage. Personally, I don't perceive him as a charismatic person. Also, he is not considered a true conservative by the Republican Party.

Sen. **JOHN McCAIN** is running second, but he is disappointed by his meager money-raising efforts. His record during the Vietnam War (prisoner of war for years) has always been an asset. But how will his steadfast lineup with Bush on the Iraq war play out? He has always been somewhat of a maverick (doesn't necessarily vote with his party), and his calm personality could be an asset - but he appears tired and seems to lack a spark of energy. He will be 71 in August, the oldest of all candidates.

MITT ROMNEY, ex-governor of Massachusetts and son of former Michigan Governor George Romney, could be the dark horse for the presidential nomination. He wouldn't be the first dark horse to win the nomination. Both Jimmy Carter and Clinton were virtually unknown when they won the nomination. Yes, he is a Mormon. So what?! Values are what is important; not brand of religion. He is also articulate, presidential looking and quite frankly, refreshing.

I remember when John F. Kennedy ran for president in the '60s and people were skeptical because he was Catholic. As if Kennedy had a pipeline to the Pope and the Pope would be instrumental in the decision making. How absurd was that thinking?

By all accounts Romney is a decent, good, family man with five children and no known baggage. He also leads the Republican pack in fund-raising.

There is speculation that **CONDOLEZZA RICE** could be on the Republican ticket as vice presidential candidate to offset the possibility of a Hillary/Obama ticket. She doesn't appear to be interested, but if push comes to shove she may be drafted. She is well-respected and articulate. She holds two trump cards: She is black and female.

Interesting how dollars may well be the deciding factor in the nomination and the ultimate presidency. Doesn't seem right, does it?

Again, hang on to your hats!. The race is certain to make history. Anything can happen.

2008 DEMOCRATIC PRESIDENTIAL CANDIDATES

Hillary **Clinton** Barrack **Obama** John **Edwards**

2008 REPUBLICAN PRESIDENTIAL CANDIDATES

Rudolph **Guilani** Mitt **Romney** John **McCain**

WEIGHT: THE DEVIL MADE HER DO IT!   March 2, 2007

Every now and then someone sends me an e-mail that begs to be seen by my readers. This one from Mary, in Texas, is especially timely since many of us are trying to shape up for spring. Now instead of blaming lack of willpower for our foiled efforts, we have a scapegoat: The Devil! Read on.

In the beginning, God created the Heavens and Earth and populated the Earth with broccoli, cauliflower and spinach, green and yellow and red vegetables of all kinds, so Man and Woman would live long and healthy lives.

Then using God's great gifts, Satan created Ben and Jerry's Ice Cream and Krispy Kreme Donuts. And Satan said, "You want chocolate with that?" And Man said, "Yes!" and Woman said, "as long as you're at it, add some sprinkles." And they gained 10 pounds. And Satan smiled.

And God created healthful yogurt that Woman might keep her figure that Man found so fair. And Satan brought forth white flour from the wheat and sugar from the cane and combined them. And Woman went from size 6 to size 14.

So God said, "Try my fresh green salad." And Satan presented Thousand-island Dressing, buttery croutons and garlic toast on the side. And Man and Woman unfastened their belts.

God then said, "I have sent you hearty, healthy vegetables and olive oil in which to cook them." And Satan brought forth deep fried fish and chicken-fried steak so big they needed their own platters.

And man gained more weight and his cholesterol went through the roof. God then created a light fluffy white cake, and named it "Angel Food Cake," and said, "It is good."

Satan then created chocolate cake and named it "Devils Food."

God then brought forth running shoes so that his Children might lose those extra pounds. And Satan gave cable TV with a remote control so Man would not have to toil changing the channels. And Man and woman laughed and cried before the flickering blue light and gained pounds.

Then God brought forth the potato, naturally low in fat and brimming with nutrition. And Satan peeled off the healthful skin and sliced the starchy center into chips and deep-fried them. And Man gained pounds.

God then gave lean beef so that Man might consume fewer

calories and still satisfy his appetite. And Satan created McDonald's and its 99-cent double cheeseburger. Then said, "You want fries with that?"

And Man replied, "Yes! And super size them!" And Satan said, "It is good." And Man went into cardiac arrest.
God sighed and created quadruple by-pass surgery.

Then Satan created HMOs.

My experience is that diet is only one component of losing or maintaining weight. Since 1975 exercise has been a huge part of my life: Running, walking and, at times, weight training. Trouble is most of us wax and wane; in other words we are either "in" or we are "out".

I can be "good" for months, exercising every day, watching my diet and then something comes along that interrupts my routine. It could be the flu or some other reason. The habit is broken. Everything is thrown out the window. I am no longer exercising and think, why bother controlling my intake?

Pounds start to add up: My clothing becomes tight. I talk about what I should be doing. And do I feel guilty? You bet I do!

Exercise has been ingrained in my way of life.

The most difficult part of exercise is beginning again! I feel exhilarated that first time back on the treadmill. I have captured that great feeling or high that I get from exercise. I think I will never forego my exercise again. And the diet thing goes hand in hand. Why would I want to work out for health's sake and fill my body with junk food? It is so counter-productive.

I admit I was much better when I spent the winter in Florida because I love to walk outside. It was a high to shop at the farms that raised fresh vegetables and strawberries, not to mention all of the fresh Gulf fish.

After feeling frumpy this fall, I joined the fray of millions on New Year's Day: I started exercising again. The incentive was to be skinny for a vacation and shopping trip in March.

My new NordicTrack is a great incentive. It has a computer that records everything: calories burned, carbohydrates burned, pace, mileage and heart rate. It even has a quarter-mile track that resembles the athletic field so you can watch yourself walk around it.

I put on my Walkman and listen to the great tapes I have accumulated over the years. My favorite artists, to name a few, are Dean Martin, Andy Williams, Frank Sinatra, Patsy Cline, Kenny

Rogers and Neil Diamond.

I am making great progress and for now I am "in." I like me "again" and feel wonderful. But in the future, if I "fall off the wagon," I have someone to blame it on. I can say the Devil made me do it!

TODAY'S HEALTH: A REALITY CHECK   March 23, 2007

Life spans in the US have been consistently on the rise for decades. The life span at birth in 1901 was 49. Life expectancy has increased by leaps and bounds in the 20th century. By the end of the century the life expectancy was 77 years - a whopping increase of 57 per cent.

But will the rising rates continue? That is the question. It is true that public health, medicine and nutrition have all played a roll in life span expansion. Now with the rising rates in obesity affecting over 60 per cent of Americans - gains in life span could began to spiral downward. Children and teen-age obesity is leading to a variety of diseases that could reduce the present lifespan expectancy.

THE WAY IT WAS VERSUS THE WAY IT IS:

There were no school buses in town to transport kids to school. I walked almost two miles to high school, rain or shine, snow or sleet. I walked home for lunch and back - then back home after school. Four trips! Six miles! In the evening I walked back and forth to Club 314 - another two miles. On the week-ends we did household chores and danced until we dropped!

Today most kids are picked-up at their door-step. If the bus stops at the corner, I have seen a mother pick up her child and drive him home a half a block. My average mileage was 8 miles. Today's average student walks zero miles for comparable activity. Instead they log a multitude of hours in front of the TV - a luxury not afforded us in the forties.

My husband's average mileage was around 5 miles back and forth to school and to the football field. Today almost all kids have a car to go to football practice. He only remembers two guys who had access to cars back then. He averaged 5 miles a day walking while today's average football player walks zero for similar activity.

In the summer we walked to the beach, to the band concert

or any other activity. Never did I ever get a ride in the car - many years we didn't even have a car.

Food habits were dictated by lack of availability and lack of money. For example, there were no pizzas in the '40s, no McDonalds, no Subway, no Taco Bell, no Big Boy and certainly not many discretionary dollars. In the summer there was A & W if you were lucky enough to know someone with a car - even then most could only afford a 5-cent jug of root beer.

Adults rarely if ever took their kids out to eat. I have no recollection of ever going to a restaurant with my mother. On a rare occasion she brought home 6 hamburgers for 25-cents from Tommy's Lunch - a rare and special treat - maybe twice a year.

Most kids today have money to visit fast food restaurants often. Burgers are bigger, french fries are super sized and everything is full of calories and trans-fat. And they drink oodles of soda - sugar galore and more calories. Most of them have access to cars. Is it any wonder that today's kids are bigger?

I can only think of a few kids in high school that would have been considered overweight - not obese. Girls were trim for the most part and not as tall as today's youth. In high school I never reached 100 pounds! And the weight and height of boys has changed significantly over the years. Today's young people are much bigger than generations ago.

For example, my husband relates comparisons of his high school football team. The average player was about 155 pounds and was less than 6 feet tall. Gary played wide receiver. He weighed 145 pounds at 5 feet 10 inches. .

Today it is not uncommon to have boys weighing over 300 pounds playing high school football with a considerable number over 6 feet tall.

Some chores from our generation are for the most part non existent today. For example: emptying wash machines, shoveling coal into the furnace; hauling the ashes out to the alley; shoveling sidewalks and driveways by hand; mowing the grass with lawn mowers that weren't self-propelled. These are just a few examples.

Alabama and Mississippi rate one and two for having the worst adult obesity record. Alabama's rate is 28.4; Mississippi's rate is 28.1; Michigan is tied for 6th with a rate of 25.2. The total average rate of all states is 22.8. Diabetes, a major complication of obesity, affects over six percent of adults in 40 states.

Federal health goals aim to drop the obesity rate to 15

percent by 2010. Sounds like quite an ambitious goal and one that most likely will not be met if current life styles of exercise and diet habits prevail.

The CDC reports that adults are almost 25 pounds heavier than 40 years ago. "Americans of all ages are 'dramatically' heavier and slightly taller than they were back then." Average weight increased for everyone regardless of age, sex, and racial groups.

In people older than 20, both men and women were a little more than 24 pounds heavier than in the early 1960s. By 2002, average weight for men was almost 191 pounds; for women, average weight was 163 pounds.

Adults weren't the only one to gain weight. Children joined the fray. Kids aged 6 to 11 are almost 9 pounds heavier weighing 74 pounds, teen boys aged 12 to 17 are 15 pounds heavier weighing an average of 141 pounds. Teen girls in the same age bracket are 12 pounds heavier, tipping the scales at 130 pounds.

The CDC doesn't address why the average weight or height of Americans has increased. They look at the hard cold numbers but stop short of pointing fingers at diets, exercise habits or lifestyles. But isn't the reason a no-brainer?

If it is any consolation hundreds of thousands of people are in the same boat.

Change is possible - if you are motivated to buck the national trend. Common sense beckons us to start on a safe, sensible diet and fitness program - for the heath of it!

CLASS STRUCTURE IN SOCIETY

May 12, 2006

According to the American Constitution, "All men are created equal," but are they? If that were the case there would be no top level to reach for, and conversely, no bottom level to escape from.

My degree in social work required me, to better serve clients, to study and examine how the class structure affects the dynamics of the individual, the family and the community. According to sociologists the American Dream of equality is a myth and societal class is divided into five categories.

The **REAL UPPER CLASS** consists of people most likely to be on the board of directors of local universities, banks or industries.

They would be considered prestige professionals: doctors, lawyers, etc. In small communities, status-quo at one time meant "old" family backgrounds. (That has evolved over time and status-quo has less significance).

The **UPPER MIDDLE CLASS** are the most energetic, confident and ambitious people who graduated from college and start their careers away from their home town. Some are professional and some are successful local business people. This group consists of hyperactive civic-minded individuals involved in local charity drives, service clubs and country clubs.

The **LOWER MIDDLE CLASS** are more conforming and proper than any other group. Most in this category have high-school diplomas, a year or two of college, or training in technical schools. According to sociologists, they are comprised of "the aristocrats of labor."

The **WORKING CLASS** very often has not obtained a high school diploma. They are the largest class (40 percent) and work at jobs that require little or no training. They mostly live from paycheck to paycheck and have boring, repetitive jobs.

The **REAL WORKING CLASS** consists of people found in slum areas and looked down upon by everyone. They are used to living on the edge of hunger and disaster. The youth are most often juvenile delinquents and the "older lowers" sink into apathy.

Individuals can climb or drop from one class to another. Class status is further defined in the entertainment and cultural areas, and in the selection of spouses and reading material. Birth rates, mortality rates and mental illness are other areas affected by class distinction.

Occupation seems to play a crucial role in determining a person's income level, style of life and status. As one sociologist defined it, "Class structure of the United States is more like a jungle gym than a ladder. To move from the lower jungle gym to the higher one, you must go outside and climb up the fire escape of higher education."

A person is born into a class structure, and children are not immune to the slights or injuries of a class system. Rich or poor have little meaning to a child before fourth grade when an awareness of class develops. By grade six, children become aware of class position based on the home, family, the father's occupation, clothes and manners.

By eighth grade children rate class very much the same as adults. Some children are banned to groups on the outside (looking in) because they are perceived different - and peers can be cruel! Their personality and self-esteem suffer. Sometimes this can be the catalyst of emotional problems, anxiety and delinquency. A rare example would be the Columbine shooting.

So what is the answer? A homogenized society? Even though the negative implications to a class society are many - the arguments for it seem to outweigh the negative aspects. Granted, we must work to try and keep the system as democratic as possible.

Put another way, this country and its system do not in any way constitute utopia, nor is utopia possible. Winston Churchill once said, "It may not be the best system, but it is the best of what there is."

Woodruff, Brain-Injury and the War   March 9, 2007

On Jan. 29, 2006, Bob Woodruff, news anchor and reporter with ABC, was on assignment in Iraq when he was gravely injured by a roadside bomb. Shrapnel and rocks embedded in the left side of his brain, neck and face, leaving him near death and in a coma for 36 days.

Painful memories of my son's brain injury returned as I watched the special report, "To Iraq and Back." It told a vivid story of Bob's struggle to recover and the horrific plight of brain-injured Iraq veterans.

Traumatic Brain Injury (TBI) can be an open, focal wound to the head, such as Bob's, or in the case of my son, a closed head injury. In Bob's case the left-side of his brain that controls speech was affected.

A closed TBI leading to oxygen deprivation has global effects. In other words, the whole brain in affected. In most cases the outcome is not as positive. I watched the TV special as it portrayed how Bob struggled with words and meanings.

Gary went through a similar struggle as he regained some of his language skills after being in a coma for six weeks. I remember sitting next to him at the Regional Major Medical Center in Wichita, Kansas: "Give me that branch!" he demanded. "What branch?" I asked. Exasperated, he pointed to a straw in a glass. I thought afterward what a good analogy.

One time when I left the room momentarily to go the cafeteria, a friend came by and asked Gary where his mother was. "I haven't seen her in five years," he replied. At the time everything was baffling. I didn't understand why he couldn't remember even for a minute.

The year was 1987 and I had never heard of anybody with a brain injury. I had to educate myself and become an advocate for him so that he might reach his optimum.

He has come a long way. Recently, at a doctor's office, she asked Gary if he had any pain. His quick retort was, "No I don't. Do you?" He is funny at times, and at times a song will jog his memory of special times in the past. He will get choked up and tears stream when he recalls how life used to be. Those are sad times for me because I feel so helpless. Mothers are supposed to "fix" things, and I can't.

I am not a proponent of the war that has gone on for over four years now; I doubt many mothers are. Many more of our young, brave warriors are surviving horrendous TBIs because major advancements have occurred in technology, medicine and battlefield know-how.

They are the unsung heroes who in many cases will be dependent on others for the rest of their lives. Life will never be the same for them, their parents, their wives, their children and their loved ones. A tragic legacy of the Iraq war will be traumatic brain injury.

They deserve the very best our country can provide. A scathing report of Walter Reed Hospital tells a different story. Why is this revelation just coming to the forefront? Decrepit living conditions with rats and mice running the halls, and walls filled with mold!

As a result of an investigation the 2-star general in charge of Walter Reed Hospital has been relieved of his command. Further, the secretary of the army has submitted his resignation. Sen. Carl Levin, D-Mich., cites "lack of accountability" and "over optimism" about the war.

Soldiers with brain-injuries are being discharged from the hospital early because the system cannot handle the stream of seriously-injured soldiers. Some of those being sent home to their small communities have no access to the cognitive therapies needed to continue to reach their optimum.

Loved ones are at a loss as to where to turn. Can't we do better than this? We should have state-of-the-art first class facilities for our war heroes who survive devastating injuries. We only hear the casualty numbers; the maimed and injured numbers are staggering but not talked about.

Bob and his wife Lee wrote a memoir called *In an Instant: A Family's Journey of Love and Healing.* I read their poignant story laced with courage, despair, anger, faith and hope. It's a powerful testimonial to the human spirit.

They are partnering with the National Brain Injury Association to help others and promote awareness. They have set up a foundation to help soldiers recovering from brain trauma. Brain-Injury for years has been called the "Silent Epidemic." How silent can it be? There are in excess of 1.4 million people affected by a brain-injury each year.

TBI victims have also been described as "the walking wounded" because to the naked eye the brain-injury and its deleterious cognitive effects may not be apparent. Iraq war victims are forced to fight the government to recognize their injury; much like the Agent Orange debacle.

When celebrities or well-known people such as Christopher Reeve, Jim Brady, Michael J. Fox and Bob Woodruff are afflicted, they help to bring awareness of the plights of millions. They have used their celebrity to help educate the public. They have become prolific fund-raisers for their cause.

I think of the dollars spent on war and the senseless killing; placing our troops smack in the middle of a civil war. I wonder what progress could have been made if these dollars were allocated to solutions for Parkinson's, brain-injury, spinal-cord injury and a host of other infirmities.

Is it any wonder we, as a nation, have become disenchanted with politics and the obvious lack of common sense? Politicians need to take their constituents seriously. They're the one who put them in office. They are there by the votes of the people and their mission should be to act in the interests of the people - not for special interests, lobbyists and their own self-interests.

A good start would be to do away with lobbyists and special interest groups. Legislators would do well to eliminate attaching "pork" to bills that need to be passed and vote their conscience instead of "left" or "right."

Term limits may be the answer, or, at the very least, a step in the right direction. But while the fox is guarding the chicken coop it's not going to happen.

Recently I heard this statement with a tongue-in-cheek double meaning: Politicians are like babies; they need to be changed often.

I am horrified and outraged by the apparent treatment of our wounded heroes: the troops.

Thanks for that colum on illegal aliens. My exact sentiments. Thanks again for yur column. You are right on the mark!

–Mary Goulet, Colorado Springs, Colorado

Dear Patt,
I wanted you do know how much I enjoyed your *Daily Press* article of July 21st, titled *Hot Topics: Politics and Religion*. I am 74 and so much of what you woted spoke to me. I found it humorous and so like the times of that period. Thanks so much. It was refreshing. By the way, I'm Catholic and Polish! :) Blessings

–Virginia Minor

COMMENTS FROM PRESIDENTIAL HOPEFUL FRONT RUNNERS...

RUDY GUILIANI: There must be public funding for abortion for poor women (because) we cannot deny any woman the right to make her own decision about abortion because she lacks resources.

BARACK OBAMA: Clinton gets in bed with big business - sells out the state she represents - and helps China at the same time.

JOHN EDWARDS: Evidently, Rudy Guliani has taken a break from reality. It is outrageous for Rudy to suggest in any way, shape or form, that he did more at Ground Zero or spent more time there than the brave first responders.

HILLARY CLINTON: We have an administration that doesn't believe in diplomacy.

JOHN MCCAIN: Republicans, once the party of fiscal discipline were corrupted by power and spent like drunken sailors.

MITT ROMNEY: It's not Rudy's three wives that will be a problem, but his 'one husband'.

Chapter 6

History / Biographies

A famous quotation by THEODORE ROOSEVELT
rendered during a speech entitled
Citizenship in a Republic
delivered at the Sorbonne in Paris on April 23, 1910:

"It is not the critic who counts; nor the man who points out how the strong man stumbles, or where the doer of deeds could have done them better. The credit belongs to the man who is actually in the arena, whose face is marred by dust and sweat and blood; who strives valiantly; who errs, who comes short again and again, because there is no effort without error and shortcoming; but who does actually strive to do the deeds; who knows great enthusiasms, the great devotions; who spends himself in a worry cause; who at the best knows in the end the triumph of high achievement, and who at the worst, if he fails, at least fails while daring greatly, so that his place shall never be with those cold and timid souls who neither know victory or defeat."

Einstein: His Genius & Humanness   September 8, 2006

My mental image of Albert Einstein conjures up a brilliant genius, an almost wild looking scientist with hair standing up on end. Of course his name is synonymous with his theory of relativity: $E=MC^2$. His over simplified explanation of the theory basically means that one person's now is another person's then.

In 1999 the law firm of Stark and Stark in Princeton, N.J., contacted me to be the keynote speaker for a Brain-Injury Symposium they were sponsoring. Among the participants were physicians, nurses, social workers, rehabilitation therapists and hospital administrators. Each participant would receive my book as part of the packet.

I readily agreed. They arranged my flight and three months later representatives from the law firm met me at the airport in Newark, whisking me away in a limousine for the half-hour drive to Princeton. They brought me to a luxurious hotel, told me to freshen up and they would return for me.

I remember that sunny, fall day with bright orange and red leaves rustling in the streets as I toured Princeton and the University. I remember driving down Mercer Street. It was typical of an Escanaba neighborhood; mature trees lined both sides of the street and seemingly formed an arch.

My escorts stopped in front of a very plain unpretentious two-story white house with a front porch. "This was the home of Albert Einstein," one of them said. No tours are allowed at his request.

It was such an eerie feeling to imagine Albert Einstein walking every day on that same street to the university. From that day forward Einstein's life held a curious mystique for me. I wanted to know all I could about this unusual genius - his humanness - the man whose brain is preserved yet today. Einstein said, "My life is a simple thing that would interest none." Talk about an understatement! His modesty only made him more loved.

His life was anything but simple. My interest was further piqued about his personal life as I read the endearing love letters he wrote to his first wife, Mileva. His parents were against the union.

Their burning love produced a child before their marriage. Their daughter, Lieserl, was adopted and to this day what became of her is unknown. Only speculation exists. A year later, in 1903, they were married. They would eventually become the parents of two sons, Hans Albert and Eduard.

Einstein met Mileva, who was four years older than him, in his physics class. Very few women were admitted to universities for instruction in mathematics and physics, giving evidence of her competence and ability. Einstein, himself, stated that Mileva used to check his mathematics.

In 1914, at the time they lived in Geneva, Albert received an appointment as a professor at Berlin University. Mileva stayed in Geneva with the boys. The move disrupted his marriage when he became friendly with his first cousin, Elsa, a divorcee, which ultimately led to an affair. He divorced Mileva in 1919 and married Elsa the same year.

There is a controversy as to how much Mileva contributed to Einstein's work. Some say she did the mathematics. Others say she was little more than a sounding board. The most convincing argument for Mileva as a co-genius is in letters that Albert referred to "our" theory and "our" work and also a divorce agreement in which Einstein promised her his Nobel Prize money. However, there was no mention of her involvement in his papers.

In 1921, Einstein won the Nobel Prize. He remained somewhat of a womanizer. Elsa facilitated his fascination with women by allowing him to see other women. They moved to Princeton in 1933 after Hitler's rise to power. His first public act in the U.S. was to buy an ice cream cone with sprinkles. Elsa died in 1936.

Einstein was always troubled by his lack of relationship with his boys. His youngest son Eduard suffered from schizophrenia. He was eventually institutionalized in a psychiatric sanatorium in Zurich where he died.

Hans, his eldest son, was severely affected by his parent's separation. He eventually immigrated to the U.S. and became a renowned professor at the University of California. After his marriage in 1927 his relationship with his father began to improve. Hans Albert gained international fame through his work. The relationship with his father continued to improve and together they traveled through America. Hans Albert spent many hours with his father on his deathbed shortly before Albert died.

Albert Einstein died in Princeton in 1955. He was cremated and the location of his remains has never been revealed.

Scientists comparing Einstein's brain to those of average intelligence think they found the explanation to explain his genius for mathematical and spatial thinking.

"In general, Einstein's brain was the same as all others except in one particular area - the region responsible for mathematical thought and the ability to think in terms of space and movement." They also said his brain was 15 percent wider than other brains studied and "that it lacked a groove that normally runs through part of this area. The researchers suggest that its absence may have allowed the neurons to communicate much more easily.

Many of the intimate details of Einstein's life emerged in July when more than 3,500 pages of letters, postcards and other documents were unsealed. My curiosity about Einstein, his genius and humanness has finally been satiated - and what a story. It was not exactly the simple life he alluded to

BRADY: LESSON IN COURAGE, HUMANITY   February 23, 2007

President Reagan has been shot! Those words shocked the nation in 1981. The three major networks also reported that Jim Brady, Reagan's press secretary, was also shot and has died! That report was erroneous; Jim Brady had been shot in the head and was clinging to life.

Sarah Brady, Jim's wife, was vacuuming and unaware of the events that would drastically change their lives. Her son, Scott, was watching TV and ran into the next room, tugged on his mother's skirt, and said, "Daddy is on TV." I can only imagine the horror Sarah felt hearing the news on TV: Jim Brady is dead!

John Hinckley purchased his gun in a pawn shop with little trouble. His deranged plan was to kill the president and become a hero to Jodie Foster, a movie star who he wanted to impress and was secretly infatuated with.

He was in the crowd as Reagan and his entourage exited the Washington Hilton. He fired six shots. Reagan was whisked away in a limousine not even realizing he had been shot. Brady lay on the cement in a pool of blood. Two law enforcement officers were also wounded. Hinckley was wrestled to the ground. Those images were shown over and over on TV.

Jim Brady, affectionately known as Bear, lost one fifth of his brain and the floor of his skull was shattered. His left side would remain paralyzed. He would undergo operation after operation to retrieve parts of the bullet that exploded the right frontal lobe of his brain. Seizures, pneumonia, infections and operations posed continuous treats. Yet, through sheer determination along with Sarah's love and expert medical attention, he would survive.

As vice chairman of the National Brain-injury Association (BIA), Jim wrote the forward for my book published in 1997. That same year I won the title of Ms. Senior Michigan and was awarded $500 to be donated to the charity of my choice. It was only natural to donate my prize monies to the BIA since the focus of my book was about my son, Gary, and his brain-injury.

I traveled around Michigan for a year promoting brain-injury awareness along with my duties relevant to winning the crown. I met with then - Governor Engler to ask why Michigan refused to apply for a federal matching grant to form an exploratory committee.

He assured me he would look into it. He did! And ultimately Michigan applied for and received the grant. I was the recipient that year of the Brain-Injury Awareness award in Michigan. The national BIA wrote a story in its national publication about my involvement and the grassroots success.

I was totally taken aback when the BIA contacted me to be the keynote speaker at the International Brain-Injury Symposium in Philadelphia. James Brady, as figurehead of the BIA, would introduce me. I said yes immediately - then frantically scrambled to prepare my speech.

It was a once-in-a-lifetime experience. Upon arrival, I was escorted to the platform and podium where I met Jim Brady. He was in a wheelchair; his left side paralyzed. He took my hand, shook it and didn't let go for the longest time. I thanked him for writing the forward to my book and gave him a copy. I wore my Ms. Senior Michigan banner across my suit and my crown adorned my head.

Jim said he liked queens and wanted his photo taken with me. I recognized a keen sense of humor - something usually lost with a brain injury. I thought he would never end his complimentary introduction of me as he read on and on. I looked over the crowd of 2,000+ and suddenly began to wilt. Then a huge applause and my 20-minute talk began. I relaxed! The response was unbelievable. And the photo ops began. What a memorable experience!

Jim, born in Illinois, was an avid Cub's fan. He had a sharp wit, was keen-minded and blessed with boundless energy. His confidence, abilities and skills had garnered him the position of assistant to the president and White House press secretary: The job he considered the pinnacle of his career. He was 40 years old. He was in essence on top of the world. But that world, as he knew it, would crumble. He was only in his job a matter of weeks when John Hinckley destroyed one-fifth of his brain with a gun purchased over the counter. No background check or waiting period was needed then.

Jim's pet name for Sarah is "Coon," short for Raccoon. Coon and Bear were on a roller-coaster ride for months while Jim's life hung in the balance. Sarah the Saint might be a more appropriate name. She watched over Jim like a mother hen and was involved in all aspects of medical decisions.

The gun control people tried to enlist Sarah as a spokesperson. "I can't do that," said Sarah, knowing that Jim would be furious. Reagan was a member of the National Rifle Association.

A year later, when Jim returned home, he read a letter Sarah had received again asking for her help. He became furious. Sarah blew up one day over Jim's rigidness. Jim finally relinquished and gave Sarah his "thumbs up" sign and reluctantly said, "Go ahead and get involved with the NRA."

On November 30, 1993, Sarah watched President Bill Clinton sign into law the "Brady Bill."

Twenty-six years later "Bear" and "Coon" cannot imagine going through the last 26 years without each other. Jim says, "Dr. Korbine saved me physically but Sarah saved me emotionally."

FITZGERALD: A MARITIME TRAGEDY   November 10, 2006

The sinking of the Edmund Fitzgerald during a massive winter storm November 10, 1975, is surpassed in notoriety only by the loss of the Titanic.

All 29 crew members perished. The Fitzgerald was the last vessel lost - and the largest - on the Great Lakes. But, it is not alone on the bottom of the Great Lakes. From 1878 to 1898 nearly 6,000 shipwrecks occurred.

November 10, 1975, is vividly etched in my mind - but for reasons other than the Fitzgerald tragedy. On that very day my husband, Gary, was in St. Mary's Hospital in Milwaukee undergoing heart surgery. In 1975 by-pass surgery was in its infancy and not much hope was given for his survival. He needed seven by-passes. My thoughts were caught up with the real possibility of becoming a widow at age 42.

I remember the daily talk by other wives whose husbands had undergone surgery; about their husbands, their families, their fears and yes, the tragedy of the Edmund Fitzgerald and what their families must be going through.

I felt frightened, alone and engulfed by my own little world of tragedy. How could these wives go to lunch, laugh and be normal? Would my life ever be the same? Well, thank God, Gary did survive!

The crew of the Edmund Fitzgerald was not so fortunate. My thoughts turned to the 29 men lost at sea. For their families life would never be the same. Their families kissed them good-bye like they had many times before - this time they wouldn't return. Their remains are entombed in the ship at the bottom of the Great Lakes.

Some say the boat was cursed from the start. When the ship was christened by Mrs. Fitzgerald it took three swings to break the bottle of champagne. Then, upon launching the ship in the water, the boat was slightly damaged when it hit a rock. Finally, one of the onlookers suffered a heart attack during the ceremony.

On her last trip, the Fitzgerald cleared Superior, Wisconsin, November 9, 1975. She was carrying a load of taconite pellets for delivery to Detroit. Traveling closely behind was the Arthur M. Anderson. The boats encountered a massive winter storm with high winds and waves over 16 feet. The Soo Locks had closed because of the storm.

During the afternoon of November 10th the Fitzgerald reported a minor list developing and top-side damage, including loss of radar, but indicated no serious problem. She slowed down to come within the range of receiving the Anderson's radar data: The Anderson, for a time, guided the Fitzgerald toward the safety of Whitefish Bay.

Then the last communication came. It was 7:10 p.m. when Anderson notified Fitzgerald of being hit by two freak waves that were heading Fitzgerald's way and asked how she was doing. Earnest McSorley, captain of the Fitzgerald, reported, "We are holding our own."

A few minutes later, the Fitzgerald sank. No distress signal was ever received. Ten minutes later the Anderson could neither communicate with Fitzgerald or detect her on radar. At 8:32 p.m. captain of the Anderson informed the Coast Guard of his concern for the boat.

A search was launched for survivors. Initially, the search consisted of Anderson and the freighter SS William Clay Ford. The efforts of a third freighter were hampered by the weather. A Coast Guard buoy tender, Woodrush, was able to launch within 2 1/2 hours, but took a day to arrive at the scene. The search recovered debris that included lifeboats and rafts, but no survivors.

The wreck was surveyed by sonar November 14-16. In May 1976 an unmanned Navy sub photographed the wreck. The Edmund Fitzgerald was lying in two pieces in 530 feet of water, deeper than could be reached by scuba.

At first it was thought and widely believed that the boat broke apart on the surface of the lake due to the storm. But a Coast Guard investigation posed a theory that the accident was caused by ineffective hatch closures. The flooding occurred gradually all through the final day. Finally, a fatal loss of stability and buoyancy caused the boat to plummet to the bottom without warning.

There was controversy over the Coast Guard report. If the boat had snapped in half on the surface the two sections would have been miles apart. Instead they were right next to each another. The alternate theory posed that without the radar operating the ship ran aground on a shoal without the crew's awareness. With bottom damage she took on water and sank so suddenly that none of her crew had time to react. It broke apart when it hit bottom. This theory is supported by the final communications between the Fitzgerald and Anderson. The Fitzgerald had settled in mud making it impossible to access for damage.

The boat's bell was recovered from the wreck July 4, 1995. It now resides in the Great Lakes Shipwreck Museum in Whitefish Point near Paradise. The wreckage is located 17 miles off of Whitefish Point.

In 1976, Canadian singer-songwriter Gordon Lightfoot (he recently appeared at the Island Resort and Casino) wrote and sang *The Wreck of the Edmund Fitzgerald*. It commemorates the events surrounding the ship's sinking. A few lines from the song follow:

"The Captain wired in he had water coming in, and the good

ship and crew was in peril.

"And later that night when his lights went out of sight came the wreck of the Edmund Fitzgerald.

"And all that remains is the faces and the names of the wives and the sons and the daughters."

TEDDY ROOSEVELT REMEMBERED   June 30, 2006

My husband visits our son, Jeff, in Washington, D.C., every year and together they visit historical sites like Civil War battlegrounds, including Gettysburg, FDR's home in Hyde Park, the Vanderbilt Home, Annapolis and West Point. They also visited the site where Stonewall Jackson and Robert E. Lee are interned, Thomas Jefferson's home (Monticello) and George Washington's home (Mount Vernon).

One year they had front row seats on top of the Citicorp building to the most spectacular 4th of July display imaginable. Our nation's Capitol really celebrates in grand style!

This year they are planning to visit historical sites in New England where some of the Revolutionary War was fought. In particular, they will visit battle sites where my husband's great-great-grandfather, who fought in the Revolutionary War, was wounded. And a must see this year is the birthplace of Teddy Roosevelt, my son's favorite historical figure. I knew Teddy had visited the U.P. and my interest was piqued to research more about about him.

People today wonder why Theodore Roosevelt's face is on Mount Rushmore alongside the three great presidents, Washington, Jefferson and Lincoln. He keeps some pretty amazing historical company, and I'll tell you why. He was one of the most remarkable men in all of history and America's most important citizen in the first quarter of the 20th century.

His resume would look like this: Harvard Phi Beta Kappa, cattle rancher and accomplished horseman, explorer, big game hunter, state legislator, seminal conservationist, Commissioner of the Civil Service, prolific author, New York City police chief, cavalry field commander and decorated national war hero holding the rank of colonel, assistant secretary of the U.S. Navy, and governor of New York. All by the age of 40!

At age 42, he became the youngest president in American history. He renamed the executive mansion the White House, refurbished it and added the West Wing, which includes the oval office where he and every president since has sat.

He saved the life of an orphaned bear cub during a 1902 hunting trip, and inspired the creation of a toy, the teddy bear, that became a nationwide craze.

He easily won reelection in 1904, and two years later was awarded the Nobel Peace Prize for his role in ending the Russian-Japanese war. He doubled the number of national parks, created 16 national monuments and 51 wildlife refuges, and set aside 125 million acres of public land as national forest. And the list goes on!

Theodore Roosevelt could have easily won a third term but voluntarily stepped aside. He ended his self-imposed retirement after watching the country slowly creep back into the arms of the trusts. But now the party bosses that Teddy had booted out of office were lined up for Taft. After losing the nomination to Taft he put together the Bull Moose Party.

Teddy was in Milwaukee campaigning three weeks before the election. Larger than life, he just couldn't resist standing up in his car to greet a cheering crowd. When suddenly a man named Schrank pulled a pistol and shot him in the chest from six feet away. The bullet broke a rib and entered his right lung after ricocheting off his glasses case and passing through a manuscript of his speech in his coat pocket, slowing the bullet and saving his life.

He insisted on delivering his speech before he would accept any medical attention. He walked unsteadily on the stage of the auditorium and began his remarks by saying, "Friends, I shall ask you to be as quiet as possible. I don't know whether you fully understand I have just been shot, but it takes more than that to kill a Bull Moose."

He opened his coat to reveal his blood-soaked shirt and received a five-minute ovation. He proceeded to deliver his bullet-ridden text for over an hour, bleeding through his shirt, and then passed out blood-stained pages of his speech as souvenirs on his way to the hospital. However, Woodrow Wilson won the election in a landslide.

In May 1913, former President Theodore Roosevelt appeared in Marquette court after filing a libel suit against the publisher of the Ishpeming Iron Ore. George Hewitt had reported that "Roosevelt was a liar and addicted to the use of alcohol." Hewitt admitted he lied and Roosevelt settled for six cents which, he claimed, "was the price of a good newspaper."

Yes, Teddy Roosevelt was a truly talented and amazing man: A patriot who loved his country. And now that I know more about him I can understand why his face is on Mount Rushmore. It belongs there among the three other great presidents.

☆   ☆   ☆   ☆

A man who is good enough to shed his blood for his country is good enough to be given a square deal afterwards.

☆

Wars are, of course, as a rule to be avoided; but they are far better than certain kinds of peace.

☆

Every immigrant who comes here should be required within five years to learn English or leave the country.

☆

A typical vice of American politics is the avoidance of saying anything real on the issues.

☆

Behind the ostensible government sits enthroned an invisible government owing no allegiance and acknowledging no responsibility to the people.

☆

The only time you really live fully is from thirty to sixty. The young are slaves to dreams; the old servants of regrets. Only the middle-aged have all their five senses in the keeping of their wits.

☆   ☆ THEODORE ROOSEVELT ☆

Chapter 7

Thomas Alva Edison

Thomas Edison
age 15

Thomas Edison
in his 20s

Thomas Edison
age 30

Thomas Edison
in his 30s

Thomas Edison
at 50

Thomas Edison
at 73

Thomas Edison's
Parents

Samuel Ogden
Edison, Jr.

Nancy Matthews
Elliott Edison

Thomas Edison's
Wives

Mary Stillwell
Edison

Mina Miller
Edison

Henry Ford, Edison & Harvey Firestone

Edison Residence in Fort Meyers, FL

A gift from Ford

Stills for making rubber from Goldenrod.

Ford & Edison in the lab

The Edisons at home

Talking with Reporters

The Phonograph

Thomas, Theodore, Madeleine & Mina

The lab at Ft. Meyers

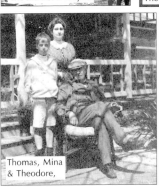

Thomas, Mina & Theodore,

In the garden

Entertaining at the Fair

Fishing

Billie & Dearie

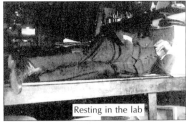

Resting in the lab

RESEARCHING THE FAMILY TREE
THOMAS EDISON: THE ESCANABA CONNECTION

June 1, 2006

 Our search began after a chance meeting at the Escanaba Library with Pat Sundstrom, director of the Family History Center. Although my husband and I had talked for years about researching our ancestors, we hadn't yet acted on it. Nor were we aware of the great research tool available in Escanaba: the Family History Center.

The journey to explore our family trees began about a year ago. Little did we know how the discoveries we would make concerning our ancestors would captivate our lives; every waking moment, every conversation.

The catalyst that began our excursion into the past was to try and document where Thomas Edison fit into my husband's family. As a boy, Gary remembered family conversations about the letter his grandfather received from Thomas Edison, his cousin. Questions loomed in his mind. Was Thomas Edison really his grandfather's cousin? Where was the documentation? Family members didn't know what had become of the letter.

But where do we start? Gary's grandfather died in Escanaba, in 1914. We knew he was born in Canada. We searched local land records, marriage, probate, birth, and death records. We checked old obituaries in newspaper articles on microfiche at the library. The local Family History Center proved to be a tremendous asset. We became aware of and contacted relatives we didn't know existed in both Ontario and British Columbia. They supplied us with folklore that was stranger than fiction. This is one of many interesting stories that unfolded:

James H. Elliott, Gary's grandfather, was born in Vienna, Ontario. He was the youngest of ten siblings. His father, John Elliott, was an Episcopal Methodist Minister and well-respected merchant of considerable influence. He had filled various offices in the church, eventually being ordained. John refused to support a union between the Episcopal and Wesleyan Methodists; consequently, he held church services in his home. The congregation increased until the floor collapsed, then services were held on the second floor of his warehouse known as "God's old barn." He was a member of the town and county councils, a magistrate, a commissioner of the Queens bench, and an associate Judge.

John Elliott dressed elegantly, including a bright red sash, and was considered a wealthy man because he owned a lumberyard and planing mill. He was very strict with his family of ten children. His sons would float his own logs down the river, fish them out and sell them to him to get a little spending money.

John Elliott's sister was Nancy Edison, mother of Thomas Alva Edison. Finally, the question of where Thomas Edison fit in our tree was answered. Nancy Mathews Elliott Edison was indeed James H. Elliott's aunt and Thomas Alva Edison, his first cousin. Now we had the documentation.

While climbing around in the family tree it was almost eerie. Ancestors came alive as we discovered intimate and profound information about their lives; their hardships and their triumphs. Elizabeth Elliott, sister to John and Nancy Elliott Edison was famous for dancing with Lafayette. Remember the famous French General, Marquis de Lafayette, who came to America to help us win the Revolutionary War? Elizabeth met Lafayette in 1824 in Connecticut at a ball given in his honor. Visions of Elizabeth in her high collared long dress bustled out with yards of underskirts and swirling around the dance floor with Lafayette in his majestic General Uniform came to life and danced in our minds.

In the 1860s two fires and a flood desecrated the town of Vienna, once considered a booming town. James H. Elliott, born in 1845, left Vienna with his new bride Louisa, at age 18 in search of work. They settled in Waukesha, Wisconsin where James worked as a tenant farmer. The 1870 census stated he had three children and a net worth of $150. Around 1890 James arrived in Escanaba. He worked as a clerk for Atkins General Store located in the 400 block on Ludington Street. According to court records, Louisa was declared insane in 1891 and sent to the Northern Michigan Asylum in Traverse City. To be sure, when you rattle around in ancient closets, skeletons can fall out. Guarded truths shrouded in secrecy screamed to be revealed. And we found many family stories handed down were just that: stories!

Several years later James acquired his own grocery store in the 300 block on Ludington Street. In 1899, James, age 55, married his housekeeper, Valerie Mapes, age 33. She came from Chippewa Falls, Wisconsin to work as a domestic. James was 57 when their daughter, Vida Elliott was born. She married Stanton Abrahamson and Gary, my husband, was born in 1931.

Perhaps even more interesting are the "branch" stories that unfolded in our initial one-dimensional quest to place Thomas

Edison in our tree.

John Elliott and Nancy Elliott Edison's father was Ebenezer Matthews Elliott, grandfather to both James and Thomas. Ebenezer, who fought in the revolutionary war, received the Badge of Military Merit and George Washington signed his discharge. Although it is somewhat mutilated, we were able to secure a copy from the National Archives. He was at the surrender of Burgoyne, battle of Monmouth; at the surrender of Lord Cornwallis, at Chemong in a fight with the Indians and in a skirmish with a party of British Light Horse at Horse Neck in which he was wounded. He applied for and received bounty land of 100 acres in Madison County, New York.

Documents retrieved from the National Archives not only disclosed his war records, but his financial status at the time he applied for bounty land at age 60. The following is taken from a sworn statement in 1820:

A schedule of the whole estate of Ebenezer Mathews.

Real Estate: I have none.

Personal: Two poor beds and scanty bedding for the same. One pair broken hand irons work mere trifle, two pigs, three geese, four hens, no sheep, cows or horses. One kitchen table and an old stand, also one snow shovel but no tongs, one broken candlestick, six harrow teeth which is all my personal property except a small quantity of wearing apparel nearly worn out and hardly comfortable to keep myself and family warm. I have no debts due to me. I owe about 35 dollars. (The document stated a property value of $14.24.)

And I do further swear that I am a farmer by profession, am afflicted with a complaint called the gravel, which renders me unable to labor more than half the time. That I have a wife who is a cripple and not able to labor. I have two children only that live with me, both girls; one aged 16 the other 12 and are healthy. That I have no children able to support me or render me any assistance. Signed: Ebenezer Mathews (Elliott)

The 12-year-old daughter referenced is Nancy, mother of Thomas Edison. How sad, poor and destitute the people that lived in those times were! Ebenezer died in 1848, just one year after the birth of his famous grandson, Thomas Alva Edison. James H. Elliott was three years old when his grandfather died.

Ebenezer received the Badge of Merit awarded for a meritorious action. Toward the end of the Revolutionary War, Continental Congress ordered George Washington to cease recognizing outstanding valor and merit by granting a commission or an advance in rank - there were no funds to pay the soldiers. George Washington, the designer and creator of the Badge of Merit, devised the award to honor the common soldier who so bravely and loyally served his country and him.

The award was the "figure of a heart in purple cloth and silk edged with narrow lace and binding." The honoree's name and regiment were inscribed in a Book of Merit to be kept in the orderly room. Lost or misfiled for almost 150 years among the War Department Records at Washington, D.C., an important paper came to light during the search for papers prior to the celebration of Washington's Bi-Centennial in 1932. Included were the dramatic accounts of the only known three soldiers who received the decoration at Newburgh, New York at Washington's Head-quarters.

The Book of Merit was lost and has not been found. However, in Ebenezer's case, three sites have been documented by the court system after the Revolutionary War that references his receiving the prestigious award. Congressman Stupak, D-MI attempted to pursue his just reward posthumously - without success

A communication from the Military Awards Branch of the Army stated that a policy ruling from the Secretary of the Army determined an act of congress would be required. Unprecedented, yes, but the Grandfather of Thomas Alva Edison and Great, Great Grandfather of Gary Abrahamson deserves recognition for his mer-itorious action and wounds sustained during his dedication and commitment to the United States of America in the war fought to obtain the freedom on which this nation was founded.

Further research revealed James H. Elliott's grandfather on his mother's side, Jeremiah Anderson was famous in his own right. During the American Revolution in 1777, at age 14, Jeremiah, a Loyalist, joined "His Majesties" service, serving in Delancey's Brigade. His father also belonged to this company and was killed at New Rochelle. Jeremiah's service included duty as midshipman on board the British Commodore's ship with Prince William [later King William IV] until 1783. A crown Deed dated July 15, 1847 was issued to Jeremiah for 100 acres in Vienna, Ontario.

Imagine the irony! James' paternal grandfather, Ebenezer, fought for the American Revolution, while his maternal grandfather, Jeremiah, fought for the British. Each received bounty land from their respective countries.

Research also revealed an interesting story about Thomas Edison's father Samuel. After Canada became a country, local folklore claims that Edison secretly trained rebel volunteers in the woods around Vienna, Ontario. He joined the Mackenzie Rebellion poised to overthrow the Royal Canadian government. But the planned revolt was short-lived. The militia had easily halted the uprising in Toronto and was now headed Southwest to meet Edison's Vienna brigade. Nine members of the group were not quick enough; they were captured and hanged in Middlesex jail in London, Ontario.

Forced to leave his wife, Nancy, and four children behind, Samuel Edison set off on foot to reach the border eighty miles away. Two years after his imposed exile and now established in Milan, Ohio, Edison sent for his family. Their seventh and last child (Thomas Alva Edison) was born in Milan on the snowy night of February 11, 1847. If only they could have known their son Tom would become famous; and considered the greatest inventor of the century.

At age seven, Thomas' family moved to Port Huron, Michigan on the Canadian border and close to the relatives they had in Vienna, Ontario. Young Tom spent extended visits in Vienna and was already showing signs of his imaginative mind. Stories abode of Tom building a model pulpit from which his playmates, the "United Brethren" could preach. His playmates were his cousins, the "Elliott Brothers." Young Thomas was fond of practical jokes and the pulpit was carefully designed to collapse by pulling a secret string in the midst of the sermon. Perhaps he was imitating his uncle Reverend John Elliott's collapsed floor while holding church services.

It has been said without exception, the world has never seen his equal. Thomas Alva Edison was named "Man of the Millennium." The "electrical wizard's" wondrous gifts of light, power and entertainment to mankind can never be matched. Of over 1000 patents, the one that gave Edison his greatest pride was the phonograph.

Interestingly, our winters are spent in Fort Myers, Florida where Edison's winter home and laboratory are located. Each year 320 thousand visitors tour the estate. The grounds are awesome. The largest Banyan Tree in the USA with a circumference of nearly 400 feet graces the grounds. Henry Ford gave the tree to the Edisons in 1925. Edison is honored annually with a huge celebration called The Edison Festival of Lights. For two weeks in February there are parades, fireworks, gala balls and celebrations galore.

One of Edison's famous quotes is, "Genius is one percent inspiration and 99 percent perspiration." Edison ("Al" as his mother called him) died at age 84 in 1931. Three days later electric lights were dimmed for one minute throughout the United States.

As we uncovered snippets from the past, we were amazed at the large families our ancestors had. Many families averaged ten, eleven and twelve children. It is difficult to imagine the hardships they endured. Or the children they lost at young ages, and their daily struggles just to exist.

A will left by James' mother reveals the value placed on such items as a feather bed, curtains, a red and gold coverlet and a clock. Just simple things, here today and gone tomorrow in our lives, but to our ancestors they were treasures; heirlooms to be handed down. Each of her ten children including James, the youngest, received a household item, and $100.

In my husband's tree, many ancestors were ministers. Reverend Isaac Elliott, a missionary, and brother to Nancy Edison and John, who lived among the Indians in the wilderness of Michigan's Upper Peninsula. Wolves could be heard howling on the cabin doorstep in the black of the night. Isaac's picture rests on a table in the Edison home [museum] in Milan, Ohio.

Today, our ancestors live on in our hearts and minds. We talk of them on a first name basis - as if James, John, Thomas, Ebenezer, Nancy, Isaac and Jeremiah were here today. And we have sparked an interest in our children about their heritage. Now our heritage will be recorded by the genealogical society in the Escanaba Library for future generations to explore. I can't think of a greater legacy!

This sign was commonly found in hotel rooms in the early 1900s.

This Room Is Equipped With

Edison Electric Light.

Do not attempt to light with match. Simply turn key on wall by the door.

The use of Electricity for lighting is in no way harmful to health, nor does it affect the soundness of sleep.

Chapter
8

Personalities

POLITICS, PACKERS & PLASTIC SURGERY   November 24, 2006

Who do you think of when you hear the name Greta? Greta Van Susteren, of course, the news analyst and host of her own show, *On The Record*. What's more she is a celebrity from our own back yard: Appleton, Wisconsin, where she readily admits her heart will always be.

Greta's book, *My Turn at the Bully Pulpit*, captured my attention and I mentioned it in my column a couple of weeks ago. Someone sent Greta the article and she personally wrote me a note that went like this:

"I was sent your nice mention of my book. Many thanks! Glad you liked it. It did not sell well because I did not mention it on my show even one time - it seemed wrong to sell my book on my own show. So, in the end, (not a lot of sales), but I am proud of the book."

I thanked her for taking the time to write. I told her my son was an attorney for the Treasury Department in Washington. He remained in Washington after doing an internship for then Congressman Bob Davis. She wrote back:

"So your son got Potomac fever? That is how I ended up here - I came in 1975 as an intern for then Sen. Gaylord Nelson (who didn't care that my father was a Republican - he only cared about helping a kid from Wisconsin - he was that kind of guy). I got Potomac fever, went back to Madison, graduated, and then went to law school (at Georgetown University) here in D.C."

Greta was born in 1954, youngest of three children, and grew up in Appleton and attended Catholic school. Her father, Urban, a lawyer and judge and one of 13 siblings, no doubt played a huge roll in Greta eventually becoming a lawyer herself. Her respect and love for her father comes through loud and clear in her book.

Greta's father was campaign manager for Sen. Joe McCarthy in 1946. In fact, when Joe McCarthy spent time in the district he stayed at the Van Susteren's home.

Greta catapulted onto the national radar screen as a legal analyst for CNN during the O.J. Simpson trial. Today, as host of her own show on the Fox News Network, she is one of America's most popular television news anchors. Don't be misled by Greta's 5 foot 3 inch petite frame. She is a real heavyweight in her business.

Her trademark is common sense talk on today's pressing

issues and a style that endears her to her audience. She is the girl next door that made it big but refuses to be affected by her celebrity.

Greta married fellow lawyer John Coale. He was her former law firm partner in Washington. John is a successful lawyer and well-known litigator in his own right.

On a whim Greta made the decision to have cosmetic eye surgery when she had a month off during her jump from CNN to Fox Television. In her wildest dreams she could never have imagined the media hullabaloo it caused. With her fabulous "new" look she was being touted as Fox-y Greta.

Greta says, "I had eye surgery because I wanted to look better for me." If anyone told her to do it she would have told them "to go jump in the lake." A reporter from a major media outlet asked Greta if she thought the surgery would affect her credibility. Greta's response was precious: The plastic surgeon had merely fixed her eyes - not removed brain matter or deleted her education or news experience.

Greta states, "appearances are important, but nothing is a substitute for doing your homework, getting an education and working hard. That is true even in television. Viewers are not stupid and they recognize credibility when they see it (even with bags under your eyes)."

Just recently, Greta interviewed conservative Bill O'Reilly about his new book, *Culture Warrior,* number three on the New York Times best seller list as of this writing. When he described himself as a traditionalist, Greta asked him how he would characterize her.

"You have traditionalist instincts, a traditional background with traditional values," quipped O'Reilly, "but you hang out with those SP's." (secular progressives). Greta asked for an example of an SP. "Like Susan Sarandon, George Clooney or Tom Cruise," said O'Reilly - taking a swipe at Hollywood progressives.

Greta, with her wide, toothy smile and brown eyes dancing, took it in stride. She held her own with the feisty O'Reilly and appeared to enjoy the tongue-in-cheek interview.

Perhaps O'Reilly was referring to the stir Greta caused when she invited her (SP) friends Ozzie Osbourne and his wife Sharon to join their table at the most prestigious annual media party in Washington: The White House Correspondents' Dinner.

The New York Times called Ozzy the dinner's most ridiculous guest - but wait, The Washington Post called Greta ingenious for inviting him.

The President's welcoming remarks alluded to Ozzy. He paused and said, "Ozzy, Mom (Barbara Bush) loves your stuff!" With that acknowledgement Ozzy jumped up on his chair and threw the president a kiss. Greta thought, Uh - oh - what's coming next? But he behaved and it turned into a great moment.

In her own words on fun: It's not a curse word. It's actually quite serious business, as it makes the hard times livable and the sad times bearable. Fun should be part of the work environment too. Stuffed shirts who can't stop and laugh at themselves should be banished!

Greta, an avid Green Bay Packer fan, makes her all the more loveable. Not exactly a Yooper, but close to it. She owns one share in the Green Bay Packers. Greta says her one share cost is $200 and entitles her to nothing but pride. She calls Bret Favre and the team "my Guys!"

On TV, when the green and gold charge on to the field, she thinks: My Guys! Then she sees all of her goofy co-owners with foam cheese wedges on their heads in zero degree weather and her heart swells. She wishes she were there! Go Pack!

Greta's affection for the Pack goes back to about age 7. Every Monday night her father used to take her to Fuzzy Thurston's restaurant, Fuzzy's Left Guard - now called Fuzzy's Shenanigans. Fuzzy is a legendary Hall of Famer.

Vince Lombardi gave the players Monday off and the team congregated at the restaurant. Greta reminisces that they would hoist her up on their shoulders and give her rides around the place. They were sweet and gentle and fun. They were her role models. They were her heroes!

I especially like and respect Greta because she is politically colorblind to Red (Republican) or Blue (Democrat). Whatever her brand of politics, it doesn't enter into her reporting. She reports; you decide! She really is fair and balanced, and that's refreshing. She admits to bias though when it comes to the Packers - her Guys!

AL JOLSON: THE KING OF BROADWAY   January 12, 2007

The younger generations may not have heard of Al Jolson or at best know very little about him. Parents of present day seniors are most likely familiar with Jolson who was regarded as the Greatest Entertainer in the World for more than three decades.

Jolson's career began in burlesque and minstrel shows in the early 1900s. He was the son of a Rabbi and cantor. The family migrated to the United States from Europe in 1894 when Al was eight years old and settled in Washington D.C. Al was born Asa Yoelson and his name was quickly "Americanized" to fit in with peers on the streets of Washington D.C.

Cantor Yoelson started to train his boys' voices almost as soon as they could talk with aspirations that one or both of his sons would become a cantor in the Synagogue.

Al's tenor voice has been described as stirring and pulsating and combined with his stage presence garnered him the cliché as The World's Greatest Entertainer. He was destined to become a legend in his own time.

Al ran away from home at age twelve to be on stage and eventually in a Minstrel Show. Some of the younger generations will say, "What is a Minstrel Show?"

The minstrel show was an American entertainment consisting of comic skits, variety acts, dancing, and music performed by white people in blackface - especially after the American Civil War.

Blacks were portrayed in disparaging ways: as ignorant, lazy, buffoonish, superstitious, joyous and musical. The costumes were loud and outlandish. The minstrel show began with brief burlesques and comic acts. It survived as professional entertainment until about 1910.

However, amateur performances continued until the '50s in high schools, fraternities and local theatres. Yes, even Escanaba had minstrel shows staged by the Kiwanis Club as a fund raiser. They began in 1947 and continued until 1957.

Minstrelsy lost popularity as African Americans began to gain legal and social victories against racism. When the NAACP got involved minstrel shows fell by the wayside.

I never attended any of the shows held at the Junior High School auditorium, but my husband did. He recalled names of the performers: Kryn Bloom, Clarence Zerbel, Guy Knutsen and Danny Danielson.

Guy Knutson, belted out *Nothin' Could Be Finer Than To Be In Carolina In The Morning*, as he soft-shoed his way into the hearts of the audiences. Kiwanis Pancake Days became the new fund raiser when the minstrel shows ended.

The first talking movie, *The Jazz Singer*, released in 1927 starred Al Jolson. By then he had become a huge Broadway star.

He was the first person to take a Broadway show on the road all over the country. Before that people traveled to New York to see a Broadway show.

Al was known as "The King of Broadway." Some of the songs he sang that people loved were: *Swanee, Rock-a-Bye Your Baby With a Dixie Melody, My Mammy, Carolina in the Morning, Toot-Toot-Tootsie (Good bye), Alexander's Ragtime Band, You Made Me Love You* and *When You Were Sweet Sixteen.*

Jolson collaborated on writing the following songs: *California Here I Come, Pretty Baby* and the *Anniversary Song.* He belted out these songs when there was no microphone or any sound system: A feat that singers today wouldn't even attempt. For instance, Anne Murray at the recent engagement at the Island Showroom had 28 large speakers.

Al's voice has been described as leathery. His blackface would remain a mask for Jolson all of his life. The magic to his work was never quite captured without the burnt cork: In black-face he would fall to his knees with arms outstretched and belt out *My Mammy.* Never will there be another Jolson.

In the thirties big bands, soft music and singers such as Crosby (who paved the way for crooners) and Sinatra began to emerge. Jolson's popularity began to diminish and he retired. He made a come back during World War II and blazed a trail as the first to entertain the troops overseas. Soon after other big names followed his lead: among them were Bob Hope, Crosby and Fred Astaire

In 1946 *The Jolson Story* featuring Larry Parks dubbed with Al Jolson's voice hit the big screen. It was a huge success and jump-started Jolson's career again. He had his own radio show. In 1949 the follow-up, *Jolson Sings Again* was released. I remember how much I enjoyed seeing *The Jolson Story* when I was about 13.

Knowing how my husband loved Jolson's music, I purchased the two movies and we spent time at Christmas enjoying them again. We shared them with our family who, of course, didn't know much about Al Jolson - but they were impressed with his style. They were only vaguely aware of minstrels.

Jolson married four times, but the wives could never compete with his love for being on stage and his love affair with his audiences. He loved applause! He loved a live audience. He was a fabulous entertainer. In his era he was the best.

To comprehend Jolson's career you have to understand how very different show business would evolve eighty years later. In his era there was no television where a performer could have an audience of more than a hundred million at a time; no radio, no movies, not even phonograph records.

There were only live performances: musicals, plays, burlesque, minstrels, carnivals and circuses. Male vaudeville actors wore loud clothes while their female counterparts often appeared on the street wearing stage makeup at a time when most women wore little or no makeup at all.

In the twentieth century the four greats known as "The Kings," were Al Jolson, Bing Crosby, Frank Sinatra and Elvis Presley.

Al contracted malaria when he entertained the troops during World War II - and suffered a reoccurrence when he entertained troops during the Korean War.

He died in the St. Francis Hotel in San Francisco in 1950 of a massive heart attack at age 64. He was scheduled to meet with Bing Crosby the following day for a recording session.

George Jessel delivered the eulogy and said, in part:

"And not only has the entertainment world lost its king, but we cannot cry, 'The king is dead - long live the king!' For there is no one to hold his scepter."

Today I was most interested in your article about Al Jolson. I will copy it and keep it for reference. I think it was 1927 when I was 13 years old, that my dad drove us to Menominee to see Al Jolson in *The Jazz Singer*. We were so happy to see that show and I often think about it being the first big movie I had seen. I must tell you I do belong to the senior age group. I am now 92 years old.

–Dorothy A. Duca

Thanks so much for your recent article talking about the career of my favorite entertainer of all time, Al Jolson. Your article was well written and it is unfortunate that you cannot hear his voice on the radio anymore. There is just no demand for it because the producers, of course, do not want it because it won't sell. People need to get the chance to her Jolie once again. Hopefully you can help out on this and assist the International Al Jolson Society with promoting the cause. God bless, and Happy New Year.

–Kirk Estee, Omaha, Nebraska

CATTE ADAMS MADE IT TO THE TOP   January 26, 2007

Singer Catte Adams is an Escanaba native - a celebrity with talent abound. Most will remember her performance on Star Search. After auditioning five times for the show, Catte went on to win the top prize of $100,000.

Nobody starts out as a successful singer, musician, writer or actor. It takes dedication, perseverance, and years of hard work. Raw talent is an important component though - and even if you are really great; you still need that big break in an extremely competitive field.

During her high school years Catte traveled with bands and played in some garage bands. She eventually made her way to Los Angeles. "I just kept singing and working in clubs and got a few breaks," said Catte. "My big break is kind of interesting."

Her big break came when she was doing a telethon for United Cerebral Palsy and her slot was at 3:00 in the morning. Catte says, "Unbeknownst to me, Liberace who was in Las Vegas had just finished his last show and was winding down, watching TV and he saw me. He said, 'I want to find that girl - find out who she is, I want to put her on my show.' And that is exactly what happened."

He taught her to perform in front of huge audiences - something she had never done before. "My debut was at the Rivera in Vegas and he took me under his wing for a year. Liberace was the kindest man in the world - he was so generous to me," exclaims Catte. "He had music created for me and had it orchestrated out with a 70-piece symphony: Orchestrations that cost thousands of dollars and he did that just for me, and then gave them to me when I did leave - he was an incredible man."

The Adams family was a musical family. Many will recall Al Adams who had a local band for many years and was an excellent musician. Catte reminisced about her childhood, "It was absolutely imperative that everybody sang and played an instrument, primarily just so they could keep peace in the house - the only way they could keep us from fighting was to make us sing.

I don't think we realized the training we were getting as kids, but my father was a very good musician and he was schooling us and teaching us how to sing. We listened to music constantly in our house - it was just natural, everybody played instruments."

Catte reminisces about a childhood dream, "wishing and

believing that one day I would be a guest and sing on the Johnny Carson Show was my biggest dream as a little girl in remote Upper Michigan. It will always be my favorite wish that came true."

Cheryl, Catte's sister majored in music at NMU and lives in Seattle where she teaches music in the school system and has won many awards. The whole family sings. Cheryl played the flute in school and local bands. She majored in the flute in college. She started out singing Jazz in Los Angeles but fell in love with Seattle and teaching music.

Catte was only about 15 when she and Cheryl, my daughter's best friend, sang a love ballad at my son Gary's wedding.

Eventually, Catte got her own show together with jazz-tunes. She started traveling all over and opening-up for comics: included are Jay Leno, Bob Hope, George Burns, Gary Shandling, Buddy Hacket and Joan Rivers. Then she began recording and touring, doing some background singing for Chaka Khan, Jermaine Jackson, Natalie Cole, Michael Bolton, Go West, Yanni, Stevie Wonder, Elton John and a host of others.

Catte, as a background singer for Natalie Cole for eleven years, accompanied her on world-wide tours along with Natalie's entourage. "It has been really amazing to travel all over the world singing background with these different groups and people who are some of my heroes - especially Chaka Khan and Natalie Cole," explains Catte.

"I was on the Unforgettable tour with Natalie: went to the Taj Mahal in India, and played in the Forbidden City in China and in Beijing," Catte reminisces.

Catte has been the voice for many international and national television and radio jingles including Coke, Pepsi, Mazda, Jeep, Toyota, Cadillac and many others.

She has written her own self-titled CD project available on her website www.catteadams.com. Her e-mail address is catte@adelphia.net. She would love to hear from friends from the past.

Some will remember when Catte appeared in the early '80s at the Terrace Ballroom. She was sponsored by the Escanaba Woman's Club after her win on *Star Search*. We attended her magnificent performance.

In a discussion with Catte she expressed interest in traveling to Escanaba with her band to perform again. I couldn't help but think the new Island Showroom would be an excellent venue. I have a contact number for an interested sponsor.

Catte has written music for film and television. She has also written for recording artists: Johnathon Butler, the Pointer Sisters, Patti LaBelle and several others in the Jazz and Pop arenas.

"It was always a big thrill to open as special guest for George Burns (my favorite), Don Rickles (the kindest), Jay Leno, and Bob Hope, who was inspiration all around - even though it bugged him every night in our rehearsed "impromptu bit" when I got a bigger laugh. He later cut the line. 'Oh well!' He was still the boss of funny," relates Catte.

Catte says her most challenging gig was *Star Search* - because it was scary. "It was pretty scary to go back every week and "WIN" - real pressure." She is funny, articulate, playful and spontaneous as a performer and when it comes to spilling out her own life before you, completely honest.

She and her husband reside in West Hollywood, California where, nearby, they own a recording studio for music production. Lest we forget this incredibly talented and successful lady hails from Escanaba - she's done us proud!

One-time Escanaba Resident has Enjoyed His Time with Entertainers

September 22, 2007

Jim Heiden's undeniable charm and charisma percolated beyond the gates of Escanaba and catapulted him to positions he would have never even dreamed of growing up as a kid. Of course, it took more than charm and charisma to land a position with Jerry Lewis and the Muscular Dystrophy Association (MDA).

Jim and his wife, the former Betty Houle, were high school sweethearts. Jim speaks glowingly of his roots and Escanaba, "My school years were truly some of the best years of my life. After all, I met my bride of 52 years in the 10th grade! In the fall we duck hunted every morning before school. How many places can a kid do that out his back door? I love Escanaba!"

After leaving Michigan State, Jim went to work, shortly thereafter, for MDA and Jerry Lewis in 1959. He recalls sitting in an Americana Hotel suite with Jerry and Bob Ross, MDA executive director, after one of the early telethons and making the remark, "Bo and Jerry, why can't we network the telethon across the country? And they got quite a kick out of the suggestion."

At that time the telethon was only seen on five or six stations out East and telethons just weren't networked. "They laughed," Jim said, "not because it couldn't be done, but rather that I was so naive not to fully understand what a huge undertaking it would be. Well, the rest is history."

Jim was born in Escanaba in 1934. His father, a veterinarian, practiced in Escanaba for over 30 years until his death in 1960. His older brother, John, and other family members still live here. Tragedy beset the family on New Year's Eve 1960 when Jim's younger sister, Janie, was murdered outside of Menominee. She and her husband of four months were on their way to Escanaba for the holiday.

Jim and Betty, parents to a daughter and two sons, live outside Philadelphia and are frequent visitors to Escanaba. Betty and I have been friends since grade school; at one time she lived next door to me. And her husband, Jim, is one heck of a great story teller. Yet, because of Jim's modesty, I was unaware of many interesting experiences he has had while rubbing elbows with the rich and famous. I did manage to extract a few for this column.

Jim has met a bevy of stars through the years. Included are Robert Duval, Suzanne Summers, Loretta Swit, Dustin Hoffman, Kirk Douglas, Mary Tyler Moore, Celeste Holm, Audrey Hepburn and Moe Howard, one of the Three Stooges. Jim relates, "While Moe and I were chatting at a cocktail party I told him what a huge fan my brother John is of the Three Stooges.

"I asked him if he would say hello to John if I got him on the phone. He laughed and we set it up. I thought I would die laughing when Moe said, 'Yuck, yuck, yuck John, where in the hell is Escanaba?' It was 1:30 in the morning and John couldn't believe he was getting a call from Moe."

"When I first met John Wayne I was so nervous I could hardly think straight, but he was so great and so nice. It was wonderful. The same with Johnny Carson, Bob Hope, Jackie Robinson and many more," recalls Jim. "Probably one of my biggest thrills was meeting Paul Newman when he invited me to sit down at his table and finish my martini."

Jim said each year when he went to New York to do the telethon he would bring his wife. "One year Betty asked if she might help on the show. My boss said, 'sure Jim, lets put Betty on the door leading to backstage where she can greet the VIPs and keep the people out who do not belong there.'"

"Betty thought that's a fine job, and did it very well until this guy comes along and starts through the back door. Betty said, 'I'm sorry. This door leads to back stage and is only for the stars, at which he looks at her and says, 'Hey Blondie, get out of my way. I am Jackie Mason (comedian) and I am a star!' Betty says, 'Sorry, I never heard of you.' Mason goes all to pieces, screaming, 'I am a star and this blonde won't let me in to do my act for Jerry!'

Luckily, one of Jerry's crew was close by, recognized him and said, 'he's OK. Let him in.' Jerry was later told about the incident and thought it was a riot. Of course, all of us at MDA never let Betty live it down."

Jim worked for Jerry Lewis and the MDA until 1973. Later he went to work for Easter Seals. Since his retirement he has continued to use his talents. "I still do voice-over work whenever I can get the work (it pays very well). I have done work for Staples, M and Ms and a host of narrations for training films of numerous companies."

Jim continues to do public service announcements for nationwide charities. Recently he was in a feature film done for the French Consulate that was shot in Philadelphia. Although his part as the town crier was brief, he did narrate the entire introduction.

High school sports were an important part of Jim's school years: His imposing frame of 6 feet, 4 inches lent itself to being an outstanding athlete and a star on the basketball team. The cherished memories Betty and Jim have of their early years in Escanaba stand out as some of the best years of their lives. Jim says, "Escanaba is the greatest little town in the world and I can't wait to get back. Friends are truly friends and we have some great ones."

MELISSA AND JOHN BESSE: March 16, 2007
CAPTURING THE AMERICAN DREAM

The small Upper Peninsula town of Escanaba and surrounding area has proudly spawned a host of talented individuals. Among them are skaters, singers, writers, musicians and painters. Some have attained notoriety on the national stage. We are extremely proud of them.

Others have purposely chosen to adopt Escanaba and the surrounding area as their home. They have given generously to the community in terms of community spirit, talent and generosity. John and Melissa Besse are an exemplary example.

We, as a community, are extremely grateful for their generosity that will continue to enrich our lives and those of our decedents for generations to come.

I said to Melissa, "I really would like to do a personal article from your point of view about you and John, about your roots, about how you met and your family."

Playfully, I added, "I don't imagine you were always 'rich and famous.'" Taking it in her stride she chuckled and answered, "Oh no! When we first married we were as poor as church mice!"

Ahhh! Now we have found some common ground!

I met Melissa and John many years ago at a political fund raiser in a private home. Melissa's elegance, grace and typical Southern charm stood out. Not surprising - Melissa was born and raised in Raleigh, North Carolina.

"As an only child, there is no other way I can say it: I was spoiled." said Melissa. "I was blessed in-as-much as so many family members cared about me."

Her grandmother, whom she was named after, was years ahead of her time. She wasn't typical by any stretch of the imagination. Grandma Melissa, born in the 1800s, was her own woman - as an entrepreneur she owned a very successful drug store in a large hotel in Raleigh.

"When she was younger she was voted the most beautiful woman in Richmond," said Melissa. "She was very progressive; a real go-getter." She certainly wasn't the typical grandma in that era.

"How did you meet John?" I asked. "John was dating my friend," Melissa explained. John had already graduated from the University of Minnesota and was attending graduate school at North Carolina State University.

"I remember that I could barely understand John with his accent." said Melissa. His accent!? I was puzzled at first knowing John was from Wisconsin. How funny - being from the Midwest we consider Southerners with the accent.

It reminded me when President Carter was in the White House. He remarked how great it was to have someone in the White House without an accent.

Melissa's aunt had baked a beautiful coconut cake for a

cake walk fund-raiser at the college she was attending. The person who won the cake inadvertently also took her aunt's beautiful cake plate home. "John offered his help in a concerted effort to retrieve the plate - and he located it!" said Melissa.

After that, John called Melissa occasionally to talk. Melissa said, "He was always trying to set me up on a date with one of his friends. Finally, I told him, "I don't need anyone arranging a date for me. I am perfectly capable of attracting my own dates."

"Oh," said John, and after a moments pause, "Well, would you like to go out with me?" Melissa said she agreed and their first date was wonderful - they went dancing. She never dated anyone else after her first date with John. They were smitten.

They married when John received his master's degree and moved to Alabama. John's first job out of college was with the Tennessee Valley Authority as a forester.

The Besses' have three children: Melissa, named after her mother and great-grand-mother, lives in Shawano; Greg, who works with his father in the family business; and their youngest daughter, Marrijo, who lives in Minnesota.

They have five grandchildren: Gabrielle, Cain, Amber, Alex, and Aprylle.

John, born and raised in Butternut, Wisconsin began his lifelong career at the age of 12. He worked in his dad's sawmill: Measuring logs, scaling logs, and building what is called a coal door on boxcars. John, in his youth, could have never dreamed where his ultimate career would take him.

The Besses' moved to the Escanaba area in 1963. In 1966, John, founder of Besse Forest Products Group (BFPG) began his operation with Northern Michigan Spliced Veneers and twelve employees. In 1983 their son, Greg, joined Besse Forest Products.

40 years later, BFPG, is one of the largest privately owned producers of hardwood veneer, lumber, and specialty plywood in North America. Today the business consists of 16 manufacturing facilities operating in the United States and Canada.

Melissa talks affectionately about the relationship of son, Greg and his father: "They compliment one another. John has his strong points, and so does Greg. John is amazed at Greg's superior organizational skills."

They each bring to the table special strengths. John's values and enterprising spirit are matched by Greg's dedication to continue building on his father's foundation and business philosophy as he leads the Company into the 21st century.

Melissa is pleased that John and Greg have such a great working relationship: "Most importantly it is built on their mutual respect." says Melissa.

Melissa and John's love story has spanned more than 55 years.

The Besses' success is the quintessential American Dream story possible with dedication, determination and hard work. It doesn't end there though.

The Besses' philosophy to "give back" and their generosity paralleling the Bonifas' (Escanaba's lumber baron at the turn of the 20th century) will benefit Delta County residents for years to come - not to mention their significant gifts to other communities as well.

On Anna Nicole and Florida Trip   February 16, 2007

WOW! I'm excited! In the past 19 years my husband and I have only had one vacation alone - that is without our disabled son who lives with us and whom we care for. Many things had to fall in place to accommodate this special happening.

My daughter, Vicki, had to take a vacation from her work in Milwaukee to travel here and care for her brother. He has many special needs, and we don't really trust anyone to care for him other than family.

He has a delayed swallow and sometimes chokes when he eats. He requires diapering and help with showers, shaving and dressing. And most of all he needs to have the structure and familiarity that a family member can provide. So that is settled; now, where will we go?

During the Christmas holiday my youngest son, Jeff, mentioned he had a conference in Hollywood, Florida, in March. He could extend his time and spend time with us if we chose to meet him there. Great idea! My husband jumped at his suggestion: Spring training and ball games! And nearby is Gulf Stream Park (horse racing). I added that the shopping is fabulous and are the beaches in Fort Lauderdale. What more could we ask for?

Now where will we stay? In January I made arrangements to stay at - and here is the kicker: The Seminole Hard Rock Casino and Hotel. Yes, the same hotel where Anna Nicole Smith died.

Many things drove that decision. First, it was close to most of the activities we were planning. Second, the entertainment that week featuring the Golden Boys, Frankie Avalon, Fabian and Bobby Rydell was a lure! They advertise something for everyone and that seemed to fit in with our senior old fogey status.

We just missed Sinatra sings Sinatra and Englebert. Darn!

I liked the idea of indulgence: A European spa for facials, massages, hair styling and make-overs. While the "boys" are taking in the ball games and horse races, I could become a new person: Well, at least on the outside! Then I can meander down to the Seminole Paradise where they feature all the greatest in shopping. Or hang out for a while in the huge 130,000-square-foot casino. Or relax by the oversized, fabulous pool.

When the "boys" return there are 10 restaurants on the premises that suit everybody's fancy. In the evening you can take your pick of 12 bars and nightlife entertainment from a comedy club to jazz to romantic mood music. The problem is they all come alive at 10 p.m. - our bedtime. But then I suppose this place isn't exactly geared to the senior crowd.

The anticipation of my trip and shopping culminated in a plan to whittle my body. I started on that venture New Year's Day. So far I have lost 8 pounds - not bad, not great! I am hoping for another 10-pound loss by trip time. My treadmill is busy counting miles. Of course my frugal husband claims with that weight loss I could fit into my two closets of clothes with price tags still on them. "There is no need for new clothes," he says. Just like a man! Doesn't he realize clothes go out of style! Surely after 57 years he should understand me and women in general by now.

Just 10 more pounds I will be in the correct BMI (body mass index) range for my height. But we all know the real trick is keeping it off! I am already reaping benefits. Amazingly, only an eight-pound loss has lowered my blood pressure.

Since Anna Nicole died in room 607 in the very place we are vacationing let me weigh in on her ongoing saga. I really didn't know much about her. I was vaguely familiar with her name and her marriage to a man 63 years older than her and the subsequent lawsuit. I was remotely aware of her reality show but never watched it. I didn't know she was a Playboy playmate, nor would I have been interested.

She first surfaced for me when her baby was born and her son died in her hospital room. In some strange way I identified with her as a mother giving birth and then losing a child. I felt empathy for her. Ecstasy and tragedy at the same time! How very tragic!

On the other hand, I can't and will never understand drug abuse. The jury is still out on the cause of Anna Nicole's death, but there is a strong possibility drugs played a part.

And this whole media circus! What does that say about our culture? What was her claim to fame? What talent did she have? She had a boob job, could shake her behind and pose - that's it. Sadly, the notoriety she loved and craved in the beginning faded and she ran to the Bahamas' to escape the frenzy.

Now men are coming out of the woodwork to lay claim to fathering her child. I confess I am like thousands of others - interested in hearing the latest developments.

Her death and the turmoil that surrounds it will be ongoing for years to come. The media will no doubt follow little Dannielynn throughout her life. This innocent child is already doomed.

Anna Nicole tried to emulate Marilyn Monroe and her life did indeed mirror Marilyn: Both sex symbols surrounded in controversy that died mysteriously in their '30s at the height of their celebrity. Both somehow became the willing victims of uppers and downers!

Her life and death are a sad commentary on where our culture is and where it is headed.

BOOKS ARE ONE OF MY PASSIONS   November 3, 2006

I can't say it any more succinctly - books are my passion, my life. Every leisure moment is spent reading, sometimes three books at a time. Finally, my kids have hit on the ideal birthday, Mother's Day, Father's Day and Christmas gift for me and my husband. A book!

They obviously spend a lot of time making their choices. I find it equally exciting to see what they think I might like to read. A few years ago my son, Jeff, who lives in the Washington D. C. area, gave me a wonderful autographed book by Sandra Day O'Connor called *Lazy B*. It became a New York Times bestseller.

It is a wonderful memoir of growing up in the American Southwest on a desert cattle ranch. In those early years amongst horses, cattle, barns and windmills Sandra couldn't have envisioned graduating from college and law school at Stanford University; nor becoming a state senator from Arizona from 1969-75 or serving on the Arizona Court of Appeals.

She was nominated by President Reagan to the U.S. Supreme Court: the first woman ever to do so. She took her oath of office September 25, 1981. Her mom and dad, whom she called Mo and Da, traveled to Washington, D.C., to witness their daughter taking her oath of office.

In her own words, Sandra said, "That terse ceremony brought tears to my eyes as I looked down from the elevated bench in the courtroom to see my husband, our three sons, Mo and Da, Alan, Ann (her brother and his wife) and President and Mrs. Reagan seated and watching the proceedings. It was a moment suspended in time, bridging the life in the harsh desert terrain of the Lazy B and the fast-paced sophisticated life of Washington, D.C."

I am sure Jeff chose that book because when we visited him in Washington some years ago, he set up a meeting for us to meet Sandra Day O'Connor. I was disappointed because it never materialized; an important situation arose that took precedence. However, her law clerk, a friend of Jeff's who had set up the meeting, took us on a VIP personal tour of the Supreme Court Justice Chambers.

I sat in Sandra's chair and my husband sat in the next chair. We gained a glimpse of what they viewed while in session. Next to each chair was a polished spittoon dating back to another era when men chewed tobacco and spit. Then a guided tour came through the back of the room - some on the tour kept pointing at us in the chairs. Guess they thought we were justices - maybe?

Behind the Chambers is a large room with a humongous conference table where the judges discuss cases. No tours are allowed in this area, nor can anyone get close to the justice chairs, let alone sit in them. We were fortunate enough to do both. Gracing the walls in the conference room were huge portraits of former Supreme Court justices. It was quite an experience!

My daughter, Vicki, gave me a book a couple of years ago called *Mustang Sallies*. I thought, now what is that all about? I found out that mustangs are the women who charge ahead, unwilling to run with the herd just because it's easier or more convenient. Mustangs were the original wild horses of the West.

According to author Fawn Germer, "Mustangs are tough, strong, agile, sound and quick to learn. Like the horse, the mustang woman experiences great rewards because her life is filled with surprise, drama and adventure. Mustang living is exciting, but can be hard."

I wondered, did my daughter give me this book because she thought I was a mustang, someone who refused to run with the herd? Or was it because she is a mustang?

Some of the ladies illuminated as mustangs by Germer in her book are Erin Brockovich, Ann Richards, author Mary Higgins Clark and Hillary Clinton.

Another good choice by my daughter! It was such an interesting read. The books the kids give me perhaps would have never entered my mind to purchase. They both spend hours in Barnes and Nobles or Borders. We do the same when we are in the city.

My husband recently bought me Greta Van Susteren's book, *My Turn at the Bully Pulpit.* As many folks know Greta has a show on the Fox News Channel. She hails from Appleton, Wisconsin, and is a huge Green Bay Packer fan. She categorizes her book as "straight talk about the things that drive me nuts." Another great read.

My husband spends hours looking up baseball statistics in his huge Baseball Encyclopedia and is currently reading the United States of Americas Medal of Honor Recipients. Interestingly, three individuals from the Upper Peninsula are recipients of the esteemed Medal of Honor Award. They were from the Sault, Calumet and Foster City.

You might say our life centers around books. We have just purchased a third bookcase for our beloved treasures. John Kennedy Jr. said, when his mother, Jackie died, "she was surrounded by the things she loved: Her family and her books." That's me!

BILL O'REILLY: LOVE HIM OR HATE HIM!   June 1, 2007

Bill holds court on his popular TV news commentary show, The O'Reilly Factor on the Fox TV channel. According to Marvin Kitman, author of The Man Who Wouldn't Shut Up, an autobiography sanctioned by Bill, there is some difference of opinion: That's a real understatement!

"For some, he is the beloved voice of reason, a font of wisdom and a man who provides diversity on the airwaves. They love his passion and concern about what he reports on.

For others, he is a semi-demented TV talk show host. He is, they say, an obnoxious, insufferable, rude, loudmouth whose view, according to the kinder analysis, is typical right-wing drivel."

Love him or hate him, Bill is unarguably the most loathed and most loved media voice of the twenty-first century.

Bill O'Reilly gave Kitman, a liberal TV critic, the green light to write his autobiography and provided him with twenty-nine interviews. "It is an even-handed in-depth look at who Bill O'Reilly is and his rise to the top that will provoke 'Spinheads' and 'Anti-Spinheads'," says Kitman.

Gary, my husband, and I watch the program but through entirely different prisms. Guess who loves Bill? You're Right! My right-winged conservative husband. As an independent I probably fall in the other category most of the time. It makes for interesting discussions and yes, sometimes it erupts into a heated change of opinions.

Bill is proud of his 100 percent Irish heritage. He grew up in Long Island, New York in an unpretentious home and   neighborhood. He discovered at age five that he was a born leader. He was bossy and opinionated even then. He attended catholic school and was the nun's worst nightmare.

Bill's dad was heavy handed when he dished out punishment - which was often. Bill couldn't keep his mouth shut. To this day Bill still speaks of his Dad's angry nature. Bill called him a "bookkeeper" who was unfulfilled in his work and brought his resentment and anger home with him. Hooligan Bill, as he called himself, caught the brunt of his anger.

And in the matter of girls! It didn't help that his father's choice of sending Bill to Marist University was an all-boys college. Bill claims he was a barbarian where girls were concerned and "hopelessly shy." Of course that would all change. By the summer of 1968 he was on his way to becoming a "dating lunatic" while working as a lifeguard.

Bill is an impressive six four with an aggressive and overbearing personality. He excelled in sports playing hockey and baseball. He was good enough to get a major league baseball team tryout.

In college, at Marist University, he played second string quarterback. By his own admission he was disliked by his coaches and teammates. His idol was Joe Namath of the New York Jets. He tried to emulate him with his long hair and white football shoes further alienating his coaches and teammates.

His cocky, conceited "know it all" attitude didn't win many over. But he didn't care. Nothing fazes him. His personality has not changed much over the years.

After college, Bill and his friend Joe Rubino took jobs as teachers near Miami for $5000 a year. According to one of Bill's female students, "We were expecting a nun when suddenly, to our surprise, a tall, blue-eyed MAN walked into our classroom." Bill made a hit. He was a student-friendly teacher.

Bill finally figured out what he wanted to do with his life and teaching was not his forte. Bill says, "I started to put it together. I said, okay, I got this gift. But I never realized I could market any of this until I got into the classroom when I saw kids actually mesmerized by my ability to tell a story." Kids were flocking to his class.

Bill started from the bottom while learning the broadcasting business. He took jobs at small stations while crafting his gift and climbing the ladder. Along the way he was fired or quit jobs. He never unpacked his boxes of stuff, that way, moving on was easy. He would pick up his boxes and move on to greener pastures.

O'Reilly decided to get his master's at Boston University College of Communication. Bill had good attributes: "He could read. He could write. He was a good interviewer. He was articulate and resourceful. Physically, he looked good on camera, had good teeth, nice hair and a nice smile." according to author, Kitman.

The personality stayed the same: obnoxious, egotistical, hilarious, aggressive, provocative and an "in your face" kind of guy. His unique brand of Bill O'Reilly sold! O'Reilly uses his journalism to see justice done. He wants to improve society by using the weight of the media. He considers himself to be a champion of the little people, "the folks" as he calls them.

O'Reilly is down-right cheap. He drives an old unpretentious car and purchased an old house to fix up. He will not pick up the tab for lunches, and pays for just himself. At an all-paid event, he freaked out when his wife, Maureen, ordered a bottle of water - the only chargeable item. She just said, "Bill Don't!" Guess Bill knew he had better "shut up."

He must be doing something right. He has risen to levels unimaginable. In 2005, The Factor lead all cable network news shows with 3.3 million viewers, almost three times as many as Larry King Live on CNN (1.2 million).

Bill's anger clock starts early in the day with the two hour Radio Factor. He blazes away in his newspaper column, (which appears weekly in *The Daily Press*) and hosts *The O'Reilly Factor* on week days! And in-between he has found time to write several best sellers.

Rodger Ailes, creator of the Fox News Channel discovered gold in Bill O'Reilly: The man who wouldn't shut up. Rodger believed he could make O'Reilly a star - he allowed him to be himself. It was the perfect job for a control freak like Bill.

Whether you love him or hate him he is raking in big time bucks and a big time audience: Even his detractors watch him. Bill, you might say, has become bigger than life with "The Spin Stops Here."

DOUG FIX: A SPECIAL 'TEACHER MAN'   October 6, 2006

Did I know Doug Fix? I knew he was a popular teacher. I knew he was a friend of my son's years ago. And I knew there was a connection to my son's wedding in 1972. Ann, Doug's wife, graciously refreshed my memory.

Doug's death brought back horrendous memories of our son Gary's tragedy. He, too, like Doug was an avid jogger. He ran in marathons and won 10Ks. Running became his passion - until one day in 1987, at age 37, he suffered sudden death while running.

He was near a hospital and EMT's were quickly on the scene. Gary was revived but not soon enough. He was in a coma for six weeks and ultimately suffered irreversible brain damage requiring care around the clock. At the time he was in school studying to be a nurse anesthetist. Life for Gary and all of his family changed in an instant. Gary has lived with us for 18 years.

Doug had just returned from Vietnam when Gary met him at Bay College - a friendship developed. Mike (Pic) O'Leary, who now lives in California, wrote a letter to the editor (9/28) about the "gang" congregating at Doug's basement apartment on South 13th. Gary was one of the "gang."

What conversations they must have had! Mike states, "We were like everyone at that time; we were defining ourselves and savoring every moment." Right on Mike! But you neglected to say that you, too, are a teacher who has been an inspiration and helped to shape many young lives.

Mike (Pic) attended our grandson's wedding in Wisconsin last fall. He helped Gary around in his wheelchair. How sadly ironic - the fate of Mike's friends: Gary brain-injured while running; Doug dying while running a marathon.

Ann was a year ahead of Gary in high school. Gary bought

Ann's candy apple red Bridgestone motor-bike. Later - when Ann and Doug first married they lived in Rock. Then Gary announced he was getting married.

Doug introduced Gary, now 22, to Reverend West from the Lutheran Church in Rock - and wedding plans were in the making. As parents from a generation of ultra conservatism we were shocked at their plans. A wedding in a field in Rock? With tuxedos, top hats and long hair? We thought God had intervened when the weather didn't cooperate and the wedding had to be held in the church.

A stream of red carpet ran down the center aisle of the unpretentious church in the country. The church filled with young people. Friends recited poems, played guitars, and sang beautiful ballads. Catte Adams and her sister Cheryl (both former residents) were in the wedding party. Catte, who went on to become the opening act for Liberace, sang a beautiful love ballad to the newly weds.

It was the most beautiful moving wedding I have ever witnessed - even with the long hair hanging out of the stove pipe hats. Ann remembers Doug and her attending the reception held at the Potvins in Schaffer. The restaurateur was probably a bit nervous when he first observed a sea of kids streaming in with long hair. A short time later, and no doubt resting a bit easier, he commented on how well-behaved and polite the young people in attendance were.

Gary does not have day to day memory without cueing. But he remembers the past. My husband and I were talking about the similarities regarding Doug's tragic death and Gary's sudden death episode. Gary understood, seemed sad and spoke up, "Doug was a really good friend of mine."

Ann said, "Gary would always recognize Doug and me whenever we would see him at the mall. And remember the time we met you at the Vierling Restaurant in Marquette? Gary came right over to talk to us." Gary's eyes would light up whenever he would see Doug. Gary, even in the abyss of his brain-injury, recognized instinctively how special Doug was.

I told Ann how coincidental it was that I was in the midst of reading *Teacher Man* by Frank McCourt, a favorite Irish author of mine. He won the Pulitzer Prize for *Angela's Ashes*. Because Doug was so beloved by his students I imagined his style paralleled Frank McCourt's who taught English for 30 years in New York schools. McCourt knew how to relate to young people: His innovative and engaging style of teaching garnered the same respect and admiration that Doug obviously enjoyed.

I am sure Doug would have been amused at McCourt's unique teaching ploys. For example, McCourt talks about the written excuse notes kids handed him after being absent: mostly written by themselves. He saved a drawer full of them. He claimed the kids found it difficult to put two hundred words together on any subject. Yet, when they forged these excuse notes they were brilliant. McCourt thought they could be turned into an anthology of Great American Excuses - or lies.

He claimed they were gems of fiction, fantasy, creativity, self pity and family problems. According to him, "here was American high school writing at its best - raw, real, urgent, brief and lying."

The toilet was plugged. The house burned down. My papers blew away. Heart attacks, strokes, births, fires and even a pet peeing on the homework were some of the excuses.

Toward the end of the school year, McCourt passed out a typed stencil of a dozen or so excuse notes minus the names. He told the kids the notes were supposedly written by the parents but only they knew the real authors.

"I want you to realize this is the first class in the world to study the art of the excuse note. You are so lucky to have a teacher like me who has taken your best writing, the excuse note and turned it into a subject worthy of study. Imagine you are writing an excuse for your 15 year old son or daughter. Now let it rip."

There was no dawdling or chewing on pens. And what enthusiasm! The students were so engrossed in writing that when the bell rang they had to be urged to leave the classroom.

McCourt had learned the key to good teaching: His unique and imaginative methods laced with compassion and understanding. The kids loved him and related to him. And I rather suspect it was that way with Doug. I am sure his students would attest to that. Doug met his destiny: "TEACHER MAN". He will be sorely missed and fondly remembered.

We have wanted to compliment you on your articles for some time. The tribute to Doug Fix and your mention of author Frank McCourt was thoughtful. Enjoyed your coverage of your teen years in the late '40s and early '50s, especially the music; the big bands, etc. Those were the years of music, the pop tunes, love songs and dances. Wow! Thanks again and keep them coming!

—Dave & Lois Nordin, Escanaba

MOBSTERS HAD TIES TO THE U.P.   August 18, 2006

John Dillinger and Al Capone were infamous mobsters of the '20s and '30s. Their names were synonymous with Chicago. John Dillinger was a notorious bank robber while Al Capone was into bootlegging, prostitution, gambling, extortion, etc. He eventually became the crime "Godfather" of Chicago.

No, I don't have a personal connection to Chicago gangsters of the past - so why am I writing about them? Well, when my husband and I first married we lived in the Uptown District in North Chicago. It was the playground for gangsters and movie stars alike in the Roaring '20s and '30s.

During Prohibition and for some years later the Uptown District was a very upscale neighborhood situated near the lake. It boasted fine eateries, fancy hotels and great show-biz entertainment. It was also near the scene of the infamous St. Valentine's Day Massacre and the Biograph Theatre where Dillinger was gunned down.

That was also the neighborhood where I worked at the world-renown Edgewater Beach Hotel. The famous Cuban band leader, Xavier Cugat, and singer Abbe Lane were regular performers when I worked at the pool-side cabanas in the early '50s.

John Dillinger, an Irish American, was imprisoned on multiple occasions for robbing banks. Once out of prison he continued to rob banks and was named Public Enemy Number One by the FBI in 1933. He was responsible for 16 killings.

In April 1934, just three months before Dillinger was gunned down at age 32, his gang came to the Little Bohemia Lodge in the Ironwood-Hurley area to lay low for a few days. The FBI, on a tip, surrounded the lodge and Dillinger escaped through a back window with fellow bank robber John Hamilton.

Dillinger more than likely passed through Escanaba in April 1934 while trying to elude the FBI. He and Hamilton were on their way to Sault Ste. Marie to hide out at the home of Hamilton's sister who lived in the Sault. Again he managed to elude the FBI - but not for long. His days were numbered.

In July 1934 Dillinger invited his girlfriend and Anna Sage, an ex-prostitute, to a movie starring Clark Gable at the Biograph Theatre near the Uptown District in Chicago. Sage, facing deportation to Romania, cut a deal with a young FBI agent to wear a red dress to alert federal agents when they departed from the movie.

An FBI agent yelled, "Stick 'em up Johnny." Dillinger, struggling to reach for his gun, ran and was shot six times in the back. Sage was eventually deported.

The year is 1928. Chicago crime boss Al Capone entered the Green Mill Cocktail Lounge. As always the band stopped playing whatever they were playing and played Capone's favorite tune, *Rhapsody in Blue*. Capone sat in his exclusive booth and enjoyed performers such as Billie Holiday, Tommy Dorsey, Sophie Tucker, Al Jolson and Benny Goodman.

Capone's booth had a view of both entrances; assassination was a real threat. The trap door used for his escape during the Prohibition era is still behind the bar. It lead through a tunnel three blocks away. The Green Mill has the distinction of being the oldest, continuously running jazz club in the country - plus being the best Jazz Club in Chicago.

The Green Mill, a Chicago Landmark, has also been the location for movies like *The Untouchables*, *Prelude to a Kiss* and the TV series *Crime Story*. During Prohibition it was a favorite hangout for gangsters and only a scant few blocks from where we lived in the '50s.

Capone and his brother Ralph owned property in Hurley, Wisconsin. Hurley barely noticed prohibition and became a summertime playground for the likes of Dillinger and Capone to escape Chicago's heat. Even Frank Sinatra was known to bring excitement to the area.

Al Capone, also known as Scarface, was finally arrested for tax evasion. In 1931 he was sentenced to 11 years and spent time in Alcatraz. He paid his fines and was released early. He lived with his wife in the Miami area upon his release. He never returned to Chicago nor to gangland politics. His mind deteriorated to that of a 12-year-old due to syphilis. He died in 1947 from a stroke and pneumonia.

As young adults we were unaware that we lived in a neighborhood with such a notorious past. We even visited the Green Mill on a couple of occasions. The Aragon Ballroom, a favorite dancing spot of ours, was just around the corner.

One day when my husband, Gary, walked to the subway station to commute to work, a huge black limousine with large whitewall tires and a spare tire mounted on the front fender pulled up in front of him. A man jumped out and ordered him into the back seat. The men flashed a police badge. Gary naively obliged and climbed in.

They wore dress hats and were garbed in dapper-looking custom suits with handkerchiefs in their vest pockets: They were dressed to kill! In retrospect, years later, Gary realized they must have been gangsters impersonating police officers.

They continued to drive and unleashed a heavy barrage of questioning. Gary, very laid-back and not fully realizing the gravity of the situation, laughed at some of the absurd questions. Then one guy said, "This can't be the guy we are looking for. Let him out!" We wonder now if they thought he was the *right* guy would they have "bumped him off" like Jimmy Hoffa?

There was still an element of organized crime in the Uptown District when we lived there in the early '50s. Coming from youthful innocence and the sheltered naivety of being raised in Escanaba, we thought it was an exciting, upscale place to live. We weren't aware of the real dangers.

This fall I am planning to visit Chicago with my daughter, Vicki, a jazz enthusiast. Our agenda will most definitely include The Green Mill, a Chicago institution. Capone's booth still reigns and the trap door is still intact behind the bar. I will also be visiting many old nostalgic haunts in the Uptown District.

I remember my mother Blanche Ritchie Petonquot telling me as a child how she was in a posse that hunted for Dillinger when he was in the UP. She was a little woman - but a spitfire. I have never forgotten the image of her with a gun searching for Dillinger. Thank you for the memory.

–Betty Petonquot LeMarble

I love your articles. Well done with a balance of information and entertainment too. Einstein seemed to have a colorful life; much more colorful than I remember. And a ladies man too - imagine that! But the information about his first wife's mathematical contributions was new to me and quite an enlightenment. Another example of how women positively influence our lives...As a coincidence I just listened to three CDs of radio broadcasts - one being *Bullets, Booze and Bandits - The Chicago Gangland Story.* Given your excellent story on Capone and Dillinger, you could have written the script for the radio series...

–Jim Buffer, PhD, Fort Meyers, Florida

Chapter
9
Relationships

THE CHANGING SENIOR RELATIONSHIPS   December 1, 2006

Relationships can become very complicated for seniors, especially after the death of a spouse. Contrary to what young people may believe, most seniors want and miss a close relationship in later life - and not necessarily sexual in nature. But yes, seniors like to hug and kiss, too.

Their hair may be white, sparse or non-existent. Their faces may be etched to reflect laugh lines, years of living, wisdom and experiences. Their body weight may have increased and be somewhat rearranged or redistributed. Nonetheless, seniors are the same inside: Feelings and memories of a close relationship are still intact. Like the song says, "People who need people are the luckiest people in the world." People need to be touched.

Years ago I remember my Mom telling me stories I thought were hilarious at the time. Now I think how sad! Her lady friends watched the obituaries and when a woman they knew died they would bring a homemade pie or casserole dish to the widower - of course in hopes of establishing a relationship.

I met a wonderful gal, Sandi, when we spent winters in Florida. She also lived in our gated community and we became very close. She is an extremely talented singer, and performed in my talent/fashion shows. I encouraged her to compete in the Ms. Senior Florida contest and she won second place.

Sandi was a retired educator from Illinois in her early 60s. Her life changed in an instant when her youngest of three sons was buried in an avalanche while skiing in Colorado. His body wasn't recovered until spring. Her husband, a physician, died of grief and a heart attack three months later. A year later, a second son died of a drug overdose.

Sandi was grieving and lonely. She missed having a partner to share her life with (dining out, dancing, attending concerts and going on cruises). She was active in her church in Illinois and finally began a relationship with an elderly gentleman who was a widower. After a year they moved in together. Kids, finances and other complications very often skew a relationship. Marriage wasn't a consideration.

They came to Fort Myers with Habitat for Humanity, fell in love with the area and Sandi bought a place. We were great friends. One day I called Sandi and her partner answered. "Is Sandi there?" I asked. "No," he replied. "When will she be home?" I asked. "I haven't seen her in days," he said. Puzzled, I later found out she had gone to church (she sang in the choir) for just an hour. Shortly thereafter, he was diagnosed with Alzheimer's and deteriorated quickly.

Within the year his care became overwhelming. Sandi called his daughter to bring him back to Illinois. They had been together for five years. Now Sandi was alone again. She joined a singles group that consisted of mostly women. Finally she met Fred, who was a good conversationalist, at one of their single dinners. She had season concert tickets for two and invited him to accompany her.

Sandi, a classy lady, dressed to the hilt for the occasion. Imagine her shock when Fred showed up for dinner and a concert in shorts and a cowboy hat! Yep! That was their first and last date.

I worried about her when she paid a huge amount to join an organization that matches people interested in relationships. She was advised that an optional video would be beneficial. The company makes a video in which the person talked about herself, education and interests. That cost another $1,100. What was she getting into? In the year her membership was current she had one date with a professional that was, in her words, "too short and a real bore."

Sandi finally met a young-acting, widowed retired business-man at church. He was 15 years her senior with eight kids. She was happy. He is "a class act," she said. She again had a partner for dinner, concerts, cruises and friendship. Last I heard he is sick and she is caring for him.

Widowed men in later life have different experiences than their lady counterparts. There are fewer of them and there is no question they are in demand! Our friends, Bob and Anne, snowbirds from Canada, also spent the winter in our Florida community. Bob is a retired commander in the Canadian Navy.

They were very gregarious, energetic and attractive, and enjoyed a busy social life: golfing and playing tennis along with holding key offices in our community. Bob, 79, is a disciplined fitness guru resembling a Greek God. He works out at the community fitness club and runs three miles a day. Life changed abruptly when Ann required surgery and they returned to Canada. The Canadian insurance precluded her from having surgery in the states.

Bob called and shocked us with news of Ann's untimely and unexpected death during surgery. Immediately friends drove him nuts trying to play matchmaker. Everyone seemed overly interested in what Bob was going to do with his life. He wasn't ready for or interested in a relationship. He plays tennis or golf six days a week

Ultimately, two years after Anne's death, Bob's fellow officers from his Navy career invited him to a golf outing in Toronto. He was partnered with a widow and friend of Anne's. While he wasn't looking for a relationship, it happened. She has her own places in Fort Lauderdale and Canada. That is the way they want it. Separate residences and separate identities.

A second marriage for seniors can become very complicated with children, finances, health insurance and myriad of other considerations. Sometimes it may be more convenient not to tie the knot, but still many do. And many more never do experience another relationship. They live with memories of the way it was.

Swiss psychiatrist Carl Jung said, "The shoe that fits one person pinches another; there is no recipe for living that suits all cases." No truer words were spoken than when Orson Welles, addressing a younger audience, said, "We both know what it is to be young, but you don't know what it is to be old!"

Art Linkletter coined, "Growing old isn't for sissies!"

Parental and Adult Children Relationships can be Delicate

April 27, 2007

I just finished reading a new book available at the library titled *Walking on Eggshells.* It navigates the delicate relationship between adult children and their parents. We all give our children advice because we care about them and our motive is usually that we want to help them.

On giving advice, the book states: They don't want it. They don't hear it. They resent it. Don't give it!

My children are members of the baby-boom generation; we're the parents that lived through a world war and felt the effects of the Great Depression. Kids were raised differently back then. Yes, we were spanked and we spanked our children.

The changes that were difficult for our generation to accept took place in the '60s. Vietnam War and drugs were catalysts instrumental in a counter-culture that made us cringe.

It was difficult for our generation to accept the Hippie movement with long hair, peace signs, Woodstock with its free love and free spirit, hole-riddled jeans, males with earrings and beads hanging from everywhere.

We came from a relatively squeaky-clean '40s generation where our parents perhaps frowned upon rolled-up jeans, saddle shoes and jitter-bugging. Chewing gum in school was our big no-no. Whoever heard of shooting classmates, drug-sniffing dogs, police monitoring at school and teacher and student sex? It is all shocking, to say the least.

Then our kids became parents and did an about turn. God forbid, they didn't want to raise their kids like their "square" parents. Out the window went what our generation called common sense. They put up with their kids strange garb. Permissiveness and discipline were at a minimum. After all, they didn't want to interfere with their free spirit.

Discipline was not their strength. They didn't want to repeat what they perceived as their parents' mistakes. Twenty years later, voila, we have a new generation of young adults.

But whatever the generation, one thing is for certain: Relationships between adult children and parents can be so complicated that even a gesture, a look, or words in anger can determine the relationship for weeks if not months or years to come.

When I wrote a previous column on mothers and daughters it really opened my eyes to how many people are suffering from soured relationships. Mothers e-mailed and called me. A couple cried about their broken relationship dilemmas. How sad!

I have concluded relationships can be extremely fragile for a variety of reasons. Relationships can be based on positive and negative perceptions by both parent and adult child. They run the gamut from love, reciprocal help and shared values to feelings of isolation, family conflicts and money problems.

The laundry list is too long to address here. For starters, children may achieve all their parents hoped for but their relationship with their parents may lack affection, warmth, respect, honesty and open communication. Adult children may also have differences in expectations for their parents and their parents' behavior.

And a couple of real "biggies!" Parents may not be able to provide requested financial support or they may interfere in their children's lives. Daughter- and son-in-law issues can enter. Differences in values and beliefs can become a source for stress.

The relationships between adult children and parents

continue throughout life and last longer today due to an increase in life-span.

Three helpful ideas to strengthening relationships are:

RESPECT ONE ANOTHER. Respect breeds respect and recognizes individuality.

VALIDATE FEELINGS AND BELIEFS. Recognize that feelings and beliefs of adult children and parents are real. Each deserves the right to their own opinions, even if they are different from one another.

We recently spent time with our youngest son, Jeff, an attorney. Many in-depth conversations ensued. I especially liked Jeff's analogy about talks that occurred between him and his father:

"Dad," he said, "We think in different terms. Your thinking reflects a world in black and white, right or wrong with no in-between whereas I see many shades of gray in humanity and certain situations."

Sounds like the differences in thinking could be a generational thing: It's the rigid thinking of the '40s and the more forgiving thinking of later generations. Both father and son have a mutual respect which is really important. They actually enjoy airing their different viewpoints.

LET GO. Recognize that each generation makes decisions and must suffer or enjoy the consequences. Allow each generation the opportunity to learn from each situation.

Walking on Eggshells is a book of ground-breaking insights and many moving, inspiring stories. The author and renowned editor, Jane Isay, charts a course through the confusing and often painful interactions parents and children face.

Jane believes her book is the much-needed road map that will keep you connected to the people you love most. It could be a great Mother's Day or Father's Day gift. As Jane puts it, "for both parents and their adult children; (it's) real-life wisdom and advice on how to stay together without falling apart."

If your relationship is not exactly that way you would like it to be, take comfort in knowing it's happening all around you and realize it is never too late to work at rebuilding that special bond of parent and adult child.

MOMS AND DAUGHTERS OFTEN DIVIDED   February 2, 2007

Often we have heard someone say, "Oh no, I'm becoming just like my mother!" I have also heard it called HTN-Heading Toward Nana. Of course, those women are worried about what they perceive as the negative aspects of their mothers. They aren't worried about being called "gorgeous or accomplished just like your mother."

Make no mistake about it. Mothers are our first female role model and the most powerful.

Mother-daughter relationships are delicate and complicated for many reasons. It would take a book to enumerate. They run the gamut of warm and fuzzy to disassociation that sometimes lasts for years or a lifetime.

Starting at a very young age, children express their desire for autonomy. They no longer want to hold your hand. You have heard toddlers say, "Me do it!" Daughters also continue to exert their desire for independence during adolescence. Her skills may not be ready for the independence we call good judgment.

Maybe some mothers may try to exercise too much control over their daughters. Maybe we dread our daughters' coming of age. What is best: Too little control or too much? At what point do we have to cut the strings?

I recently read that when a young bear reaches adolescence, its mother, having taught it everything it needs to know to survive, will just walk away. At one point we have to do the same, even though we feel at times we must rescue our daughters from the consequences of poor choices and actions.

It is difficult to zip my mouth when I see my granddaughter make poor choices that have dire consequences that affect her life and may affect her children.

As mothers who have gained experiences from years of living, we still try to guide our kids - even if they, too, are now grandmothers. Parenting never ends. Advice is not always welcome. Biting one's tongue is perhaps wiser at times than creating a rift.

Relationships can be complicated. However, it is truly sad when one or both parties participate in martyrdom, guilt, self-sacrifice or resentment. Sometimes - and many daughters will attest - mothers can push buttons. Some daughters lack respect. Both lose so much. You just can't wallow in resentment and stay healthy.

If you have to say no to a request by your mother, then do it. Every time you feel guilt or shame about your personal needs and give in to your mother's demands, your own health is at stake.

From a daughter's perspective some mothers may be resentful because they never had the opportunities their daughter's had.

My mother was the youngest child of a well-respected, middle-class family. She was idolized by her father and probably a bit spoiled. I remember what I perceived as a sometime sassy tone when she spoke to her mother. Yet, she loved her mother dearly.

She was 32 when her mother died. A week later, as a self-indulged teenager in my own little world, I turned on the radio to practice jitter-bugging. My mother went into a rage: How could I possibly listen to music when my grandmother had just died? Years ago a mourning period was observed and customary in respect of a loved one.

In her later years my mother often mentioned her lack of opportunities. It seemed as she neared the end of her life she seemed sad and resentful her life was winding down and she didn't feel fulfilled. She spent a lot of time sleeping - no doubt from a combination of medications and depression.

I understand now more fully how she must have felt. I probably didn't have the empathy I should have had. At the time I ran four miles everyday. I had a business and my life was exciting and full. I would think why couldn't she get out and walk? Why couldn't she help herself? She complained I didn't visit her enough. Yes, I was busy, and yes, I felt guilty.

Many times as an adult I wanted to lash out at my mother over something said. But I didn't. I did hang the phone up in tears one time because I was so exasperated. I would not talk back. Why? Because I had respect for my mother.

My husband would tease me and say, "Why doesn't that respect carry over to me?"

Unlike my mother, I have such a full life I now wonder when I would have had time to work. I guess we always feel our children should visit us more.

In my opinion I think many of the kids born to '60s parents lack respect for their parents. Maybe there was too much of a buddy-buddy relationship with their kids. There are times that I witness in my grandchildren that lack of respect. I hear the same complaints from my peers about their grandchildren.

It was different a couple generations before us. The saying

was that, "children were to be seen and not heard." Parents were stern and readily handed out corporal punishment. There did seem to be more respect.

My husband tells me of accompanying his father on Friday evening to visit his Norwegian grandparents from the old country. He sat in a chair and was very quiet while his father carried on a conversation with his parents. No one spoke to him. After two hours they left - no words, no hugs, no kisses and no acts of kindness, like offering him a cookie, and never did they once call him by his name. No warm and fuzzy memories.

Right or wrong those times commanded respect, Perhaps out of fear? I don't know.

The ideal mother-daughter relationship is built on love, compassion and respect. Yet so many are built on guilt and obligation and perpetuate a chain of pain. You may have heard the saying, "When Mama ain't happy, ain't nobody happy."

A closing prayer from *Mother-Daughter Wisdom* made so much sense.

"That we learn to honor and respect each other without requiring undue sacrifice. That we become willing to forgive each other for the pain and hurt we may have unwittingly caused each other. That we honor each other as powerful teachers."

And finally, that the mother-daughter relationships of the future become so steadfast and supportive that when a woman says. "I'm becoming just like my mother," she will beam with pride. And her friends and family will proclaim, 'Well done!'"

HAVE FUN, JUST FOR THE LOVE OF IT!   February 9, 2007

Did you know that, except for Christmas, Americans exchange more cards on Valentine's Day than any other time of the year? Approximately 192 million greeting cards are exchanged annually, not including packaged cards exchanged by children in school. In the U.S., Esther Howland, an American printer and artist from Massachusetts, is given credit for publishing and sending the first valentine cards in the mid 1800s.

The town of Loveland, Colo., does a large post office business every year around Feb. 14. The spirit of good continues today as valentines are sent out with sentimental verses and children exchange valentines at school.

Remember the anticipation of Valentine's Day in grade school? Everyone brought their valentines to school and deposited them in a huge box provided by the teacher and decorated by the students. The teacher called out names as she handed out the valentines. It was such fun opening them and hoping to get a special one from that special someone - perhaps someone you admired from a distance - even in second grade!

Other times the teacher let each kid hand out his or her own valentines. Looking back, I remember some kids didn't get many valentines while the desks of others had piles of them.

In particular, I remember a boy with longer, unruly, greasy hair (years before long hair was cool) who didn't have any valentines to give to classmates nor did he get many. Back then long hair was synonymous with a poor family; most boys had a crew cut. He probably lacked the pennies to buy a few valentines.

I am sure even at a young age he felt the stigma of being "left out," embarrassed and shunned. That "boy" died a few years ago. I remember him at a class reunion: Even 50 years later he didn't seem to "fit in." One wonders if his personality was altered from exclusions he might have experienced as a kid. And if so, how very sad!

In the fifth grade my husband remembers skating at the 19th Street rink with a girl that was very athletic. He had a crush on her. She had racing skates and won events, so that endeared her to him. He remembers spending 25 cents and buying her a heart filled with chocolates at Tony Wahl's Drug Store.

The folk lore, legends and rumors about the origins of Valentine's Day are many. But most agree that the special day has a tie to Christianity. Legend has it that St. Valentine was a priest who defied the emperor's ban on marriages by marrying young people in secret. He was discovered and put to death.

And why were marriages banned? According to legend, in the third century after Christ, the Emperor Claudius did not want any of his soldiers falling in love and marrying because he felt women and families distracted the soldiers from their duty to him - and in some cases made the men not want to go to war at all. He needed more soldiers so he declared marriage illegal. Therefore anyone performing this ceremony would be killed!

Pope Gelasius in 469 decided to put a Christian spin on the celebration by declaring that it was time to honor St. Valentine, who was said to have died on February 14, 270, for refusing to give up Christianity.

The legends are many, but one thing we are all familiar with is the icon Cupid, the little cherub who was the son of Aprohodite, the goddess of beauty. The young, playful god was known as the god of love and is depicted in art flying around with a bow and arrow shooting love into the hearts of the unsuspecting.

Of course Cupid and the heart became symbols of love on Valentine's Day. Chocolates are the traditional favorites, also known as a love trigger.

And did you know that nearly 60 percent of all Valentine cards are purchased only six days before Valentine's Day - a procrastinator's delight. You still have time!

Valentine's Day is synonymous with love stories. Harry and Bess Truman had a special love that spanned decades: nine years of courtship and 53 years of marriage. More than 1,300 letters from Harry to Bess survive in the Truman Library collections.

He first saw her in Sunday school. He was 6 and she was 5. "She had golden curls and beautiful blue eyes," Harry recalls. They graduated from high school together in 1901. They went their separate ways until becoming acquainted again nine years later. He wooed her with letters for years before she accepted his offer of marriage - even declining once.

Growing up in the era they did, they preferred letter writing to phone calls and even 60 years later the letters were filled with the same terms of endearment as when their love affair began. They were very private people and preferred one another's company to the exclusion of others, even during their years in the White House.

I remember the last Valentine's Day dance we attended at our community clubhouse in Florida. Of course everyone wore red and the decorations were lovely: red and white streamers were suspended from the ceiling, cupids and hearts hung all around and tables were adorned with red and white bouquets of flowers. There just seemed to be an aura of love in the air. The band members, decked out in red vests, played love songs that beckoned everyone on to the dance floor.

Valentine's Day is like any other special day; it is what you make of it. This year why not make it something special for that someone special.

Loving the 'World of Gabrielle'   June 9, 2006

For the past four summers my 10-year-old great-granddaughter, who lives in West Bend, Wisconsin, spends a most-welcomed week or two visiting us in Escanaba.

The reason for her visit is two-fold: It clearly gives us an interesting and different perspective as we enter the "World of Gabrielle." And for Gabrielle's mother it's a welcomed vacation from the endless questions of a 10-year-old inquisitive mind while she's busy diapering and feeding her 1-year-old twin boys as 5-year-old Noah vies for attention.

Surely, being with us for a week is quite an education for her, too. Gary, our son with a brain-injury and a memory problem, lives with us. It can be a real circus at times. It is truly heartwarming though to see her pure interaction with Gary, and how she picks up cues on how to treat him. Her young intuitions are better than most adults. She recognizes he is not like her other uncle. And yet, she treats him with respect and kindness.

Gary recognizes her kindness and he likes having her around. A recent conversation went like this: Gary: "Are you my daughter?" Gabrielle: "No, I am your great-niece." Gary: "How great are you?" Gabrielle: "You're my great uncle." Gary: "How old are you?" Gabrielle: "I am 10." Gary: "How old am I?" Gabrielle: "You are 53." Gary: "Who knocked your front tooth out?" Gabrielle: "Nobody, Gary, it just hasn't grown in yet."

We went shopping one day, and rather than get the wheelchair out of the jeep to take Gary into the store, I muttered to myself, "Gary can wait in the car. We will only be a few minutes." In an effort to reassure me Gabrielle said, "GiGi, don't worry about Gary. Who would want to steal a 53 year-old man that can hardly walk?"

I couldn't stifle the laugh. But then I realized these are different times and she has, no doubt, been instructed by her mother and at school to beware of strangers "stealing someone."

She is all girl and very feminine. She loves our shopping trip to buy her a couple of new outfits for school in the fall. She is unselfish and with the few dollars her mother gives her for spending money she looks for small gifts to bring home for her brothers. She hints that her Mom loves Sayklly's candy. We buy the candy, but I have an idea *she* is the one that eats most of it.

Her creative abilities are amazing: She can take colored toothpicks, a colored note pad and straws or just about anything and make something interesting. She watches me make strawberry jam and memorizes the steps so she can show her mom when she gets home.

Her navigation on the computer is unbelievable. She pulls up Barbie.com and designs clothes, plays games and spends hours clicking on links. Her knowledge of the states and capitals is equally amazing. She tells us what books she reads and about her school's "battle of the books" (a prize for the person who reads the most books during the summer).

She thinks we are rich because our house is big and I don't check prices when I buy groceries. She tells me the brands her mother buys and how to save money with coupons. She soaks up information like a sponge. Her two favorite words are "gross" and "cool."

And we become more child-like and lighthearted with her around. She is full of hugs and kisses - and new revelations by the minute. Then she returns to West Bend. We will miss the "World of Gabrielle" and the lessons that she teaches us. Hopefully, her visits with us will be fond memories when she becomes an adult.

Love is a strange thing
it is a flower so delicate
that a touch will bruise it
and so strong that nothing
will stop its growth.
Think how often we miss
love in a lifetime - by a wrong gesture
- by an unspoken word
- by not keeping silent at the right time.
We lose it by the interference of others,
-by a lack of money,
by a quarrel over a trifle,
and yet we cannot live without it.

Love is
the greatest gift
a mother can give her children
and the greatest gift
they can give her in return.

Chapter
10

Places

FLORIDA VERSUS ESCANABA   September 29, 2006

It won't be long before the "snow birds" begin to pack up, board up, winterize and head for warmer climates. We used to be one of them. For the past 10 years we have spent six months of the year in Florida. I won't pretend I didn't enjoy the weather and the ease of living in Florida during winter. There is so much else to consider though.

I hated the packing and closing up one house for half a year. And there's the worry about the house we just vacated. Not to mention the double expenses of taxes and insurance and everything else that goes with maintaining a house. In Florida we also had a pool to be maintained even while we were gone - and consider the hurricane worries.

We lived in a gated community for 55 and over in Fort Myers. The community spirit was great. We were all basically in the same age group with so much in common.

Folks congregated at the community pool in the morning for exercises, and in the afternoon to socialize and partake in cook-outs. I walked daily around our center lake, mesmerized by the egrets, blue herons, cranes, storks - and yes, an occasional alligator.

The nature of the community lent itself to being active. I got involved by coordinating the yearly fashion show luncheon, which included a senior talent show. I also organized an energetic Red Hat Group called Vintage Vamps. Volunteers chaired the dinner dances. I always chaired the St. Paddy's Day event - yes, I am half Irish!

For the most part we were all in the same economic range. Most were content to just enjoy the sun, dinner dances, tennis, golf, camaraderie and join in the many structured activities the community offered.

It was an eye opener when we met a few of the "condo commandoes" as they were called - usually from a city in the East. Personalities really varied. Apparently, in their pre-retirement life they had positions where they were in charge and growing up in the city can foster some pretty aggressive personalities. Luckily they were in the minority; however, they made a lot of "noise."

I loved the great cultural activity offered in the area. The dinner theatres were a favorite of mine. And the shopping was second to none.

There was no end to the fabulous places to dine; so many

places offered outdoor seating overlooking the Gulf. And the beaches - what can I say! We didn't have to beg the kids to visit us; they readily came in the winter.

Grocery shopping was quite an experience. Everyone, men and women from 9 to 90, wears shorts - we are talking January and February. The check-out and carry-out "boys" were men retired from their corporate or college professor jobs in another lifetime. And loving it!

Our experiences trying to get reliable respite help a couple hours a day for our son with a brain injury were not so great. One agency sent out a young woman who brought along her two kids (a no-no). She took our son to a playground for her kids and left our son in a rattle-trap of car without air. It was 90 degrees. He was dangerously overheated and lethargic when they returned.

Another agency sent a black woman who couldn't speak English. When I complained - they said I was discriminating. What parent wouldn't be discriminating when their child's welfare is at stake? Yes, I stand accused. I wasn't about to leave him with someone who wouldn't understand his needs due to a language barrier.

We have been blessed with the fine service we have for our son in Escanaba. The same young man has been with us over six years. He treats our son with the utmost respect. And the community knows Gary Jr. People are so nice to him wherever he goes.

You never really get used to the differences in the city versus a small town. In Florida, it could be dangerous to go to the shopping center at night. You need to be very aware of your surroundings. Walking out to your car, after dark, when other people are also leaving is a good idea. For some years the Edison Mall had security on horseback policing the grounds during the holidays. And the traffic is horrendous!

The bank we did business with in Florida has a sign on the door: Take off sunglasses and caps before entering. Puzzled, I asked the teller about the sign. "Banks are robbed frequently and with sunglasses and caps we can't get a clear view of people on our video camera," she explained. Then she related they had been robbed two weeks previously for a second time in less than a year. The crime rate is high.

I think about those differences when I wear sunglasses in the bank or shop in the evening in Escanaba. It is comparatively safe and low-keyed here, plus, most everyone knows you. We have a history here. As a matter-of-fact, our families date back to the 1880s in this area.

The summers are delightful. In the spring I love watching the buds on the trees open up and produce their new season of leaves. Fall is great too, with its crisp air and colorful leaves. I love the three seasons. But, personally, I admit I am not fond of winter. After missing a winter in Florida due to my husband's health issues, he has decided we will at least spend March in Florida next winter even if he has to travel there in a hearse. Yes, his sense of humor can be a bit dark at times! Overall, the choice is no contest. Escanaba wins hands down! Pity the unfortunate city people who have never experienced the great life of living in a small Midwestern town.

TRIPPING TO OTHER COUNTRIES   August 4, 2006

Our first trip out of the continental USA was to Hawaii in 1973. It was a 10-day trip: Three days in Los Angeles at Disneyland and seven days in Hawaii. The $449 price per person included the air fare from Chicago and nine days of first-class lodging. Unbelievable today!

I loved the beaches, wearing the colorful muumuus, the exotic drinks with fresh pineapple, the pupus (Hawaiian appetizers), the grass skirts, leis, Hawaiian music, fields of Poinsettias, dining and dancing under the stars and the Luaus. The folklore and unique culture all added to the mystique of our first trip overseas. The Hawaiian saying is "hang loose," and that is just what we did.

Talk about a small world! The first day we were in Kona on the big Island we checked into our room and meandered down to the bar for one of those exotic drinks before dinner. Low and behold, a young guy with the call name "WDBC Escanaba" on the back of his jacket walked by. We couldn't believe our eyes!

"Hey," my husband called out, "we're from Escanaba!" as if Escanaba is a household word. The guy stopped in his tracks. "So am I! My name is Mike Nelson and I am part owner of the radio station here. I used to work for WDBC." And so it goes.

Acapulco was our next destination in 1974. The taxi ride from the airport was like being on a roller coaster; driving down curvy, hilly dirt roads at 100 miles an hour in a car without windows. We met up with a cow lying in the road and, without slowing down, the driver swerved off the road to a cliff's edge, almost giving us heart failure. Then I saw my first lizard ever - in my room! Sleep was uneasy after that.

A really unique experience was going to a bull-fight held in a huge, circular arena. The pageantry, matadors and music were great; but I was appalled at the way they weakened the bull by sticking swords in his neck before the ritual started. I left there dejected after seeing the bull tortured and defeated; not my idea of entertainment or anything I would want to see again.

We did enjoy seeing the famous Acapulco cliff divers plunge from a cliff that seemed a mile high. And the beaches were awesome. Carlos and Charlie's on a roof-top was a favorite rib place to dine. We took a bus into the village. Some of the natives had live chickens on the bus. Women and children with their feet covered in saran wrap begged tourists for money. I bought an alligator purse with a baby alligator on it before finding out I would have to smuggle it through customs. Alligators are a protected species.

Jamaica, our next vacation, was in 1975. We arrived in Jamaica in February with winter sweaters, boots and coats. The natives lost my luggage! It didn't arrive at the hotel for two days. I went barefoot and wore my husband's jeans with a rope belt for two days while I whined and cried in 90 degree heat about how my trip was ruined.

I bartered with a Jamaican native who was carving a huge head all week; they expect you to barter. I finally bought it for $50 on the day we were scheduled to leave.

The unusual Jamaican head carving is two feet tall, solid wood, very heavy and worth much more than the price I bought it for. It stayed in my arms for safety on the plane and as we maneuvered through customs in Chicago. We had a long walk through a tunnel and my husband slowed down due to his beginning heart problems.

As a result we fell behind the group being led through customs. We reached the screening area and suddenly custom officials told me to step aside - then they confiscated my head. "We need to x-ray this head," he said. "What for?" I questioned him naively. "Drug smuggling," he replied. Shocked and irritated I said, "You had better not scratch it. I want it back in perfect condition!" Did we look like drug smugglers?

Jamaica also has a unique culture. The music was neat.

The limbo-stick dances were part of the scene and *Yellow Bird* was a popular song while we were there. We climbed a tree with steps to reach a unique bar. A bar in a tree 40 feet off the ground? Yes, that was unique. Doubt I would venture up that tree now. We had planned on horseback riding, too, but when we saw the mangy horses covered with a million flies we opted out.

Puerto Rico was another destination in 1976, and I remember a prevailing wind at all times. Our accommodations were not the best. We spent every day in Old Town exploring the historical fort, El Morro, and its surroundings. We dined in a magnificent church hundreds of years old that had been converted into an elegant restaurant called the El Covente. However, Puerto Rico wasn't my favorite place to vacation.

The grand dame of vacations was our 50th anniversary in 2000. We booked our first cruise ever and took our family. We took the Eastern Caribbean route to the Virgin Islands. It was most memorable. Our granddaughter, Mary Pat, performed a tap dance on talent night. Our son, Jeff, and his wife Peggy performed the Sonny and Cher song *I Got You Babe*. My daughter, Vicki, and her husband Dave hung out with famed comedian Marty Allen after his show. To culminate a wonderful event we exchanged our vows - and so did our children. The ship's captain conducted the ceremonies.

The trips we have experienced all hold very special memories. The one place I would like to revisit is Hawaii. I loved the culture and folklore. I hope to go back there someday. Guess it had better be soon though -- time is running out!

ISLAND BRINGS BACK OLD MEMORIES June 16, 2006

Mackinac Island is a favorite summertime place to visit. People from around the world, including presidents and movie stars, have visited the Island. It is like a throw back to the 19th century. The absence of cars slows the pace. Visitors and residents travel by bike, horse drawn carriages or by foot.

In the early '60s we lived in the Sault and a highlight in the summer was visiting the island with three kids in tow. They loved the exciting excursion from St. Ignace on the ferry to reach the Island.

We brought a picnic lunch, rented bikes and circled the nine-mile road around the island. From a high vista along the route we marveled at the magnificent view of Lake Michigan. Souvenir stores and Mackinac Island fudge shops lined the main street. You could watch the fudge being made in the windows and the tempting aroma found its way out the door to beckon you.

Years later, as a graduation gift to our youngest son, we visited the island in a style not afforded us when we were younger. We stayed at the Grand Hotel.

It was truly a grand experience; a five-course dinner served in the huge dining room with violins softly playing, then louder, including some moving patriotic songs that stirred our very being and made our hearts swell with pride.

Waiters catered to diners and guests dressed to the hilt (the nines as they say today.) Demitasse was served in the parlor in the early evening.

Wow! Such elegance!

We felt like the rich and famous. My husband and I returned for the unique experience several more times on special occasions.

The Grand Hotel opened in 1887. Vacationers arrived by lake steamer from Chicago, Montreal and Detroit and by rail across the country before the invention of automobiles. The rates were $3 to $5 a night. Victorians made Mackinac Island one of the best summer resorts. Guests danced to Strauss' waltzes and dined on whitefish. Visitors strolled on the broad 660-foot front porch, boasted as the largest in the world.

The famous movie, *Somewhere in Time*, starring Christopher Reeves and Jane Seymour, was filmed on the island in 1980. It is still shown at the Grand Hotel on certain evenings. Also *This Time for Keeps* starring Jimmy Durante and Esther Williams was filmed in 1949 on the island, including the Grand Hotel.

A bevy of presidents has visited the island and stayed at the Grand Hotel. Suites have been named in honor of many first ladies and designed to reflect their taste. For example, Nancy Reagan's walls are covered in her signature red; Rosalynn Carter's features wall coverings of soft Georgia peach; Jacqueline Kennedy's suite features the gold presidential eagle on a navy blue background. Each first lady helped design her suite.

Each suite includes the official White House portrait of the first lady and a brass plate on the door with her signature on it. Needless to say, these rooms are extremely pricey and access is very limited. Named rooms start at $360 per person and commemorate places, people and eras. Other rooms start at $230 per person. There are 385 rooms and no two are alike.

The Grand Hotel experience requires evening wear for dinner and in all areas of the hotel. And guess what? No tipping is expected or permitted anywhere in the Grand Hotel. Instead, a charge is added to your daily room rate. Perhaps tipping is less painful if it is charged to your room?

Lest we not forget the historical significance of Mackinac Island. Jean Nicolet, a French-Canadian, is believed to be the first white man to see Mackinac in 1634. The Island has been under control of three different countries: France, England and, finally, America. The British chose the high bluffs for the site of Fort Mackinac. Guided tours complete with cannons and original barracks is a very interesting tourist attraction.

I don't mean to sound like a travel agent, but truly the Mackinac Island experience is family oriented and unforgettable - and it is in our own backyard!

FEELING YOUNG AT THE HARD ROCK CAFE   April 6, 2007

Vacations definitely change through the years. What might appeal to a person in their 20s and 30s would drive today's senior up the wall! Most of today's music is not the kind you can sing along with, like the great melodies and soft ballads of yesteryear.

I doubt many seniors would be interested in sky diving, water-skiing, snorkeling, rock climbing or, for that matter, partying even until 10 p.m. Yet I recall visiting cousins in Indiana in my 30s. A highlight was water-skiing, the night club scene and dancing until dawn. Yes, believe it; at one time we were young and energetic!

We have just returned from a vacation in Fort Lauderdale. Our plans to stay at the Seminole Hard Rock Hotel and Casino were in place long before the death of Anna Nicole on the premises. The amazing AAA Four-Diamond resort appealed to us. It has everything you need at your fingertips.

Last year we had heard about the magnificent complex. It took three years to build and opened in 2004. It was everything we imagined and more. Connected to the hotel and casino with over 2,000 gaming machines was a huge lake. The complex features 17 restaurants, 11 clubs and lounges to suit everyone's taste in entertainment, not to mention 22 retail shops!

Can you imagine a place named Bad-Ass Coffee Shoppe? Guess I am out of the loop. Seems my kids' need their Starbucks fix a couple of times a day. My son, Jeff, was attending an Anti-Money Laundering Conference and stayed on to spend time with us.

When we arrived we collected our luggage and ventured out to grab a cab. My husband, Gary, eager to begin his vacation and minus his glasses, ran over to jump in - can you believe - a sheriff's car!

Our room on the fifth floor was exquisite. It overlooked a four-acre lagoon-style tropical pool complex with a bridge to the Beach Club Restaurant where we enjoyed poolside luncheons.

I left Gary in the room while I explored the premises. Again without his glasses, he got in the elevator by himself and stood for 5 minutes until somebody rescued him. He couldn't read the floor numbers.

The history of the Seminole Indian Tribe was most interesting. In a series of wars against the Seminoles in Florida about 1,500 U.S. soldiers died. The Seminoles never surrendered; hence the Seminoles of Florida call themselves the "Unconquered People."

Many Indians were exiled to Oklahoma: They were forced to march on foot sometimes referred to as the "Trail of Tears." Less than 200 Seminoles retreated to the Everglades where they repopulated. They lived on the fringe of society.

Seminoles are the only American Indian Tribe never to sign a formal peace treaty with the U.S. Today they have sovereignty over their tribal lands and their economy depends on tobacco, tourism and gambling. Seminole Casino Hollywood was the first high-stakes operation in the country, opening in 1979 just blocks from their four-star complex today.

"Seminoles" is also the nickname of the athletic teams at Florida State University. Of course the Seminole Tribe agreed to the use of their name in writing.

In 2006 the Hard Rock business was sold to the Seminole Tribe for $965 million. Included in the deal are 124 hard Rock Cafes, four Hard Rock Hotels, two Hard Rock Casinos and two Hard Rock Live! Concert venues. The casino in Biloxi, Mississippi, was scheduled to open in 2005, but Hurricane Katrina delayed that opening until this summer.

How fun to explore the premises and all of the great memorabilia, which are either purchased at auction or donated by celebrities. The decor was a very pointed Rock and Roll theme. Even the door handles were in the shape of a guitar. There were huge glass encased displays dedicated to Elvis and the Beatles: clothing worn by them, guitars used by them, gold records and many rare photographs.

There were literally hundreds of display: One of Prince and the purple jacket he wore in the movie *Purple Rain*; a guitar and shirt worn by Jon Bon Jovi; Chuck Berry's guitar and gold record, *See You Later Alligator*; Hank Williams Jr. colorful short jacket worn on a world tour; and an interesting history of Allman Brothers.

One of our favorite times was early evening in the lobby promenade. Every evening before dinner a casual band played tunes by Frank Sinatra or Tom Jones. People (including us) spontaneously danced all over the place while the lobby bar served up tropical drinks. Everyone was happy!

Another feature is a European spa for facials, massages and just about any kind of pampering you would want. Many of the slots had a Rock and Roll theme. My favorite was the Blues Brothers machine that rang out their songs with every quarter. Of course winning a jackpot did help it to become my favorite. Another favorite was the Cleopatra slot.

And now home at last! Vacations do make us appreciate what we might have perceived as a mundane life at home. It is great to be home; however, I do feel richer for the experience and memories.

Chapter
11

Christmas Traditions

Christmastime at Grandma Laura's was so very special that I can conjure up in my mind Christmas Eve, Midnight Mass and the wonderful aromas of her "French" meat pies baking in the oven while her homemade wine delighted the adults.

French Meat Pie (Tourtiere)

4# lean ground pork	Simmer slowly for 2 hours
1# ground beef	Add 2 tsp. cinnamon
3 onions chopped fine	1 tsp. cloves
1 cup water per lb. of meat	1/2 tsp. allspice

Thicken with a little flour or 5 slices stale (dry) bread crumbs. Simmer 1/2 hour longer. Put into pie crust and bake at 350° until Crust is browned. Can be partially baked and frozen.

Grandma Laura's Special Orange Cake

1/2 cup butter	2 cups flour
1 cup sugar	1 tsp. soda
2 eggs	1 orange
1 cup sour cream or buttermilk	1/2 cup raisins
	chopped nuts

Squeeze juice from orange and save. Put orange and raisins through grinder. Cream butter and sugar. Add milk and soda. Stir slowly into flour. Add orange, raisins and nuts. Bake at 350° for about 40 minutes. Add 1/2 cup sugar to orange juice. Pour on cake while hot to form glaze.

CHRISTMAS MEMORIES OF LONG AGO   December 8, 2006

I wish I could say that all memories of Christmas when I was very young were like the poem *T'was the Night Before Christmas* with visions of sugar plums dancing in my head while I was all snuggled and nestled in my bed. They weren't!

But let me put the Christmases of my early childhood in context. It was the late 1930s and the country was coming face to face with the Depression. Jobs were scarce. Money was scarce. Escanaba was no different than the rest of the country.

Prohibition had ended. Drinking, now legal, resumed full scale. Escanaba's west end, the area along Stephenson Avenue, was noted for bars. It seemed every other business in that corridor was a bar. In fact, Escanaba was named in Robert Ripley's national syndicated column, *Believe it or Not*, for having the most bars per capita in the United States. And they were all thriving!

At the time bars were open on Christmas Eve. Many a husband and father spent Christmas Eve in the bars. Later the bars were mandated to close on Christmas Eve. (A good move by the state.) The deadly duet of drinking and domestic violence was rampant. Why? Was it because there was little money and no jobs? Were people depressed? Did the drinking mask the problems?

Dime beers, jute boxes and conversation with laughing and joking were perhaps an escape from the grim reality of the times. Many children would grow up with memories of drinking and the violence it would lead to. Mine was no different. Some of those memories haunt me today.

But there were good memories too. The anticipation of Santa Claus was exciting. I remember getting a Shirley Temple doll that I had for years. I got a desk with a roll top when I was 10. My daughter has it in her home today. There were blackboards, tea sets, sleds, tricycles and many other things I remember. My grandmother helped with that.

The stockings we hung were a big deal. They were always filled with a banana, orange and apple plus a few pieces of candy. I wonder what kids today would think of such a meager stocking? My ice skates were bought for a dollar at a skate exchange. They were black and I was embarrassed because they weren't white figure skates. I tried to put white shoe polish on them but it would come off when they got wet.

I yearned for white figure skates. Perhaps that is why I bought myself a pair after I was married and lived in the Sault. We skated together as a family at the Pullar Stadium where the Detroit Red Wings trained.

Of course, in the '30s and '40s there was no TV. A favorite pastime was going to the skating rink every evening after Christmas. The 19th Street rink (Royce Park) provided music to skate to. We warmed up in the shack with its pot bellied stove.

I loved going to the Coliseum just before Christmas. Everyone got a huge bag of candy and the program with Santa Claus and all of the Christmas songs were wonderful memories. It was all free! And the movie Theatre: The huge Christmas tree on the stage and the wonderful wholesome musicals with Sonja Henie, Betty Grable and Bing Crosby. Those were great times!

There was no shopping center and the Escanaba downtown was brimming with people. Santa parked at the Fair Store. The Salvation Army rang its bell on the Fair Store street corner.

There was something magical about downtown during the Christmas season with all the decorations, beautifully-decorated store windows (especially the Fair Store), and the bustling of people shopping. Stores were only open one night a week: Friday. Christmas shopping hours were only extended the week before Christmas.

For a number of years my mother was a single parent and we were fortunate to have her mother who helped out. I spent most of my time with my grandmother and slept there at night. My grandmother was deaf and when my grandfather died she felt more secure with me there even if I was a little person. She perpetuated many Christmas traditions in our family.

She and her six children would spend time together at Christmas. She baked cookies and always made at least a dozen of her most delicious French meat pies. Relatives and friends alike from Bark River and Schaffer would stop for a sip of her homemade wine and a piece of meat pie.

I remember hearty laughter and everyone happy - and also sitting in the stairway trying to listen to the adults when we should have been sleeping!

As a teenager I loved going to Midnight Mass. There was an enchanted feeling of the wonderment of celebrating Christ's birthday, worshipping and singing hymns in St. Pat's choir that stirred my heart in ways that would be difficult to describe.

Taking photos was rare in those early years. The cost of film and developing it into photos were luxuries. Many folks didn't have cameras. Some had a small Brownie camera. Technology wasn't like today with hundreds of cameras to choose from - and money to purchase them.

When I married and had children it was important to me that they would have good recollections of their childhood and Christmas. My daughter, Vicki, picked up on the little things we did with our young family, like attending church services.

I remember one church service when my youngest son, Jeff, was about four. He kept talking aloud and asking questions. I tried to quiet him by telling him, "This is God's house and we can't talk now." While standing on the pew with his arms outstretched he loudly exclaimed for the whole congregation to hear, "Well, if this is God's house then where is he!?" People turned around smiled and laughed. We still talk about it.

CHRISTMAS TRADITIONS: THE INSIDE STORY

December 22, 2006

Here's a look at some Christmas traditions, origins and memories:

THE CHRISTMAS TREE

The Christmas tree originated in Germany in the 16th century. German people decorated fir trees with roses, apples and colored paper. The Protestant reformer, Martin Luther, is believed to be the first to light a tree with candles.

The first Christian use of the Christmas tree symbol is credited to the 16th century. German born Prince Albert, husband of Queen Victoria, is credited with starting the trend in England in 1841 when he brought the first Christmas tree to Windsor Castle.

The first record of a Christmas tree in America came in the 1820s. It was brought here by the Pennsylvania Germans. But many people in early America saw them as Pagan symbols, which in fact, is their origin. By the 1890s Christmas ornaments were being imported from Germany and Christmas trees were in high fashion.

In my lifetime I have seen many changes in Christmas trees and decorations. Early on I remember strings of popcorn garland on the tree. Candy canes hung on the tree. Tinsel resembling icicles hung from the tree. The strings of lights were large and colored: red, blue, green, yellow and white. A tree cost about $2.

The first artificial tree I remember was in the '50s. They

were aluminum (silver in color) and a color wheel rotated at the base. We bought one and only used it one year as it nearly drove us crazy. We reverted back to traditional trees with blue lights only for a number of years. The cost ran from $10-$15.

In the '70s we didn't have little children at home and we bought more sophisticated trees. We traveled to Green Bay to get a popular white flocked tree - and still used blue lights. They cost $25 to $50.

Artificial green trees began to come into vogue. We bought several of them in the seven-foot range. Ornaments became very creative and color coordinated. The lights became tiny. Artificial trees have distinct advantages. You buy just once, there are no needles to fall, no watering, or frustrations to get the tree home and saw the trunk to make it level.

Artificial trees are perfectly shaped and come in all sizes. It is not unusual to have a nine- or 12-foot tall tree with the high ceilings in homes today. What I hope will be our last tree is a nine-foot Chicago slim tree.

The theme is woodland and the colors of crimson and gold match my decor with many bird houses and birds. I also have crimson wreath picture frames personalized with a photo of each family member displayed on the tree.

Our tree goes up the day after Thanksgiving and stays up until the first week in January. Interestingly, according to statistics, a third of families have artificial trees, a third have traditional real trees and a third does not display a tree.

THE CANDY CANE

Candy canes have been around for centuries, but not until around 1900 were they decorated with red stripes and bent into the shape of a cane. They were sometimes handed out at church services to keep children quiet.

An Indiana candy maker came up with the idea of bending a white candy stick into the shape of a candy cane. He incorporated several symbols of Christ's love and sacrifice through the candy cane.

The color white symbolizes the purity and sinless nature of Jesus. Then he added three small stripes to symbolize the pain inflicted upon Jesus before His death on the cross. There are three to represent the Holy Trinity.

He added the bold stripe to represent the blood Jesus shed for mankind. When you look at the crook on top, it resembles a shepherd's staff. If you turn it upside down, the letter J symbolizes the first letter in Jesus' name.

RUDOLPH THE RED-NOSED REINDEER

Can you believe that Rudolph was born in 1939 as an advertising gimmick? Robert L May, a 34-year-old writer for Montgomery Ward, was asked to invent a Christmas story. The company gave copies of the story to customers during the holiday season as a promotion - and a song was born! I remember Gene Autry's rendition of the song in later years.

CAROLING

The custom of singing carols is said to have come from 13th century Italy where a man named St. Francis of Assisi led songs of praise. It is said to be very bad luck to send carolers away empty handed. It is customary to offer food, drink or even a little money.

EGGNOG

Did you know that at one time eggnog used to be made with beer? In the 17th century strong ale called nog was very popular in Britain around the holidays. It was made from beer, sugar, egg yolks, lemon rinds and cinnamon. In the 19th century North Americans took the French version made from sugar, milk and egg yolks and added brandy, rum or sherry. The modern day eggnog has been the same for over 150 years.

CHRISTMAS LIGHTS

The very first person to have Christmas lights on their tree was Edward Johnson who worked for Thomas Edison (my husband's first cousin three times removed). It would be some time before the general public could purchase similar lights. The first strands to be mass-produced came from Eveready in the early 1900s. By the 1920s General Electric had improved upon the invention.

Christmas has a rich history of tradition. They all add to the enchantment of the season. Researching traditions and origins of Christmas memorabilia has certainly broadened my knowledge and hopefully yours.

Merry Christmas, and peace be with all of you!

CHRISTMAS GIFTS THROUGH THE YEARS   October 27, 2006

It seems every year Christmas shopping begins earlier and earlier. Some years ago the stores would wait until after Thanksgiving to launch their Christmas merchandise. Now you are apt to see Christmas merchandise before Halloween - even in September.

People shop early for a variety of reasons. More women work now and like to shop early and at their convenience. Perhaps families like to spread out the cost of Christmas gift giving. Some folks use lay-away to insure choices and pay at they go. Some people do their buying on the Internet. And still others shop when they see a great sale.

Every year there are new gadgets and new toys for kids and adults alike, so there is never a need for duplication. Wrong! I've talked to many senior friends only to find out that they receive the same gifts that we do from our kids. Pictures, pictures and more pictures in all sorts of frames! You guessed it - *all* of the grandchildren.

Every year it's more photos. It is not that we don't appreciate our grandchildren, but there is a limit. If I were to display *all* of the photos and frames we have received through the years every flat surface and every wall space would be covered. I would have to buy another house just to display the almost 40 years of photos from our adult children, or I could stock a frame shop with a variety of frames that would put specialty shops to shame.

Mary Pearson, a friend and former resident, visited here from Texas last summer. Mary had a brilliant idea. She has five kids and is motivated to replace the photos of grandchildren in frames they have received through the years with photos of themselves. They would display them on every available flat surface: tables, kitchen cabinets, bathroom vanities, dressers and desks. When the family visits at Christmastime the reaction of their kids would be priceless! Perhaps they should also present each kid with a photo of themselves for their gift - of course minus the check many of us give our kids!

One year I gave our kids, Vicki and Jeff, each a popcorn popper for Christmas - minus the usual check. They called one another to see if the other one had received a check. They thought maybe their check was accidentally not included. Believe me it got their attention. The surprise was a cruise that included them for our 50th anniversary.

Men are notoriously late shoppers. They wait until the week of Christmas - and sometimes even Christmas Eve Day. My husband, although a romantic in some areas, never displayed that side of him when buying me a Christmas gift. And I hope he is embarrassed when he reads this. Predictably, he'll probably howl with laughter.

We were living in the Sault and married for about 10 years with three small children. I put my heart and soul into Christmas: outdoor and indoor decorations, thoughtful and beautifully wrapped gifts for everyone under the tree, delicious homemade Christmas cookies and candies and a wonderful Christmas dinner.

Everyone was so pleased with their gifts - then it came time to open mine. I was all hyped up. He had just placed it under the tree Christmas morning and wouldn't let me touch it. I ripped the wrappers off and received the shock of my life: A six pack of beer! He and his brother, Glenn, who was visiting, laughed themselves silly. I ran into the bedroom in tears. How could he be so cruel! After Christmas I laughed last. I bought myself three new expensive outfits.

That Christmas didn't stop him from presenting me with gifts that were hilarious to him. I got used to his sick sense of humor and went along with it. No more tears.

One year he gave me a tool chest. It wasn't such a bad choice since I hang all of the pictures and do the needed repairs. He is helpless in that area.

Another year he gave me a fire extinguisher. Another hysterical laugh for him! The kicker was the year he gave me a check for $500,000. He cracked himself up laughing. I should have cashed it and he could have laughed himself all the way to jail.

One Christmas there was nothing under the tree for me from Gary - not really a surprise. Everyone sat around drinking eggnog after opening the gifts. Gary left the room and came back with my heaping basket of ironing. Now what is this all about - what kind of laugh is he drumming up now?

He dug down to the bottom of the basket scattering clothes all over the floor and pulled out a beautifully wrapped small gift for me. Another joke I thought. Much to my surprise and delight it was a beautiful gold necklace. He had really out-done himself. He claimed he never worried about me finding it because I had never ever reached the bottom of the ironing basket.

It would be fun for a future article for readers to e-mail me about the most ridiculous Christmas gift they ever received - or even the greatest. Be my guest! Just add your name.

HOLIDAYS EVOKE JOY AND SADNESS
December 15, 2006

It is true that for most people Christmas is a very joyous time. Families get together for a traditional holiday dinner, exchange gifts and celebrate family traditions. Memories of those happy times are priceless. There is no question for most people Christmas brings back our most vivid memories and tugs at our strongest emotions.

For some - Christmas is painful. The memories of a difficult childhood, the death of a loved one or a divorce can be overwhelming. Christmas for some is dreaded. The Christmas music and hymns, the glitter, the surrounding excitement and the anticipation of Christmas enjoyed by most intensify feelings of sadness in others. Depression is real.

My mother claimed she didn't like Christmastime. It reminded her of early years when she couldn't give her children things she thought they should have. It conjured up sadness, memories of being poor and being alone after the death of her husband.

Christmas is family time, but the reality is not all families get along. But at Christmastime, suddenly and miraculously, families are supposed to regroup in a unity that may feel insincere to them. Worrying and thinking about the upcoming union may fill people with guilt - or even worse, remind them of being alienated from family members altogether.

I know we should all try to resolve our differences. And in a perfect world that may be true, but this world is not perfect and neither are relationships. People are out there suffering over their stubborn refusal to extend an olive branch - or to accept it. The guilt and hurt intensifies at Christmastime.

A sad commentary on our society is that Christmas is one of the catalysts for domestic violence and suicide. It is a busy day for police who settle family disputes.

I read about a new collection of short stories by New York Times and USA Today best-selling author Barbara Russell Chesser titled *Keeping Christmas*. The main focus of the book is to help people wrestling with holiday grief. The 26 stories will remind us, "while we may have much to mourn, we have more to celebrate," says Chesser.

"We all long for the perfect holiday as the year ends and a new one begins. To savor the peace and joy of the season, we must reconcile the disappointments, the tragedies of the past year -

indeed our entire lifetime - as well as the triumphs, large and small," she writes.

For several years after my son, Gary, dropped dead while jogging, (he was revived and eventually emerged from a coma), it was difficult for me to come to terms with his severe brain injury.

I hated the holidays. It reminded me of the wonderful Christmases we had when Gary was the "before-injury" Gary - then I would contrast it with the way it had become. Tears would flow spontaneously. I was haunted that Gary would never realize his dreams or our dreams for him. He was only 37 when the tragedy occurred 19 years ago. Christmas was painful. I thought I would never be at peace.

Years have passed, and finally I have reconciled with the devastation of his unfortunate tragedy. Now I focus on how lucky we are that Gary is still with us, and we are able to provide him with security and love. He is funny, loving and extremely perceptive at times. He has a big heart and thanks us every day for caring for him. We thank God for him. He keeps us young - at heart, anyway.

We are looking forward to 20 family members (children, grandchildren, and great-grandchildren) ascending upon us at Christmas. Gary just purrs when his siblings, nieces and nephews are here.

I think of Christmastime when our family was young. Younger mothers place a real burden on themselves wanting everything perfect. I know! I've been there. Many work a full-time job. They run themselves to a frazzle, decorating inside and out, shopping, wrapping, baking and cooking in addition to their everyday chores of running a household.

Overspending and budget worries plague young families. The Christmas season becomes rushed, hectic and exhausting. By the time Christmas arrives they are spent emotionally, financially and physically - and almost relieved when it's over.

A passage I read in *Living Artfully* spoke volumes: "the best and most treasured gifts are not found in the store, enclosed in a box, or discovered under a tree. The best gifts are the people in our lives and the moments we share."

Still there are so many lonely people in our community that we need to care about.

Mrs. McGregor, editor of *FIFTYplus*, commented on my recent article about relationships. She said her readers have told her that loneliness is almost worse than bad health. And certainly the feeling of isolation is magnified during the holidays.

What can we do as individuals? Small, insignificant acts of kindness can make a huge difference to someone hurting. We can wrap a few cookies and visit a lonely neighbor; let them know we care. We can visit places like Christian Park, Bishop Noa and other facilities, bring some cookies and spend time with residents. You can invite a lonely neighbor for dinner, or bring them a special meal if they can't get out.

We are blessed with wonderful, caring neighbors, Mike and Nicky Wangrud. They mow our grass, weed our flowers and shovel our sidewalk and driveway. We are humbled by their acts of kindness. They even share their little girl, Annika, with us. And their friendly dog, Scrappy, greets us with a vigorous tail wag.

If you are unable to fit some "hands-on" caring into a busy schedule then a generous donation to the Salvation Army would go a long way toward providing people in need of food, warm clothing and other necessities. It is a way of saying, "I Do Care!"

Make sure your church knows of people that may be isolated and lonely. There are always Good Samaritans willing to visit shut-ins and bring them some fruit or cookies along with comforting and kind words.

If we all do some small caring action this Christmas season our hearts will know the real meaning of Christmas. A community effort says, "We Do Care!"

READERS SHARE THEIR MEMORIES   December 29, 2006

The holidays are winding down. Some folks are saying, "Whew, thank goodness!" A New Year (2007) complete with resolutions, hopes, dreams and yes, bills is about to commence. The memories of Christmas will fade for now and come alive for today's younger generations in 40 or 50 years when they begin to reminisce. What will the world be like then? Will there be a world? Will today's youth look back at these times with fondness like the seniors of today?

Nostalgic memories from the past have really hit home with many readers judging from the e-mails, letters, phone calls and people I meet in the community. It seemed befitting to close out the year with a sprinkling of letters and excerpts from readers.

FROM KEN SCHUBRING, DUNWOOD, GEORGIA

Enjoy your "remember when" type columns so much. They are a pleasant trip back to an era that has long since passed into history. It is fun to go back and reminisce about them - and still share them with those who didn't have the privilege of living back then.

I am a native of Manistique although I have not lived there for over a half of century. I was a member of the MHS Class of 1940. Your reference to the repeal of prohibition and its effect locally reminds me of those days in Manistique.

We had three banks and with the bank panic in early 1933 one of them (the Manistique Bank) went belly up. Well, lo and behold, that bank's location at the corner of Cedar and Walnut subsequently became the state liquor store premises.

There used to be a gentleman I knew who during the days of the 18th Amendment had been a regular customer of the moon shiners. With legal liquor back, he switched to a then name brand on the store shelves: Sweepstakes. I don't think the stuff is available anymore.

Your mention of the Fair Store brought back memories. Our family used to shop frequently in Escanaba at the Fair Store and Montgomery Ward's (affectionately referred to by some of us as Monkey Wards).

Your reference to ice skates, family Christmas get-togethers, Christmas Eve church services and even the old Brownie box camera rang a clear bell with me. Thanks for providing in your columns a healthy serving of Americana, Upper Peninsula style!

FROM TERRY AND KATHY BURAK, ARIZONA

As long time Escanaba residents (1943-1985) we still call Escanaba our home...and I look forward to your column in the Daily Press. I really enjoy your column especially when you talk about the early years in Escanaba. It really brings back great memories.

One of my early highlights was a weekly trip to an ice cream store at the corner of 10th and Ludington. I think it was called the Boston Shoppe: that along with Ely's potato chips and roller skating at the Coliseum were great early memories.

We still spend two months in Escanaba each summer and look forward to heading east for the summer. Keep writing. We sure enjoy your column.

FROM JOAN GRAVELLE, ESCANABA

I read your piece in the paper every week. I really enjoy it. I read it to my husband who is legally blind and he says you really got it together on seniors. Keep up your writing.

From AUDREY (BEACH) CARLSON, Colorado

I loved your column on Christmas memories. Some are similar to mine. Until I was 10 years old, we lived in a two room shack in McFarland. My mom always called it a shack. We had two cows. Most years, one cow had a bull in the spring.

My dad bought a pig early in the summer and fattened it up to butcher in the winter. He also butchered a bull. We had plenty of meat to eat. We never went hungry but I wonder if we were short on food the nights we had bread and gravy for supper. We never thought about it as it was one of our favorite meals. So were pancakes.

My dad didn't drink or go to the tavern. We had cousins who were not as blessed as we were. We know how the entire family suffered when the dad drank. My childhood memories are mostly good ones. The bad ones are the times I misbehaved and got spanked.

We got an apple, an orange, unshelled nuts and hard Christmas candy in our stocking. We always got some type of clothes. A favorite when I was five was a brown skirt and yellow sweater. One year I got a maroon snowsuit that I loved.

We got stuffed toys, games, books, paper dolls, color books and crayons and kids skis. The games were for all of us. We played cards a lot and Chinese checkers when we were kids.

We went to Midnight Mass in Gwinn. When we got home, we went to sleep and that's when Mom and Dad put our gifts from Santa under the tree.

I remember going to the Coliseum and I remember the Salvation Army ringing their bell by the Fair Store.

I, too, skated at Royce Park. We were probably there at the same time but didn't know each other. I also had black skates that someone outgrew. I hated those black skates too. I think I was in ninth grade when Patt (Garrett) Marenger gave me her white figure skates as she had foot surgery and couldn't skate anymore. How I loved those skates!

Movies then were nice. They told a story free of violence and terrible language. Seeing a movie was relaxing and good entertainment.

We had lots of relatives and they were a huge part of our lives. Our years in the little shack were happy and stress free. We knew everyone in McFarland and it was comfortable.

There were the folks who drank too much and there was an occasional bum that came down the road. My mom must have kept a pretty close eye on the road because I remember her calling us kids in the house and she locked the door. Apparently she knew who the bums were.

Wouldn't it be great to just be able to go back for a day and see what we would think of that life now? For one thing, I know that my plain ordinary house is a mansion to what we had then.

FROM MARY (NOYES) PEARSON, HARLINGEN, TEXAS

Your ice skate story hit home with me. I also had black skates, but I found some white enamel paint and I painted them. It held up pretty well, but cracks formed during the first year I wore them. I got a pair of white figure skates when I was 16, but they were always too big for me.

FROM BARBARA LACROIX, GLADSTONE

I just wanted you to know how much I enjoy reading the articles you are writing for the Daily Press. I surely can relate to a lot of them - especially the one of Nov. 17 (health and technology). You always "make my day" with your articles. They are so well written. Keep them coming.

FROM DAVID AND LOIS NORDIC, ESCANABA

I have wanted to compliment you on your articles for some time now. Lois and I have enjoyed them. The tribute to Doug Fix, your mention of Frank McCourt - we have read the first two books and now will look forward to *Teacher Man*.

Enjoyed your coverage of your teen years in the late '40s and early '50s, especially the music - the big bands. Those were the years of music, the pop tunes, love songs, dances - Wow. Thanks again and keep them coming.

FROM YOURS TRULY:

May your New Year be everything you want it to be. And, God willing, I will keep on writing. Thank you Rick Rudden, editor, for the opportunity to express what many seniors feel, think, worry and reminisce about - along with giving the younger generations a glimpse into the past.

Chapter 12

Miracles, Faith and Acceptance

Thy fate is the common fate of all;
Into each life some rain may fall.
≈ Henry Wadsworth Longfellow ≈

You have to accept whatever comes and
the only thing is that you meet it with
courage and the best you have to give.
≈ Eleanor Roosevelt ≈

*Embrace your strengths and continue
to grow from life's experiences.
Never ever stop dancing!*
≈ *Patt Abrahamson* ≈

A Miraculous Survival? You Decide! November 18, 2005
(Feature Story, Published in the *U.P. Catholic*)

Heart problems first reared its ugly head for Gary Abrahamson in 1975 at age 44. He had heart by-pass surgery in Milwaukee when that type of surgery was in its infancy. Fortunately, a world renowned surgeon, Dr. Dudley Johnson agreed to operate when Green Bay surgeons thought Gary's specific risk was too high. Dr. Johnson, who holds patents on many of the tools used in heart operations, performed a 5 by-pass procedure and Gary's death sentence was lifted.

Years passed and Gary experienced a very active life, even winning local 5K races in the over 50 category. His persistent heart problems would eventually catch up with him. In 1998 he was rushed to Green Bay in an ambulance where he underwent angioplasty (insertion of a stent into a clogged artery) successfully. Life was good again until 2002 when he became increasingly short of breath. A test revealed stenosis of the aortic valve. While open chest surgery was recommended–he opted for medications to manage his problems. His shortness of breath became increasingly debilitating and there was another problem. One carotid artery was totally occluded and the other was 70% blocked.

In 2004, sensing the precariousness of his condition, Gary (now age 73) decided a trip to Mayo Clinic was imminent to reassess his current problems. The tests revealed his condition even more critical. His aortic valve was calcified to such an extent that doctors said they had only seen a couple of cases so severe. He was at risk for sudden death. Again, surgery was his only answer but now it posed other problems. The danger of a stroke was a very real possibility with the carotid artery blockage — that needed to be corrected first. The decision seemed very risky and overwhelming – again he declined. The fact that he had a disabled son at home drove his decision. "I don't want my wife to possibly have to care for two invalids," he told doctors.

That was all to change the summer of 2005. The first episode happened at home. He reached down for a shoe, became short of breath and it didn't resolve like it had in the past. He got up from his chair - let out a sigh and collapsed! At first he appeared to not be breathing. By the time the ambulance arrived, he had moved on his side. That was his first hospitalization in June. He would have two more episodes. He collapsed in the parking lot of the Stonehouse Restaurant. Again the ambulance rushed him to the hospital. Life was swiftly ebbing away and surgery seemed to be his only last ditch attempt to buy some time. It was extremely risky, but then....so was doing nothing. He claimed, "I am backed against the wall." In desperation he began to explore where other people have gone for the type of surgery he needed. Time was of essence.

Gary had heard Mel Taylor recently traveled to Texas for a serious operation. He found out Mel was critical, died on the operating table, and survived! Mel's advice was, "Gary, go to the Texas Heart Institute. Dr. Coselli, a surgeon, is world- renown. It's your only hope." The survival mode took over. A computer check revealed that St. Lukes Episcopal Hospital in Houston was home to the Texas Heart Institute with an international reputation in cardiovascular research, education and patient care. The world-renowned Denton A. Cooley, MD had founded the Institute and recently had appointed Dr. Joseph Coselli to the position of chief of adult cardiac surgery.

Dr. Cooley has contributed to the development and techniques for replacement and repair of diseased heart valves. He performed the first successful human heart transplant in the United States in 1968. In 1969, he became the first heart surgeon to implant an artificial heart. The heart is now on display at the Smithsonian Institution in Washington, D. C. Dr. Coselli specializes in the evaluation and treatment of diseases of the aorta—performing more than 5,200 repairs of the aorta and more than 2250 repairs of aortic aneurysms and is considered the most successful surgeon in this field. Convinced he was going to the "best of the best," Gary was able to obtain an appointment with Dr. Coselli.

But the ongoing duties of caring for a brain-injured son meant that leaving home was not without problems. The plan was to have the Abrahamson's daughter, Vicki and her husband Dave, who live near Milwaukee, share the 24-hr care needed for their severely brain-injured son. That meant getting a green light from their employers. Their youngest son, Jeff, a Washington D.C. attorney for the Treasury Department, would juggle his schedule to meet his parents in Texas for the consultations and proposed operation. Jeff's presence was essential. There was a real risk that Gary would not survive and his wife would need emotional support.

PART II

Three days later on July 12th the Abrahamson's were on a Houston— bound flight. "I wish I could fast-forward a couple of weeks," remarked Gary, filled with apprehension of what lay ahead. Gary's extreme shortness of breath just before boarding the plane was a cause for concern. He worried he might pass out or worse... die...because no medical help would be available.

The next day, with a plethora of medical records in hand, the Abrahamson's arrived at Dr. Coselli's office in St. Luke's. The initial meeting was with Dr. Coselli's nurse. An exhausting day of tests preceded the consultation. It was late in the evening before he was seen by Dr. Coselli.

A robust and imposing tall man with a pleasant face entered the room. He had already been briefed by his nurse. Dr. Coselli sat on his stool and wheeled it over to within inches of Gary. He looked directly into his eyes and asked, "How much of a risk taker are you?" Gary starred back at him, paused for a moment, and then said, "That depends on what the stakes are." The doctor shot back, "Gary, you are here because your condition is critical. I wish your heart wasn't so weak. Your ejection factor (a measure of the heart's pumping strength) is now at 35%. It was at 50% a year ago. Your lungs are not in good shape. You have pulmonary hypertension and fibrosis. I can do the surgery with 15 to 20% risk...the difficult part will be the recuperation process." More queries and answers followed. Finally, the doctor said, "we will need an angiogram first and there are risks with that test in your case. When we have those results, I can tell you if we can proceed."

Gary's son, Jeff, arrived that same evening. As Gary briefed Jeff with the day's events there seemed to be hesitation about going forward with the angiogram. "Dad, the reason you are here is to take that risk. You have to remember if you choose to do nothing, you have a real risk of sudden death at any time." After a pep talk from Jeff, Gary decided to go forward and the angiogram was scheduled the next day. Dr Coselli wanted his most experienced cardiologist to perform the angiogram.

At 7 am Gary arrived at the hospital with his support team (his wife and son.) He looked anguished but resolved to go through with it. Dr. Hogan examined him. His demeanor and apparent skill immediately helped put Gary at ease. The test took longer than anticipated and Patt's thoughts ran rampant. However, all went well, except the results were more devastating than was anticipated. Gary's ejection factor (now down to 20-25 percent) meant that Gary's heart was even weaker than anticipated. The aortic valve was calcified and fixed. There was a previous unknown heart attack, plus it confirmed that one carotid artery was totally occluded and the other was 70 percent blocked. Also, for some unknown reason the first surgeon in 1975 had crossed the mammary arteries in his chest now making entry into the chest without losing one or both virtually impossible.

That evening, Dr Coselli entered the hospital room with his nurse. He explained the difficulty with the surgery and the fact that they were not dealing with a virgin chest. "Is the risk still the same?" Gary asked. "It's about 20-25 percent." he responded His nurse quickly added, "Remember that there is a 75-80 percent chance you will pull through!" Sensing Gary's reservation the doctor said, "Why don't you sleep on it, discuss it with your wife and son, then call my office on Monday with your decision." After he left, Gary turned to his wife and said, "Honey, why don't we just go home and return to our life in a cocoon?" Jeff, sensing his Dad's reluctance and his mother liking that idea said, "Dad, you need to focus on the 80 percent, not the 20 percent. After being hospitalized twice in just a few weeks, one fear we all had was that the surgeon would conclude that you're too risky to operate on. The good news is that you have a choice. We don't need to make a decision today – let's continue to talk over the weekend."

Gary was discharged from the hospital Saturday. He felt better than he had been feeling, but it was not to last. At 3 am Sunday morning he awoke with his heart racing, and pounding in his chest. Situated on the 12 floor of a hotel was not an enviable place to be in. All three rushed to the emergency room where Gary was in atrial fibrillation. Apparently the angiogram had caused a disturbance. He was admitted to the floor that monitors heart rhythm. Early Monday evening the doctor's nurse called the room. "We had a cancellation on the surgery schedule for tomorrow morning. Do you want that spot?" "Can we discuss it?" his wife asked. "There isn't time. We need an immediate decision." she responded. Gary was vigorously shaking his head "NO." He knew that opting for surgery meant he might die, become paralyzed, or suffer neurological problems. Despite these risks, Gary had consigned himself to going through the surgery at this point, but he was counting on a few more days before he had to face his destiny. He just wasn't psychologically ready yet. Having refused surgery for the next morning, Gary was at the mercy of the doctor's surgery schedule, which seemed to change by the day, depending on the needs of patients and new emergencies that arose. In the meantime, Gary's shortness of breath worsened. He could no longer use the bathroom. He was pale and on oxygen.

At 8:00 pm Tuesday evening the doctor appeared after a full day of surgery. "I understand you weren't ready for surgery. "OK 'chief' just let me know when you are ready." he added softly, with his unique brand of humor. He turned as if to leave the room. "Wait a minute," his wife said. "He IS ready now." "OK!" said Dr. Coselli. "I will talk to you tomorrow evening and tentatively put you on the schedule for Thursday. Of course, that can change if there is an emergency."

Wednesday evening Dr. Coselli brought in the papers and explained the risks...plus presented Gary with an additional list of risks two pages long. A bevy of questions ensued. Surgery was scheduled for 8 am Thursday morning. Gary thought they would do the surgery without operating on the carotid artery. He was worried about a stroke. Patt asked, "Isn't there a greater risk when one carotid artery is already occluded?" "You're right, "the doctor explained, but there is at least an equal risk of stroke on the heart-lung machine if the carotid artery is not cleared of plaque, so it would be better to error on the side of doing something, rather than nothing, with the carotid artery." Gary, his voice cracking and choked with emotion, addressed the doctor, "I have been praying for God to guide your hands tomorrow." "I pray for that everyday." Dr. Coselli responded. Gary knew the cat and mouse game was up. No more vacillating. No more indecision. No more going back. Tomorrow was D-day.

PART III

Gary asked his wife to spend the night with him before the surgery. The priest came to his room. All three prayed together. He blessed Gary and departed. Phyllis LaBranche, proprietor of the Swedish Pantry Restaurant in Escanaba had given Gary a medal that had been blessed when she was in Medjugorie. Patt pinned it on his hospital bracelet. Tears streamed down Gary's face as he reminisced about their life together, their family and happier times "I have had a great life." Gary began, his face wet with tears, voice choked with emotion and fearing this might be his last day on earth, "I can't talk any more, but you know how I feel." Patt, holding back tears read him a booklet on courage...then, silence—as they held hands into the night. Finally, Patt climbed into the hospital bed and Gary rested in the chair unable to lie down because of his condition. Neither slept as they anticipated what lay ahead.

6 am Thursday 21 July: The nurse entered his room and gave the necessary instructions. Gary was unable to shower — Patt bathed him. Soon a male nurse came to prep his chest and neck for the surgery. Their son Jeff arrived from the hotel. The mood was solemn while waiting for Gary to be transported to the operating holding room. A cap was placed over his hair, and he was wheeled swiftly to an elevator with Patt and Jeff scurrying behind. The holding area was lined up with people waiting for surgery separated only by curtains. A short time later, a nurse announced they were ready for Gary. They took his medal off of the bracelet and explained he couldn't have it on during the surgery. They would take care of it for him. Jeff held his hand and Patt bent down, kissed his cheek and holding back tears assured him, "Everything will be alright. I will be here when you wake up. I love you!"

Patt and Jeff retreated to the waiting area. They were told a liaison nurse would brief them every hour as the surgery progresses. The first briefing would be 9:30 am. A cart with breakfast sandwiches was nearby so family members did not have to leave the area. Food was the last thing on their mind.

9:30 am the liaison nurse called out family names. "Abrahamson!" She approached Jeff and Patt. "They haven't opened the chest yet. The carotid artery is being operated on now and everything is going well." Jeff and Patt sighed with relief and dug in to wait for the next update.

11:00 am "The chest has been opened and surgery is in progress. His carotid surgery took only eleven minutes. His brain waves were monitored during the procedure. Everything is progressing well. I will be able to tell you more at the next briefing." reported the liaison nurse. Minutes seemed like hours.

12:30 pm This time the liaison nurse sat down next to Patt and Jeff. "There is a problem with the right ventricle." she announced. "But I thought it was the left ventricle that was troubling and more important?" queried Patt with anxiety in her voice. "You're right" she explained, "but you need both." Puzzled and concerned, Patt, who typically is inquisitive, didn't ask any other questions. It was as if she didn't want to hear anything negative. The time seemed endless before the next briefing. As if summoned by God, Mary Green, a hospital pastor appeared and sat next to Jeff and Patt. "Please join me in prayer for Gary." she said. They held hands knowing Gary's fate was in God's hands. The pastor continued, "Please keep Gary safe during his surgery and grant Patt and Jeff the strength to accept whatever God in his infinite wisdom decides for Gary." The excruciating wait continued. 1:30 pm came and no briefing. At 2:00 pm Patt said, "Something is wrong! What is taking so long? Why haven't they been back to brief us?"

2:15 pm The liaison nurse approached Patt and Jeff. Again she sat down. She had a look of terror in her eyes. She peered at Patt and said, "I am so sorry. They are not able to get your husband off of the heart-lung machine. His heart is too weak to beat on its own. Patt burst into tears. Jeff's eyes widened with concern. "What are you telling us...that he is dead?" Patt sobbed in between words. "The plan is to wait an hour or so and try again to wean him off of the heart-lung machine." she explained with a look of compassion and concern not fully addressing Patt's question. Pastor Mary Green again appeared from nowhere. "I have a private consultation room opened for your family." she said. "Please follow me." Did that mean when they tell Patt and Jeff he is dead they could cry and grieve in privacy?

4:00 pm The liaison nurse returned, "I have better news!" she exclaimed. "They have now weaned him off of the pump, but the tubes are still attached. He has a balloon pump inserted to assist the heart beating. He is not out of the woods yet, but things are looking better." With that astounding news Patt and Jeff hugged one another. Jeff left for the chapel to pray. Patt prayed and waited for the nurse to return.

5:00 pm Vicki, the Abrahamson's daughter called for an update. She was unaware of the most recent developments. Patt tried to brief her through sobs and tears. "Mom, our faith is what has sustained us so far - we need to keep the faith." Vicki said trying to console her mother. Jeff returned from the chapel and took over...he was more composed and promised to inform Vicki as soon as they had more information.

6:00 pm The nurse came back and exclaimed, "They have pulled the tubes. And as soon as they get him situated in ICU you can go in and see him. He won't be awake. They have decided to leave his chest open for a couple of days with a sterile drape. The doctor is concerned that closing the chest would place undue pressure on the heart in its weakened condition." With that the doctor came into the consultation room, pulled up a chair and went over the events. The doctor stated that he implanted a St. Jude Medical mechanical valve and Gary's condition was critical. "What are his chances for survival now?" Jeff asked. "Perhaps 50 to 75 percent. He didn't give me much to work with. His heart is very weak. And of course, he has many other problems including his lungs. I will keep him asleep for two days and probably close his chest on Saturday. I don't want him moving at all until his chest is closed. Be prepared for a roller coaster ride." Despite the recent positive developments, it was clear the doctor was being very guarded in his answers. He knew the risks all too well and Gary was nowhere near out of the woods yet. Before parting, he advised, "Patt, after you see him, I want you to get some rest. Too often the spouses end up in the emergency room too. You need to rest and conserve energy for when he is awake. There is nothing you can do now." With that he patted Patt on the shoulder...his warm way of showing compassion.

7:30 am Patt and Jeff entered ICU. They were lead to a wash basin and told to wash their hands; a ritual each time you entered ICU. They proceeded through more than 32 beds, each separated by curtains and occupied by mostly men - with respirators taped in their mouths, beds propped up and competent nurses tending to them. The ICU housed two units with 64 beds in all. Gary was in a private isolation unit that was completely glassed in, where the most serious of the ICU patients are kept. Upon reaching the unit the gravity of the situation became evident to Patt and Jeff. There were a dozen or more doctors, nurses and residents surrounding the bed. Tubes and monitors were suspended from everywhere. The pulmonologist beckoned Patt and Jeff closer to see Gary. Dr. Casar explained they extracted two quarts of fluid out of his lungs during the operation. Patt felt wobbly as she viewed Gary: a respirator taped to his mouth, IV's in his arms and neck, hooked up to bottles of fluid with his face and neck swelled up. She patted his hand and wished that this was all just a bad dream. "He is bleeding very profusely" Dr. Casar explained. "We will know more in the next 24 to 48 hours. Right now he is critical and bleeding at the rate of 1200 cc's (over a quart) an hour." The nurse explained later that doctors like to see 100cc's an hour or less.

At the motel, sleep was not an option for Patt. She called

hourly for updates. The bleeding continued throughout the night. Chris, a male nurse with a litany of credentials and experience was assigned to Gary the first night. Surely this was not by accident. And Dr. Coselli's resident spent the night literally picking blood clots out of the tubes. The resident doctors had the pulmonologist on the phone all night. Later, a resident explained that rarely anyone comes out of surgery with an open chest—if they do— infection could be a problem. He personally had never witnessed an open chest after surgery. He said Gary was the "prime topic of discussion among the residents." Gary received 16 units of blood. Normal for that surgery is 6 units or less.

Gary was on three IV "drips," a slang term to denote the drug regime he was on to sustain his blood pressure at artificially sustained normal levels...and "drips" for heart irregularities. As part of the rules of this specialized care unit of care Patt and Jeff could visit Gary for three designated periods of 30 minutes every 24 hours. Patt asked for Gary's medal blessed in Medjugorie and pinned it back on his bracelet. Surely his fate was in God's hands. Friday night the bleeding lessened. Saturday morning, two days after the surgery, Gary was wheeled back into surgery to close his chest. Later that day his urine output slowed. Lasix, a diuretic, was administered to help the kidneys rid the body of fluid. The doctor came by and said he was going to let Gary wake up. Was there any neurological damage? Soon the family would know. Saturday evening, although still hooked up to myriad machines, Gary began to wake up. Jeff planned to fly back to Washington on Sunday. He had been in Houston 10 days and needed to get back to his family and job. He was glad to see his father open his eyes before he left. Tears trickled down Gary's face as Jeff bid him goodbye.

PART 4

Patt missed Jeff's comforting presence as she traveled back and forth on the shuttle provided by the Holiday Inn Medical Center. Now she was able to comprehend the immensity of the Texas Medical Center. Hospitals and related facilities were suspended in space everywhere, one after the other, each for a specific discipline. One for cancer, one for children, one for heart, one for orthopedics etc. She was amazed at the rich ethnic diversity - Hispanic, Afro-American, Asian, and Middle-Eastern. Later she found out that whites are in the minority in Houston.

In addition to the diversity in local population, it was evident that people from all over the world had come to the medical center for one ailment or another. Many were outpatients all wearing the telltale hospital bracelets. Some that departed at the MD Anderson Hospital for cancer wore masks. And many young people wore hats or baseball caps to cover their hairless heads. One attractive young lady sporting a pink baseball cap wore a tee shirt that said *"CANCER SUCKS."* One elderly couple struggled to get off and on the shuttle. She was on oxygen and he had a walker. They were in their 80s and apparently had no family to help them. Most of the Muslim women wore the wraps and long skirts - some covered their faces. One young Muslim woman wore the conventional shawl - like wrap to the waist. But her bottom half sported designer jeans...tight at that!

Gary was still on a respirator. He tried to communicate in writing and became exasperated when Patt couldn't understand his sprawling. One time he wrote "flem" and wanted his throat suctioned. Another time he wrote "cloth" and wanted a cold cloth on his head. His temperature fluctuated. And Patt still didn't know whether there was any neurological damage. One by one they weaned him from the drips and removed the pump assisting the heart. Finally, they weaned him from the respirator on day 6 post surgery.

Patt wasn't prepared for what was to come next. Happy to be able to verbalize with Gary, she began orientating him on the days since the surgery. He interrupted, "I was tired and you didn't bring me a sandwich. You didn't even come and see me. Why are you pulling this? I am going to write to Jeff and report your strange behavior. There are rats and spiders all over the floor and wall. What does the paper say about this place? Why am I in this 13 dollar-a-week flea bag?" He continued, "We went to England last night and saw John Lennon's house." Patt summoned the nurse. "Something is wrong with him! He isn't making any sense!" she said, bewildered and frightened that perhaps he did have a stroke. "Being in ICU on morphine and not knowing if is day or night can cause ICU psychosis. I have seen this often. I am sure he is OK." she explained, trying to quell Patt's fear. "I brought you USA Today to read." Patt said, trying to ignore his off-the-wall statements. "What does it say about me? Does it say anything about this place? They are clever here. Joe is the boss. I heard them talking about your jewelry. They are sizing you up. Will we sleep here tonight? The bed floats. Are we on a boat?

Can we leave? Let's get out of here!" Patt left frustrated and deeply concerned.

When she returned the next day, Gary seemingly began to understand that he had been in a drug-induced state (on a "bad trip") and none of this was really happening. He proceeded to tell Patt how, in his mind, the medical staff wrapped him up in plastic like a picture and said "they wouldn't take the bag off until we came up with the money and paperwork. Jeff was on the table with me and held my hand - then he looked down from the cubicle in the ceiling. Last night I begged them to kill me but they wouldn't. I hassled with them to take this thing out of my mouth but they wanted 500 dollars. I told the guy to call Vicki - but they wouldn't. I didn't trust you. I thought you were in on it." Patt left for the motel...again deeply troubled and concerned. Was this really something called ICU psychosis or was there some neurological damage?

During the night Patt received a call from the nurse. "Gary became agitated again and complained of seeing rats and ants. He went into ventricular tachycardia and started to turn blue. I called the resident and he put him on a higher dose of oxygen and administered a tranquilizer. He seems fine now. I just wanted you to be aware of what had happened." Gary had come close to being re-intubated (i.e., put back on the respirator).

One day a group of doctors were at the foot of Gary's bed discussing his case. Gary recognized Dr. Denton Cooley, who still visits the hospital early in the morning several days a week. Dr. Cooley, at age 85, performed surgery until the last couple of years. An imposing, tall man, he prides himself on eating less than 2000 calories a day; no doubt the reason for his longevity and high energy level.

But then, upon calling the hospital to see if Gary had been moved out of the ICU unit to another floor, Patt received an absolutely shocking response. The nurse said, "Didn't anyone call you? Your husband was taken to surgery at 3:00 AM -he was bleeding." "Oh no!" exclaimed Patt, "I'll be right there!" She called Jeff and Vicki to inform them of the latest happening —then rushed to the hospital, her heart racing. After all he has been through - now this. She raced through the hospital halls, up the elevator, and ran into ICU. Then an even bigger shock...she was bewildered and lost for words to find Gary sitting up in a chair talking on the phone to Vicki. "What is happening?" she screamed at the nurse. "I am so sorry," replied the nurse. "I thought you were the wife of my other patient." "I'm OK honey." Gary chirped cheerfully. Another example of the roller coaster ride—one that could have been avoided. Apparently the nurse was in training.

Finally, Gary improved enough to be moved to the heart monitoring floor. The feeding tube was removed and he was started on clear liquids. He was still seeing those awful creatures, but now he was fully aware they were hallucinations. "I see rats in the corner and over there," Gary said as he pointed. Patt, now less concerned, saw humor in the situation. She ran over to the area Gary pointed out and stomped and jumped up and down. Just then, the nurse stopped short, as she entered the room, looking bewildered as she watched Patt doing her stomp "dance." "I'm killing rats!" Patt exclaimed. Surely she thought these two people from Michigan's Upper Peninsula must be "loco."

Dr. Casar, the pulmonolgist, came to check on Gary. "He is depressed today." Patt told him. "Gary, you have no reason to be depressed." he responded. He demonstrated with his thumb and forefinger - barely a trace in between "You were this close to the OTHER SIDE!"

The next day was Sunday August 1st. Gary was relaxed and watching a ballgame. Patt decided to go back to the hotel to rest. She was there about 10 minutes when the phone rang. It was the nurse. "Suddenly Gary's heart rate jumped to over 225 and he is being taken back to ICU Recovery in the Cooley building. His heart beat is irregular."

Patt left immediately on the shuttle. The roller coaster ride she was promised wasn't over yet. Gary was again hooked up to IV drips to stabilize the heart rhythm. He apparently had a reaction to the drug given to stabilize the top chamber of the heart. It caused a disturbance in the bottom chamber (ventricular tachycardia)...a much more serious rhythm problem.

His heart "flutter" continued. Worried, Patt queried the nurse about the rhythm problem. "How is the problem treated—with a pacemaker or drugs?" She rather glibly responded, "The flutter is not unusual. The heart is irritated from surgery and a rhythm problem can occur in about 40% of the cases. I know you would like to think your honey is unique—but he is not." she said jokingly. The nurses were exceptional, cheerful and competent. One African-American nurse coined Gary "old blue eyes!" Turning to Patt she said, "I see what got you - dem blue eyes." Looking now toward Gary, she said, "And you still got 'IT' honey!"

The electrophysiologists were called in on the case. They

called themselves "heart electricians." Gary continued to be short of breath. An x-ray showed fluid in the area between the heart and lungs. Specialists performed a thoracentesis (removing fluid with a needle from the back). Almost a quart of fluid was removed. An echocardiogram revealed Gary's heart now had an ejection fraction (how the heart pumps) of 45 to 50 - back where it was in 2004.

The nurse explained that two more tests were on the schedule for the next day. One was a transesophageal echo (TEE) where a camera is dropped down the throat to check for blood clots behind the heart. The other was a cardio-version. The paddles are placed on the heart to try to shock it into a normal sinus rhythm. Gary didn't sleep all night worried about the scheduled procedures. Finally at 5:00 AM he summoned the nurse, "I am not having those tests. I didn't sleep all night."

Patt arrived before 8:00AM in anticipation of the newly scheduled tests. "Did you sleep well last night?" Patt asked. Irate and without much finesse Gary answered, "No, I didn't and I am NOT having anymore tests." "Does the doctor know?" queried Patt. "Yes", continued Gary in an irritated tone. "Dr. Coselli said there was nothing to it and I told him if it's so easy, you have the tests." Humorously, he placated Gary and answered, 'OK chief.' Dr. Hogan, the cardiologist arrived and was visibly unhappy with Gary's decision. After more coercing and reassurance from the nurse, Patt, and the doctor—Gary reconsidered. He signed the papers and once again they wheeled him off. Jennifer, the nurse, accompanied him and held his hand as his bed was whisked down the hall. In addition, Dr. Hogan's nurse practitioner promised to be there for moral support. Soon it was over! Gary's heart was shocked into a normal rhythm. IT WORKED!!

Two days later Gary was transferred to the heart monitoring floor. After three additional days of physical therapy, Gary was discharged from St Lukes. Holding a pillow to protect his chest, he was helped into a vehicle for his flight to Green Bay where he would enter St Vincent's hospital for rehabilitation. The flight was draining. Gary was exhausted and shaky upon arriving at St. Vincent's. He would spend a week there and surprise therapists with his progress.

On August 17, five weeks after his ordeal began, finally, Gary returned to his home. Labor Day week-end the Abrahamson's attended and danced at their grandson's wedding in Milwaukee. Especially significant since Gary and Patt first met at a dance in high school and have shared their love of dance for 56 years.

The recuperation process will be ongoing for months. When asked about his ordeal, Gary responds, "There is no question in my mind—my survival is miraculous! I give credit to my faith, prayers and support from family and friends, and of course, God, who guided the hands of the top surgeon in the world, the dedicated and renowned Dr. Coselli...hand picked by the world renowned Dr. Denton Cooley. And certainly credit is due for the astounding specialists that represent Dr. Coselli's team." Gary sincerely believes that there is no higher calling than that of the dedicated doctors and nurses who care for and repair God's greatest creation--A HUMAN BEING!

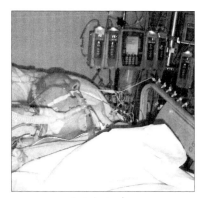

Intubated

"Old Blue Eyes"

Leaving the Hospital

Dancing at the Wedding

FAITH AND ACCEPTANCE   Never Before Published
BY RUTH ALKIRE, (PATT'S FIRST COUSIN) AS TOLD TO PATT ABRAHAMSON

The year 1970 will forever be etched in my mind. I graduated from college in January. My eldest son married in February, the same month I was hospitalized with pneumonia. In March I entered the hospital with a possible heart condition and in April I delivered my fifth child. Most devastating, on July 10, my second born son passed away after heart surgery. His death forever changed our family. In September, I started teaching school, facing thirty-six children with a broken heart and spirit. Then, in November, my granddaughter was born.

My story is about John and the events leading up to his death and our family's attempt to make sense of the loss of our son and brother.

At age seven, John underwent a delicate open heart surgery to correct a constricted valve in the artery of his heart which had restricted his activities since his condition was discovered at age 5. Johnnie had a congenital subvalvular aortic stenosis.

John was a delightful child excelling in whatever he undertook. He played hockey, was the best diver and a star on the golf team at the school he attended. He served as manager of both the football and basketball teams. John touched the hearts of all those who knew him. His memory will serve to inspire - epitomizing accomplishment in the face of adversity.

On June 22, 1970 (John's 17th birthday) we entered the University of Chicago Clinic. I went through all of the "red tape" admitting John into this monstrous, cold, gray building not realizing that he would never return home. Not realizing that life would never be the same and a part of me would die with John.

It was afternoon before John was finally taken up to his room. He changed his clothes and we toured our surroundings. Upon returning to his room he spotted his nametag on the door. It stated John Eric, Age 16. In a flash he changed the 16 to 17. Today was his birthday and he was a year closer to manhood!

John's surgery was scheduled for June 26; that meant I had three days and nights to spend with him. We shared the tenderest of moments reflecting on the fun, we, as a family shared.

We also agreed on a means of communication. A tube would be inserted in his throat for the first three days after surgery preventing him from talking. We agreed that when I asked, "how do you feel?" or "is there any pain?" he would give me the "peace sign" if he felt ok.

I returned home in the evenings and the same familiar cold chill would consume my body. John stood in his ceiling to floor window overlooking the parking lot and waved good-bye. Whenever I return to that hospital I can still see my John waving.

The morning of June 26th came too quickly. The nurse came in with John's relaxant injection. Soon afterwards, a man dressed in green garb entered pushing a squeaky gurney. I said a small prayer for the strength I needed to hold back the tears as I bent over John, kissed him and whispered, "See ya in a couple of hours, John."

A couple of hours? John was taken to surgery at 7:00 am. We prayed and waited for what seemed like an eternity. My thoughts drifted. John was so special and so was our close relationship: no doubt spawned by the nurturing, caring, and perhaps over protectiveness a parent feels when a child's activities pose a treat to his life. It was now 5:00 p.m. They notified us in the waiting room that John was on his way to intensive care.

I remember feeling a sense of relief that the surgery was over as we entered to elevator to go to the ICU. The elevator door opened and I can barely describe the scene I witnessed. It was John being wheeled down the corridor in a propped up bed! He was attached to a host of machines with five doctors assisting him. It was frightening and I felt weak at the sight. The surgeon said they needed a short time to set him up in ICU.

We entered the unit. It resembled a scene from a Frankenstein movie; a sinister laboratory with tubes and wires suspended everywhere. The wires connected to his wrists and ankles lead to a monitor that emitted a continuous beep, beep, beep. The tube down his throat was the most troubling to me.

I tried to choke back the sobs, painfully masking my grief with a thin smile and refrain from my instinctive compulsion to run and put my arms around him. Instead, I walked as calmly as I could to his bedside. John's eyes were opened and he seemed somewhat irrational. "John", I said choking back tears, "you are doing great. How do you feel?" He spread his two fingers and gave me the "peace sign." A sign that said, "I'm O.K. Mom!" His eyes closed and I bent down, kissed him and reassured him everything was going to be O.K.

We retreated to the waiting room. The surgeon told us the operation was a success. He had removed a bicuspid aortic valve (the normal aortic valve is tricuspid) which was completely insufficient. He continued to explain that he inserted a fresh homograph valve. A homograph valve is a human valve thought to be better than artificial type constructed of plastic.

The doctor continued, "The first six to twelve hours are crucial. If John can hang on, he'll make it." The time is now 8:30 pm. I began to pace the floor and the corridor. As I left the waiting room to walk down a hallway I saw a man in the all too familiar green garb literally run into the ICU. I turned around and stumbled into the waiting room groping for help! I turned to my husband, "I know something is wrong with John!" I said as a strange feeling engulfed me. How did I know? I just had that instinctive, intuitive feeling that only a mother can have.

Unfortunately I was right. An hour dragged by and the surgeon finally approached us, "John's blood pressure is dropping, but I am perplexed as to why!" The night seemed endless. I continued to walk the corridors and pray for John's life. The dedicated surgeon spent most of the night attending to John while his life hung in the balance.

About eleven the following morning the team of doctors made a decision to take John back to surgery. His blood pressure had still not stabilized. Upon reopening the chest cavity the surgeon discovered a vein that had not been sealed off. It had produced a sportier and his chest cavity was filled with blood causing the low blood pressure. According to the doctor John had tolerated the second surgery well and his pulmonary function was much improved.

We were allowed to see John five minutes every hour the first day and a half and I saw some improvement. He was able to communicate to me with his eyes and the "peace sign". It was excruciatingly painful to walk down the corridor and see my John still attached to the myriad machines that kept him breathing and living.

Forty-eight hours post surgery he developed complete renal shut down. The kidneys lost all function. On the sixth day after surgery, the surgeon instituted peritoneal dialysis to function for the kidneys. It worked for forty-eight hours. Then the BUN rose above 300mg. percent and the potassium levels were too high.

On the seventh day post surgery I noticed his left leg was bandaged. Upon questioning the doctor I learned that there was severe swelling. At seven o'clock that evening as we were ready to go home the doctor asked us to stay. A blood clot had broken loose from John's leg and entered his left lung causing an embolism. At the same time the right lung collapsed. Again, I walked the halls praying for John's life.

On the eighth day post surgery, even with the lung complication, John was again wheeled into surgery. This time doctors inserted an anterior-venus shunt and hemodialysis was started. Within ten minutes John suffered a cardiac arrest. The team resuscitated him and immediately stopped dialysis.

Reality set in as I contemplated just what was happening, what John was going through and how futile it all seemed. Suddenly, I realized, I had to change the way I prayed: My prayers now were for God to help me accept his will. God had kept John alive long enough for me to accept his death. In all reality, John died June 26th. The machines kept him breathing two weeks longer.

The following day his BUN was up around 350mg. The surgeon explained the tremendous risk in undertaking another dialysis, but death would be certain in a few hours without it. He was dialyzed daily for the next four days. On the fourteenth post-operative day his potassium was 4.6 and his BUN was 70mg. His cerebral status was questionable, although, he did respond but was not alert.

Suddenly on July 10th, fifteen days post operative; he developed a ventricular tachycardia, then ventricular fibrillation and could not be resuscitated.

A quote from the surgeon the morning John died: "It almost seemed to me as if John's name was in the book from the start. I have never had so many complications in a row with one person in all of my years of practice."

Filled with untold grief I continued to search for some meaning in John's death. A friend of mine sent a card with the thought that when you go forth into a rose garden to pick a bouquet, you never select the withered and drooping flowers, but always look for the brightest and gayest buds and blossoms. She wrote, "Maybe God does that sometimes too." It was a beautiful thought, but my grief was too new for anything to be helpful.

For a long time I prayed that John's passing would not be in vain. Somehow, somewhere, and in someway I waited for Him to help me make sense of this horrific tragedy. The answer did not come overnight.

Then a tragedy took the life of a friend of John's. He died in a car accident. The circumstances were tragic; the young man kicked his way out of the car, which had landed in a culvert. Stunned from the accident, he veered into a two-foot pond on a golf course and drowned. Ironically, the teen was buried next to John with an identical stone marker.

John's death gave me untold compassion and empathy for others experiencing the loss of a loved one. As I reached out to the family of John's friend with profound understanding and sympathy for the grief they were enduring, I knew God gave me the answer I was looking for. Indeed, John's death wasn't in vain.

The following quote by Helen Steiner Rice speaks eloquently: "Feed not your loneliness on empty days, but fill each waking hour in useful ways. Reach out your hand in comfort and in cheer. And I will comfort you and hold you near."

Since John's death I have reached out and empathized with the parents of three youngsters whose lives were cut short. The loss of John taught me compassion and empathy for my fellow man. I just know John is looking down and proudly saying, "way to go, Mom!" You see, even before he entered the hospital he had participated in a community effort; Walk For the Retarded.

I am grateful for having known John during the seventeen years that God lent him to me to care for and love. John's death has helped mold the person that I am today. My memory of John will never dim, nor will my love. I had him for just a short time, but better than not to have known him at all.

Of course I wonder about the man John would have become, the profession he might have chosen, the children he might have had. I grieve that John's hopes and dreams were cut short. That's only natural. Then I think about my many blessings: My four other children, my grandchildren, and a loving husband of over fifty years; someone with whom to share the tears and joy.

I know as long as we are alive, we will move in and out of crisis and adversity. Eleanor Roosevelt once said, "You have to accept whatever comes and the only important thing is that you meet it with courage and the best you have to give." My faith is strong and I have accepted God's infinite wisdom - His plan with His help!

PATT'S INSPIRATIONAL STORY

It is now almost 20 years since the day (October 25, 1987) our world was turned upside down. We were called to Kansas where our son lived with his family. "Come quickly, the family needs support!" the voice said over the phone. Gary, age 37, suffered a cardiac arrest while jogging. He was barely clinging to life. We prayed for his survival. We thought if he wakes up everything would return to normal. That wasn't to be. Deprived of oxygen, Gary's brain was severely damaged. Brain injury, at that time, was a foreign word to us. In the weeks that followed: coma, seizures, pneumonia, bizarre maniacal behavior, and the breakup of his marriage would change Gary's world...our world. They are painful memories we try to bury in the deepest recesses of our mind.

It is 18 months since his trauma and the psychologist at the mental health clinic is saying, "Gary's wife can no longer "keep" him. Last week he threatened to kill himself. She must get on with her life for her sanity and concentrate on raising their two sons."

The alternative was a nursing home for the aged devoid of the therapies he would need if he were to progress. No, I'm his Mom and I will fight to get the "system" to provide for his long-term rehabilitation. Naive, I was driven by a maternal force that lacked reality, and a mentality that wouldn't allow me to comprehend that Gary might never be a contributor to society again. I waged war against the system, the doctors, hospitals, my husband or anyone else that thwarted my efforts to bring my son back to "normal." It would take years of anguish and desperation to deal with the gruesome reality of severe brain injury.

We all reach forks in the road of life. What road we choose ultimately affects not only us, but also everyone we are remotely close to. Self-pity Alley is paved with anger, hostility, depression and bitterness. I finally chose Positive Avenue Boulevard lined with hope, faith, humor, love and purpose. I needed to stay positive, have a healthy mind and remain strong to be able to cope with the devastation. I needed some outlets, some diversions, other than my caregiver role.

I enrolled in a class at our local college. The next year I became a full time student and graduated with an associate degree. The following two years I traveled to Northern Michigan University (about an hour from my home) and received a Bachelor of Social Work Degree with honors. At age 59 I walked across the stage to receive my diploma while my family beamed, screamed and cheered with delight. Even Gary in his abyss clapped and yelled "Way to go Mom!"

A couple of years later I was asked to compete in the Ms. Senior Michigan Pageant. Why would they want me? I had neither talent nor experience in this sort of thing. I was told the focus of the pageant was the search for the gracious lady who best exemplifies the dignity, maturity and INNER BEAUTY of all senior women. Reluctantly I agreed. I could tap dance a little and a professional dance instructor helped me put together a Charleston tap. Again, I viewed this lark as a diversion and a fun experience. But a pageant at my age? I was in a state of shock when I won the local competition and was poised to compete in the state finals. You can't imagine the exhilaration and bewilderment when I was named Ms. Senior Michigan, 1997.

During my reign as Ms. Senior Michigan, I used my platform to create awareness and educate people about head injury. I was also pleased and humbled to be considered an inspiration and role model to senior women.

1997 was banner year. My book about head injury, *Brain Injury: A Family Tragedy* was published and I competed in the National Ms. Senior America. No, I didn't win the national competition but I won the national Ms. Senior America Inspiration Award and received a two- minute standing ovation. That was so heartwarming and much more meaningful to me.

The next year I received the Education and Awareness Award from the Brain Injury Association of MI. That fall I was asked to be the keynote speaker at the National Brain Injury Convention in Philadelphia introduced by Jim Brady (President Reagan's Press Secretary.) And since then, I have been asked to do inspirational speaking.

I can say, as a family, we have found a recipe for survival. It has taken years to get to this point. Gary is most comfortable living with his parents. He welcomes a dash of humor - we call it comic relief. He is very aware that he is the object of a generous portion of love. We have a sprinkling of satisfaction from finding the right ingredients to survive as a family. We came to the realization that there is no Wizard, like in the Wizard of Oz, and the yellow brick road is mythical. And Gary will require 24 hour care the rest of his life. And yet, we feel rich and blessed living each day to the fullest filled with that special love that bonds a parent and child.

Appendix: Emails from Readers

Patt, great story on the 400s. I have always been a rail buff, and now I live in Perkins, a couple of miles from the track that would have taken the 400 north out of Escanaba. Now it is used almost exclusively to haul ore from the mine south to Escanaba. Sincerely, **~Ron Miaso, Perkins, Michigan**

Hi Patt, I recently read your fine article in the Esky paper about the 400. It brought back many fond memories as I traveled back and forth from Milwaukee and Chicago. I bought my first 35 millimeter camera in the late sixties and the very first shots I took with that camera was of the 400 and another train that was on display for the public...I am looking forward to your next article in the paper, you have quite a following here in Lansing, as your memories of the past are very much the same as ours seeing we all grew up in Esky around the same time.

~Don Ashland, Lansing, Michigan

I just finished reading your article on Theodore Roosevelt in the Escanaba Daily Press. Your article will hopefully open a few eyes as to just how great of a man Roosevelt was. As a former history teacher, I was often asked why Roosevelt was included on Mount Rushmore with three of our greatest presidents, Washington, Jefferson and Lincoln. I wish I could have handed them your article at the time so their question could have been more adequately answered. I hope to have the pleasure of reading future articles from you.

~Bob Erkkila, Calumet, Michigan

Dear Patt Abrahamson, My cousin Velma Meyers Jones, formerly from Schaffer sent me your article on Tom Swift. My mother Sophie Kwarciany was the cook for Tom Swift Sr. for many years...As a young boy, on one occasion I did see the slot machine in a hallway off the bar area but had no knowledge of the heavy gambling. **~David Kwarciany, Wauwatosa, Wisconsin**

Dear Patt, I'm Karen Peterson, a member of the Delta County Genealogical Society. I also help write the Delta Pedigree our quarterly newsletter. I enjoyed your article published July 6, 2007 in the Daily press, Genealogy is a Favorite Hobby. We would like to re-print your article in the next Delta Pedigree which will be the September issue. And ask your permission to do so. Looking forward to reading more of your work. Could you have another book in the works??

~Karen Peterson

Just wanted to tell you how much I enjoyed your article on your recent trip to DC. I have long felt that it is one of the most wonderful areas in the nation (the UP coming first). We lived in Silver Spring for nineteen years and I taught in Chevy Chase. Our greatest enjoyments were to visit the sites in DC and surrounding regions - the shore, mountains, rolling meadows and historical places. Thanks for the article. **~Marlene Winter-Johnson, Garden,Michigan**

Hi Patt, I enjoyed reading your article in the press today. I remember the Minstrel Shows very well. I seem to remember that the Escanaba lettermen had what they called "The E-men Minstrel." I was interested in reading that you bought The Jolson Story and Jolson Sings Again. Where did you find them? I would love to get them, too. We had the recorded albums (78s) and, needless to say, they are of no value today. Thanks for your writings. They are always of interest to me.

~Marilyn (Molin) Olson, Palm Harbor, Florida

Hi, Read your article about the streamliner. Brings back memories as I rode it to Escanaba every summer to stay with my grandparents, Minette and Eric Froberg. My granddad was an engineer on the liner and Gram and I would pick up grampa at the station. I was up late and really thought I was something! We would stop at Sandberg's bar where Gram and I had an orange pop and Gramp had a beer - then home to bed. Fond memories! Thanks for the article.

~Barb Marlin, (Yooper in Illinois)

Patt, As a childhood friend of Ann Fix, I've been reading from a distance (we live in Nevada) all of the accolades to Doug - I loved your article, but saddened by the similarities in the circumstances with his fate and your son's. I have read many of your stories relative to what your family has been through with Gary - I admire who you are and have been doing. My family has been the care-giver for our parents through cancer and stroke, but as difficult as it was, I don't believe it could compare to dealing with the same circumstances with a child. Just thought I would drop you a line to let you know what a nice tribute to Doug and Gary - you're a classy lady, but even more important - a class act!! God Bless.

~Mary Ross, Nevada

I just had to tell you how uplifting your writings are in the Daily Press. Thank you for being such a great writer and sharing it with all of us. Love and prayers always.

~Barb Nelson, Escanaba, Michigan

Dear Patt, Dan and I are vacationing in Uaymitun, Yucatan, Mexico which is about 200 miles west of Cancun. We are all "connected" now via the internet, and of course I wanted to read all of the news from the Press. As usual, I enjoyed your article and especially because it was about Catte! Dan and I were very much interested in what has happened to her. Thank you so much for bringing us up to date. Again, thank you for another great article! Sincerely,

~Kathy (LaPorte) Creten, Escanaba, Michigan

I have enjoyed reading your column on local people, ancestry and history for several months. You certainly have a talent and wisdom earned from your years of experiences in both family and business life. Well done! I hope you are willing to continue to share your thoughts and stories for many years to come.

~Mickey (Coyne) Wieciech

I just wanted you to know how much we enjoy your columns, you are a great writer. Keep it up and thanks for the enjoyable reading. They all seem to hit home, and a lot of good memories.

~Evelyn and Sam Poquette, Escanaba, Michigan

About the Author

LaPorte Studio, Escanaba, Michigan

Patt Abrahamson, author, columnist, speaker, political activist, and Ms. Senior Michigan, 1997 title holder is widely respected and appreciated for her weekly columns in the Daily Press. She graduated cum laude from Northern Michigan University with a bachelor of social work degree at age 59.

Her boundless energy, life experiences and accomplishments Through the Years have contributed to the success of her weekly column. Patt continues to pull the strings in the fabric of life that we all share a common thread. She writes about a variety of issues and subjects with a focus on "The Golden Years" and history.

Her published work, *Brain Injury: A Family Tragedy* (1997) has sold in many countries. It is still currently in print.

Patt lives in Escanaba, MI with her husband Gary and son, Gary Jr. She can be reached at P.O. Box 344, Escanaba, MI 49829 or her e-mail address: pattabe@charter.net